The Flat and House Hunter's Guide to London

The Flat and House Hunter's Guide to London

Patricia and Robert Ross

Photographs by
Leonardo Ferrante

District maps by
Geographia Ltd.

November 1973

Dear Ray + Alma.

We thought you'd enjoy having a copy of our London guide book.

Best regards,

Pat + Bob Ross

LONDON
GEORGE ALLEN & UNWIN LTD
RUSKIN HOUSE · MUSEUM STREET

ISBN 0 04 914051 5

Printed in Great Britain by
Lowe & Brydone (Printers) Ltd.

ACKNOWLEDGMENTS

The authors are deeply indebted to the following people and organizations for the help and advice they gave so generously: Clifford Krieger, of Gross, Fine and Krieger, Chalfen; Byron Theo of City Assurance Consultants; Morris Hearne, David Coward, Rachel Taylor, John Brown, Richard Ronald, Rosemary Taylor and the members of various amenity societies; Liz Cohen, for research; Christine Watt for typing; and Madeleine Barretto. And to the friends who gave inside views of various areas of London—Maggie Burnett, Penny and George Pulver, Venetia Thompson, Sherry Marti, Joan Lovell, Sally Oliver, Annabel Bowman-Vaughn, Michael Hearne, Hilary Leek, Charlotte McGowan, Teri McLuhan, Jane Safer—thanks.

The authors also wish to thank Geographia Ltd for their generosity in allowing them to reproduce the district maps, which form such an important part of this book, from *London Street by Street* and Geographers' Map Co. Ltd for permission to reproduce the map of London borough councils which appears on page 60. All these maps are Crown Copyright and are based on the Ordnance Survey, with the sanction of the Controller of H.M. Stationery Office, whose help was readily given and greatly appreciated. The motorway maps which appear on page 274 are reproduced by courtesy of the *Evening Standard*.

CONTENTS

INTRODUCTION

How does one set about finding a special place to live in a great city where there are 7,400,000 people living in an area of 620 square miles? That's what this book is about.

The book does not guarantee that you'll find your dream cottage in a Chelsea road, or your ideal anything. It will definitely be a valuable companion through all the various stages of your flat or house hunt, but you will also need lots of energy, a willingness to work hard, and some good luck as well—if you are to find just what you want.

We particularly dedicate this book to those people who cannot live happily far from the heart of London; who like living with all the conveniences and drawbacks of the city centre at their fingertips; who have a special affinity with city sights and sounds. It should help the house and flat hunter who already knows London; and it will be a special bonus to the newcomer, who doesn't know Barons Court from St John's Wood.

We are not unaware that at least 10 per cent of London's population is inadequately housed: the names on the waiting lists for council housing number 190,000. Middle-income Londoners, on the other hand, face a dilemma, not a crisis. Both groups need help—but whereas the G.L.C. anticipates that everyone on its lists will be decently housed by 1981, the only prediction for the middle-income group is that the housing situation will get worse.

One might start feeling more sympathetic towards the apparently comfortably-salaried middle-income man once one realized that the absolute minimum he will have to pay for a house in one of London's main residential areas—not centre, but off-centre—is £10,000 (£15,000 to £20,000 and in need of repair in the centre). It is also almost impossible for a family to find a decent flat or small house to rent at less than £25 a week. And prices are rising at a rate of 10 to 15 per cent a year.

Actually house prices in the second half of 1971 and through the first half of 1972 increased at an annual rate of 20–25 per cent. The minimum price for a new house in any part of London is over £10,000 and still rising.

New flats are also in great demand. Flat hunters queued for five days in February 1972, in St John's Wood to buy one of 80 Wates flats priced between £14,000 and £32,000. All were sold in two hours. A few weeks later a few of the flats were put back on the market by their buyers for a few thousand pounds more.

Reasons for the 'residential property boom of 1971–2' include the easy supply of mortgage money from building societies; a rapid increase in wages; shortage of land for development; and an inadequate supply of new flats or houses, a fact blamed on developers slow to react to the increased demand.

Some say that by the end of 1972 or by mid-1973 prices should stabilize. Major reasons for this view include the decline in money coming into building societies. This would result in less money available for mortgages. Interest rates may rise which would make mortgage repayment more expensive. Wage increases may slow down. And the allowance of tax relief on loan interest for purposes other than house purchase may divert some speculative money into the stock market and away from the house market.

Other possible developments which may result from the spectacular rise in property prices.

1) Building societies may be allowed to raise their ceiling on home loans from £13,000 to £20,000. Or they'll be allowed greater flexibility in giving special advances. The government may also impose controls on the amounts building societies can lend.

2) Greater controls may be imposed on furnished flats especially on rents and security of tenure.

3) Flat break-ups may be supervised more closely. Service and maintainance charges may be audited. A fair price for long leases may be established for all tenants in a block where flats are being offered for sale.

4) The rateable value limit of £400 in London may be raised to bring more flats and houses under the control of the Rent Acts.

5) Capital gains tax may be imposed on the gain made when one sells a house within a short petiod of buying it. This would slow down speculators and take away some of the attractiveness of 'trading up' to a bigger home using the profit made on the last house.

6) Gazumping (see glossary) may be banned by an act of Parliament.

Some people would argue that the only long term cure to the housing problem in London is to get more houses and flats built. Perhaps the government could give special grants to developers in a similar programme to that which created the hotel building boom of 1971—2.

One thing is certain—house prices won't be going down in central London. And as long as people with money want to live in the more fashionable parts of London house prices will continue to rise. The supply is fixed, yet the demand continues to increase.

When you compare the cost of paying off a mortgage or renting a flat in central London with the average salary of the young business executive, you wonder how anyone but the wealthy can afford to live in central London. Also, central London's population is decreasing because business and industry are taking over so much of the residential property, forcing out the man of modest means who wants to live near his work, and the conveniences of the city.

London is rapidly dividing into two types of area: one with housing decay trapping the poorer people; and the other with rampant house-price inflation attracting only the wealthy. In America this modern disease—the movement of middle-income people from the central city to the suburbs—has been termed 'Urban Decay'. If the same thing is not to happen in London someone must give serious thought to the plight of the middle-income house hunter.

Looking at London

The World's Most Livable City

New York is madness. Tokyo is too crowded. The Parisians aren't friendly. London is civilized, but by no means heaven on earth—not enough housing for the poor; handsome houses in states of gross neglect; traffic snarls; its well-known share of grey and rainy days, and its lesser known share of brilliant spring sunshine. . .

London does not have the sense of urgency about getting things done, and getting 'ahead' that New York does, nor does it have the beautiful boulevards of Paris. But in what other city would you see so many spots of green—squares and parks and gardens—which give an impression that someone actually planned the place and thought about people who would be living here. What London does have is a very happy combination of youth and gaiety, and age and sobriety—not the gaiety of Rome, or the sobriety of Moscow, but a healthy combination.

The London Fog? The World Press reported recently that 'at the modest cost of 36 cents a year for thirteen years, each central Londoner bought himself 50 per cent more winter sunshine, an 80 per cent reduction in smoke, and the total elimination of his city's proverbial black fogs.' All this happiness is due to Britain's Clean Air Act of 1956, at which time the government provided 70 per cent of a householder's cost in modifying his furnace or fireplace to take smokeless fuel.

Anyway, the purpose of his book is not to discuss the merits of London, but housing, the concern of many people who have already discovered that London is a lovely place to live. People are coming to London in large numbers, from all over the world, to live for three months or three years or indefinitely—much to the despair of many Englishmen who don't believe there is room enough for all. And if you look at Islington's housing waiting list of 10,000 needy people living in inadequate conditions, you may agree with the protestors.

Then look at the preliminary 1971 census report, which records an exodus of families from London. London, like other central cities of the world, is becoming a place for either the wealthy, who can afford to live in luxury close to many of the conveniences a city has to offer; or the very poor, who live in poverty (or perhaps the splendour of a new council flat), and enjoy few of those conveniences London has to offer. Business is moving in. And there simply is less and less property available for the middle-income man—what he wants is still there, but he will have to work hard to find it.

Two mass movements in London will have an important influence on house hunters in the early 1970s:

1. The Break-up

All sorts of property owners who formerly rented their flats are now engaged in the full-scale selling—or breaking up—of flats. This movement is so strong that some estate agents are predicting a London with only two types of flat dwelling:

1) furnished flats for rent
2) flats for sale, on long leases.*

This may seem a frightening prospect to a city dweller who has always signed a two- or three-year lease, and paid his annual rent by the month or quarter. But it is not as frightening as it seems, for with property in as great demand as it is in London, it should always be possible to sell your lease should you decide to move on. An investment in London property is one of the wisest buys a man with money can make, at present.

But while the flat market is in such a state of flux, there are serious difficulties for the man who wants a three- to five-year lease on an unfurnished flat. They are not easy to find. In fact, the government's Francis Committee Report on Rent Acts has pointed out that in 1963, the flat hunter in London would have found 767 unfurnished flats for rent, had he scanned the letting columns of the *London Weekly Advertiser* for a five-week period. By 1970, the number of flats to let had dropped to 66, for a similar five-week period. That's a reduction in the unfurnished flats-to-let market of *92 per cent*.

The Managing Director of Freshwater, largest landlord of rented flats in London, has said: 'Unless the present government introduces urgent, even emergency measures to encourage the development of more homes for renting in London, there will be little point in flat hunting in five years' time—unless you have a spare £1000 to pass under the counter for non-existent fixtures and fittings, or can afford a flat for £10,000 or more.'

Another quote, from *The Financial Times*: 'More and more rented accommodation is being withdrawn from the market as institutional landlords sell off their properties in an operation known as "break-up".... The flat-owning companies can make a lot more money by selling off their flats to sitting tenants or gaining vacant possession and then selling them. Capital is then released for more profitable operations . . .'

2. Hotel Boom

The second movement affecting the London flat or house hunter is what Londoners call the Hotel Boom. Every summer, London literally runs out of hotel beds. For that reason, British travel authorities insist that London will require sixty new Hilton-style hotels within the next five years, to accommodate tourists.

So what does all this mean to the house hunter? It means that some of the flats or houses he would have been interested in renting or buying are gone, or scheduled for demolition. In spring 1971 two complete garden squares were demolished near Gloucester Road tube station in Kensington—to make way for two massive hotels. Between September 1968 and April 1970, Westminster council dealt with about sixty applications for conversions of properties to hotel use.

The Councils do have zoning restrictions, but they are caught, of course,

*This mainly stems from 'The Rent Acts' which, in effect, precluded the building of new flats for rent at an economic level.

between this conflict of 'preserving the beautiful' and improving their revenues from tourism and trade conferences, which requires large amounts of hotel space.

The price you'll pay to live in Central London?

One man who left his wife in Surrey and came to London to seek bachelor accommodation describes his fully self-contained one-room flat as 'no bigger than a cupboard'. He pays £10 a week to live in that room, which is part of a charming cottage in an eighteenth-century row. He believes he's fortunate, for £15 a week is the minimum rate for any self-contained unit in central London (self-contained meaning it has kitchen, bath and toilet). Most single people get round the high cost of living by sharing, and thus halving the rent.

To live in the so-called prestige areas of central London, a family requiring a one- or two-bedroom furnished flat will face a rental of, at the minimum, £25–30 a week.

Annual rents for unfurnished flats are lowest in mansion blocks, with no central heating, and highest in purpose-built luxury blocks, such as those you'll see round Regent's Park and Hyde Park. A flat in a mansion block may be rented for as little as £800 a year in Maida Vale or a similar area chock-full of these blocks. The minimum rental for a flat in a new building overlooking a park is probably £2000 a year. Of course there are the 1930s-type blocks, which are somewhere between the Victorian mansion block, and the brand new posh block, in price scale.

You will seldom find any unfurnished flat on the market bearing a premium of less than £1000 for 'fixtures and fittings' (see *Glossary Guide,* p. 30).

To purchase a lease on a flat in inner London, expect to pay £8–12,000 for a one-bedroom flat, on a fifty or sixty-year lease. If you require three to four bedrooms, £15–30,000 is the range. Be alert to the extras:

a) rates—the tax on property values
b) ground rent—rent charged on long-lease tenant by freeholder or ground landlord
c) service charges—payment made to help maintain the building.

To buy a house, £15–20,000 is the absolute minimum for central London's posh pockets, and £10–15,000 just 'off centre'. And estate agents aren't likely to bend over backwards for you when they learn you're interested in low-price housing (which comes on the market so rarely).

Short leases, of course, come more cheaply. A short lease, though, is more difficult to mortgage, and to dispose of, should you decide to leave London, or move house within London.

Because of the extremely high cost of living in the very heart of London, many house hunters will find it worthwhile to look just on the fringes—in Parson's Green instead of Chelsea; in the villages of Blackheath or Greenwich, south of the river. If you do not insist on living ten minutes from the West End, then you will find prices lower than the minimum outlined here for living in London.

The London Skyline

Types of Buildings in which to Make Your Home

One scarcely needs reminding that London was once a series of villages—the oldest being the City, Westminster and Southwark. Almost all the other present-day boroughs were once outlying villages, for residing or resting.

Happily, this is a city where people of even modest means can live in 'period properties'. ('Period' is a favourite word in the jargon of the estate agent, who often uses it to refer to anything that is not brand new.)

The period houses you'll hear most about are Georgian and Victorian ones. The Georgian era covered 116 years (1714 to 1830), and the Georgian influence, of course, carried over into early Victorian times. If you look at the work of builders to this very day, you might say the Georgian influence has not subsided.

The Regency period, about which you'll hear a lot, and dream about once you've become familiar with all the Nash terraces around Regent's Park, began at the turn of the nineteenth century. It was thus a part of the Georgian period, but the Regency years were filled with extravagant circular design, a break from the simplicity and predictability of standard Georgian architecture.

Though many people observed that the bulk of Georgian building was monotonous, the Victorian heyday which followed highlighted some of the merits of Georgian times—well-planned squares and terraces blending together to form a very handsome townscape. In Victorian times, the total look of a street or square was overlooked, and the individual house was of primary concern. Thus the resulting 'Birthday Cake' villas occur, such as those in Melbury and Addison Roads in Kensington; or the smaller, yet highly-decorated two-storey red brick terraces of the Victorian suburbs. Within the descriptive word 'Victorian' come the early, mid and late Victorian styles. There is the tiny two-storey Victorian terrace; the family size Victorian terrace house, and the giant size Victorian terrace house, with its garden square.

Whereas in Georgian times only the gentry could afford a town house, Victorian times and the Industrial Revolution brought equal opportunity for all. The men who made money from their factories moved to the outskirts of London and built large brick houses, mostly in imitation of the Gothic style. In the heyday of Victorian times, when the start of the railways brought a new kind of prosperity to the country, there was a great demand for the grand house, wherein the owner would employ a domestic staff of six or seven people and entertain in the rather lavish way, which had formerly been the privilege of the upper classes. The grand houses of Bayswater, Notting Hill and Kensington are examples of this type. Victorian architecture is notable for its confusion, with influences from the Dutch, the ancient Greeks, the Turks, and many others.

The humbler of the Victorian buildings went up near the factories, for the working people. Some of these small Victorian houses are often called cottages. A terrace of two- or three-storey Victorian houses is sometimes called villas, and you'll find such villas all over London. They bear no resemblance, of course, to a real villa, the large detached house or mansion with its own front and back spacious gardens. Between 1881 and 1891, 45 per cent of the outer ring of London suburbs grew. So if you think that outer London looks the same no matter which direction you drive, you have some basis for your belief.

Today, residential London is a maze of many varieties of architecture. And the house hunter can probably work his way through the maze more effectively if he sorts London housing into size scales:

1) The miniscule—mews houses and workmen's cottages. Very popular, in great demand.
2) The family house—Georgian, Regency, Victorian or modern. Also very much in demand.
3) The monsters—the six- and seven-storey giant houses, which require far too much money for upkeep by a single family. Most of these tall houses are subdivided into family flats.
4) The modern—brand new, purpose-built blocks of flats, a few in tower proportions, but most just big and rectangular.

What is probably the most appealing thing about living in London is the feeling of city life which has a bit of country air about it. Anyone who lives in a small house in one of the small streets off Walton Street, on the borders of Chelsea and Knightsbridge, certainly lives with the 'now and then' feeling of being in a small village. All the shops he needs are cosily placed in Walton Street, which is a sort of village 'High Street', yet cosmopolitan Brompton Road is only five minutes away.

The charming streets of workmen's cottages which appear in all areas of London are excellent examples of village life within a city. The toilet has been brought from the outside to the inside, flower boxes have been added to the front windows and a pretty paint job covers everything. Shopping is just round the corner in the 'High Street'. This 'Chelseafication' of former humble workmen's cottages to middle-class homes is another favourite way of life in London.

Just as typical of London life, but not as intimate, is the grander life style of a flat in a gigantic house in Eaton Square or Rutland Gate. There is a regal entrance hall with chandelier, antique sideboard and fresh flowers in a vase, a lift to all flats (sometimes only one flat per floor, or perhaps two) and a porter living in the basement, caring for tenants' needs.

The Mansion Block movement, stimulated by the development of the Cadogan Square area in the late 1800s, has made mansion block living a way of life for many Londoners, though it is not basically the most attractive life style. The red brick is generally cold and imposing, and few of the flats were built with sunlight or an attractive view in mind. They were built because they accommodated many families in a fairly small space; and they were attractive at the time to the Victorians, who had some sort of passion for orange-red brickwork.

A typical mansion block is overflowing with middle-income tenants, paying less rent than they could afford, in order to save money to buy a house or flat in the near future. Then there is the super mansion block, which is a refined and elegant place to live, even if you don't own the flat. These have great spacious rooms, in an elegant location, such as Albert Court, behind the

Albert Hall in Kensington, Rutland Court, by Knightsbridge Barracks, or Orchard Court, just up from Selfridges.

Economizing on space was something that the builders of Georgian terrace houses had in mind, long before the Victorian mansion blocks came along. But the Georgians economized in a masterly way. The concept of terrace and square, square and terrace or garden is one unique to London. And it is certainly an appealing way to live, with a communal garden in front of the terraces, or private or communal gardens in the back. Georgian terrace houses are all family sized; the Victorian terrace houses come in all sizes, the classic being the two-storey red-brick row, and the Edwardian terraces are generally massive, not suitable for single family living.

The villa, or detached house, way of life is not so common in central London, mainly because of lack of space, which has always been of concern to builders and city planners. London land is, and always has been, of high value in comparison to the provinces, and it is not often used frivolously for rambling houses with acres of garden. St John's Wood is villa land. Castelnau, the part of Barnes which lies just over Hammersmith Bridge, is beautiful semi-detached villa land (the villa joins another villa at one side). So is Addison Road in the Holland Park area of Kensington. You will happen upon the occasional Regency or Victorian villa in almost any area of London. Highbury has some Victorian villas; Holland Park some Regency villas. Regent's Park is, of course, the pinnacle of Regency London's achievements. A few villas remain in York and Chester Terraces.

Because of the increasing value of London land, villas can disappear before one's very eyes, to make room for smaller, modern family houses. Wimbledon is a perfect example of dwindling numbers of old villas and increasing numbers of new houses.

Though London is perhaps overloaded with devotees of old houses and old anything, she is not without proponents of the modern life style. The modern movement has brought all sorts of 'town houses', usually built in a neo-Georgian or Regency style, rather than in true modern design. Many of these are to be found in Hampstead, Highgate and Primrose Hill.

The luxury Tower Block movement, however, has never reached significant scale in London. You can almost count them if you try:

The Water Gardens, Edgware Road
Portman Towers, Baker Street
The Barbican, the City
The Quadrangle, Cambridge Square
The Hilton Hotel, Park Lane—second Hilton will open in 1973, in Holland Park, Kensington
Household Cavalry Barracks, Hyde Park, Knightsbridge
A fair number in Wimbledon and Putney.

Tower blocks have an unfortunate reputation since so many have been put up by local authorities as council flats.

An important London life style is embodied in those big blocks of flats, built in the 1930s, which fall somewhere between the Victorian mansion block, and the brand new tower block. The best of these blocks will have polished brass name plates, doorbells and door knockers, and attractive gardens, visible from the road. The worst have absolutely no personality or anything about them which you could call attractive, except of course the reasonable rents.

Pros and Cons of Some of the London Life Styles

MEWS HOUSE Though it presents the epitomy of charm from the outside, it has miniscule rooms and low ceilings inside. A mews house usually has very little natural light, for its back presses against the 'master house', of which it was once a part. Most likely, the mews house was once the stable for the horses. But look at all the plus's a mews house has: great for newly marrieds who can correct any mistake in decorating with a few flashes of the paint brush and very little expenditure; very little outlay needed for furniture as well; and privacy—no people above or below you complaining about loud music, parties or newlywed arguments.

COTTAGE It may be part of a row, à la Chelsea, or it may stand on its own. You may see the occasional cottage around London that looks like a gate-keeper's house—this type is called a lodge. Cottages are general as small as mews houses.

MODERN HOUSE You cannot judge a book by its cover, nor can you judge a modern town house by its outward appearance. Some new town houses in Primrose Hill, selling for £16,000 and upward, started falling apart the minute the builders left the premises and the owner-occupiers moved in. It is not at all unusual to hear the buyer of a new home, or the resident of a

Mews houses in Knightsbridge   Modern houses in Holland Park

newly-built block of flats, complain about poor structure, thin walls and faulty plumbing. It is just as important to hire a surveyor to look over a new property as it is an old one.

GEORGIAN HOUSE The beauty of a Georgian terrace house is its efficiency —so easy to manage because of its layout—an arched doorway leads to the dining room and kitchen (brought up from the basement) on the ground floor; the main drawing room and study are on the first floor; bedrooms are on the top floors. But speculators led a big building boom in Georgian times, so not all Georgian houses are of the same high standard of structure.

LARGE BLOCK OF FLATS Security can be very poor in some large blocks of flats. In others, security is superb, with a twenty-four-hour doorman and a porter running round all day servicing tenants' flats. These days any city dweller has to be security conscious—so look before you leap into that beautiful new block of flats.

MANSION BLOCK Many mansion blocks have no central heating. And though the vast amount of space in most mansion blocks is particularly appealing, a long cold winter is not!

PRE-WAR PURPOSE-BUILT BLOCK OF FLATS Generally speaking, the newly-built block, or old block built specifically as flats, is much more livable in than a conversion block, i.e. a grand old home divided into small

Georgian row houses

Tower block in Chelsea

units for small or large families. The bathroom is almost always at the other end of the flat from the bedroom in a conversion block. Before you are bowled over by the large amount of space in such a flat, think about your daily life there. If all the rooms are entered from a hallway which looks like a bowling alley, fatigue is apt to set in before half the household day is over.

TOWER BLOCK London has a remarkable skyline of turrets and towers, roof gardens and chimneys. The great diversity in London's buildings makes the view from a tower block a very special asset.

HOUSE WITH GARDEN Is a private garden a vital part of your life? Then avoid the mews house, small cottage, or mansion block, all of which are sadly lacking in garden space. Georgian houses generally have lovely gardens; Victorian terrace houses have very small gardens. If you choose a flat or house with a garden, you'll never have to worry about selling your property in the market place. The value of a property with a garden is considerable, anywhere in London.

Do Not Touch

If you happen to choose for your home a house or building which is under a government preservation or conservation order, you are fortunate in one way—for you know the area will stay the same, and you face no risks of being moved out of the way by builders and developers of property. But you face one possible disadvantage, which is that you cannot make any changes in the facade or in some cases even in the structure of your house.

The borough council of the area in which you choose to live will give you further information about your street; or you could try the Historic Buildings Board of the G.L.C., County Hall, S.E.1.

The Royal Borough of Kensington and Chelsea and the City of Westminster have the largest number of buildings designated to be saved. Sadly some boroughs and builders are destroying houses which many belive should be saved.

Council Housing

The greatest number of council houses and flats, all built this century, are in these boroughs:

Southwark   41,506
Lambeth   32,116
Lewisham   27,273
Greenwich   27,116
Wandsworth   26,528

So keep these figures in mind, if you object to living in a house which is dwarfed by a massive council estate.

Be your Own Landlord

Buying a Freehold or Leasehold House or Flat— Why it Makes Sense

'Who wants to support a landlord for the rest of one's life?' goes one philosophy of home ownership. 'Ah yes, but who needs all the headaches of a house? It's better simply to pay rent and let the landlord have all the worries.' —that's the other argument. Just what are the advantages of owning? Well . . .

Building a Capital Asset and Beating Inflation

Property has traditionally been an excellent hedge against inflation. The increasing cost of putting up new houses forces up the price of existing houses. And of course the demand for houses is on the increase, while the supply is hopelessly inadequate. As a result houses and flats, especially in central London, are going up in value at an astronomical pace. An acquaintance of ours bought a house in St John's Wood a few years ago for around £20,000. He claims he could get easily £40,000 for it today. That's good capital growth. The same story could be told over and over again by house and flat owners all over central London. A house in the right location is your most valuable asset. The money you put into it improves its value. This is not so in a rented flat. And now the government gives grants to improve your house (see *Improvements Grants*, p.   ).

Some shrewd 'equity-orientated' investors prefer not to tie up too much of their capital in a mortgage or their income in outgoing. They prefer to rent their home and invest their capital and part of their income in stocks and shares. Each to his own.

The Gearing Effect on a Mortgage

The return on your invested capital can be amazing with a mortgage. Say you buy a £15,000 house and you put up £3000 of your own money and borrow £12,000. Let's also assume that the house appreciates in value at 10 per cent a year (not too difficult these days). In two years the house has gone up by £3000, and your invested capital has doubled in value—not a bad return in two years. Gearing works best, of course, when you put up the least amount of your own money.

Substantial Tax Advantages

When you buy a house or take a long lease and pay for it with a mortgage you get tax relief on the interest payments. The government is in effect subsidizing the house owner or mortgage payer at the expense of the rent payer, who gets no tax relief on his rent payments.

High tax payers can get further tax relief by paying off their mortgages with an endowment insurance policy and getting tax relief on the premiums. Under discussion in Parliament is a plan to relate tax relief directly to income and size of mortgage, in an attempt to give more relief to younger home buyers. A further tax advantage comes when you sell your house or the lease on your flat at a profit, in that you won't be subject to Capital Gains Tax, provided the house or flat was your principal residence.

Earn Income on Your Own Property

Here's a very worthwhile aspect of home ownership. Many people build a self-contained flat into their house, either in the basement or on the top floor. They then furnish it with second-hand or quasi-antique furniture and rent it to young single people. The reason landlords like to rent furnished is to avoid the main problems of the rent acts; and young people are less likely to stay for long periods. A young married couple may be quieter, which the landlord likes, but they may have a baby and decide not to leave for a while. Also landlords believe that if they want to sell the house they may have trouble getting a family to leave.

The rent you get from your tenants could help pay off your mortgage *and* your rates. Some building societies will not permit their cheints to rent any part of the mortgaged house, however. In any case it's a good idea to obtain prior permission before letting all or part of your mortgaged property. Of course houses constructed so as to provide self-contained flats carry a high premium. Conversions are also expensive, although you could get an improvement grant from the government.

The income you earn on tenants is taxable as earned income, if you provide service for the tenant and collect the rents yourself. (If you let an estate agent manage the property the income is taxed as unearned.) A point to remember when you let out part of your house concerns capital gains tax. The house must be your main residence, if you hope to avoid the tax on the sale. If the house is considered part investment, because you are earning income on it, you could jeopardize your situation when it is time to sell. The same problem might result if you take boarders in your house or flat.

There's also the chance of earning income on your house or flat by subletting it furnished while you're away: £75 to £100 per week for furnished houses or three- and four-bedroom flats is not unusual in central London.

Intangibles

There are certain things about owning a house or a flat that can't be measured in money terms. There's the pride one gets in owning something—a possession that no one can take away. As long as you continue to make the mortgage payments or until the lease expires, it's all yours. Then there's the independence you get when you own your own property: no landlord to bother with, and freedom to do with your property as you wish.

Lastly, there's the status and ego fulfillment aspect. Your image changes when you are a home-owner, both in your own mind and no doubt in the minds of others, as they view you. You're a better risk if you've got an asset in the form of a house.

Some of the Pitfalls

1) Financial Miscalculations

For some people, buying a house could be a financial disaster. Most people underestimate the real costs of buying a house. If you borrow £10,000 on a £12–13,000 house your interest payments alone could come to between £850 and £1000 per annum, depending on the source of the money. Add to this the premiums on the endowment repayment policy. The actual cost would depend on the person's age, the length of the policy and whether it is a with or without profits policy. On a £10,000 without profits policy maturing in twenty-five years, the cost annually is about £260. On a with profits policy for the same period the annual premiums are about £370. This assumes a man is aged thirty at the start. The basic difference between the two is that the without profits policy is designed just to pay off the mortgage at maturity. The with profits, which is more expensive, is designed to give a nice capital sum at the end, in addition to a mortgage. The total outlay before tax reliefs on a £10,000 mortgage is, therefore, between £1100 and £1400. The sum could be greater for an older man.

Even on a building society mortgage repayment plan, the annual repayment outlay would be around 10 per cent of the sum borrowed before tax reliefs. A mortgage protection policy, to insure the mortgage is repaid even if the money earner dies, can add £15 per annum to protect a £10,000 mortgage.

When you add to this the solicitor's fees, stamp duties, land registry fees, surveyor's fees, moving costs, and possible conversions and renovations, you've got quite an outlay—and one that most people underestimate.

Once in your home you've got heating and electricity costs, maintenance, decoration, insurance and other related outgoings. It could become quite a headache for those who don't have adequate resources. A good accountant can work it all out for you in money terms. It might be a worthwhile exercise.

2) Wrong House, Wrong Site, Wrong District

The number of people who buy houses that are overpriced, too small, poorly constructed or, even worse, falling apart are legion. There's the case of the man who put his life savings into a house without checking with the local council whether road construction was planned for the area. Sure enough, a major road was constructed within a few streets, too close to give his house any resale value but not close enough to get anything from the council for blight. He then found he had to move because of his livelihood and couldn't find a buyer at any price. Then there is the multi-millionaire who spent more to 'do up' his mansion than he did to purchase the freehold. He 'over invested' and could not sell the house at the price he should have in order to gain any return on his investment.

So even if you've found the perfect house analyse the site and what's happening or may happen in your immediate vicinity. Buying a house or a long lease on a flat in the wrong district could also make you regret your purchase. If the location's bad from the transportation point of view, with no bus or tube line, you'll have to depend on having one or two cars at your disposal. Or you'll be forced to use taxis all the time. And what about schools and other amenities? Does the neighbourhood depress you? Do you enjoy walking through the streets? What about crime in the area? These are all important questions that you've got to consider.

A final problem in choosing a home is the consideration of a house if offered with sitting tenants. These tenants are protected by the rent acts and are almost impossible to remove. The house may seem a bargain, but stay away. Unless you are very young and are interested in the house primarily as an investment, not as your residence, only settle for a house with vacant possession throughout—even the oldest people can live for another twenty years. Our neighbour is ninety-six—and she goes out to market every day and is as fit as anyone years younger.

3) Having to Move Too Soon

A serious problem could harass the house or flat purchaser who finds he has to move out soon after settling in. Unless your house or flat is in a very desirable location where prices skyrocket every few months (and there are few such areas) you may find that moving in a rush can cost you money. All the settling in and mortgage costs would be lost. Some mortgage lenders impose a penalty for paying off a mortgage in the early years of the loan. And if it's an endowment mortgage your first two or three years of payments probably won't have built up a cash value, so you may lose your first few premiums.

If your life is such that you may have to pick up and move house at the drop of a hat, choose a place to live which provides easy exits at low costs.

4) Restrictions in the Deed or Lease

If you are going to the expense of buying a freehold or a long lease you want to be sure you can use the property as you see fit. Before going ahead with any purchase get your solicitor to review the deed on a freehold purchase, or the lease on a leasehold house or flat. If you are taking over someone else's mortgage be sure to understand the terms contained therein. You'd be surprised at what you might discover you are bound to do in some of these legal documents (see the section on *The Legal Maze*, p. 275).

Pros and Cons

In the search for your ideal home you'll be faced with some alternatives. Here are some things to consider:

House versus Flat

All things considered a house makes more sense than a flat. Houses tend to appreciate in value faster than flats, because the demand for family houses is greater. But in central London a house may just be out of the question cost wise, so if you can't afford a £30,000 or £50,000 house in central London you'd be better off spending £15,000 on a house in an improving area, rather than choosing an expensive but smaller flat in an area that has already 'arrived'. If the address is all that important to you, and you can't afford a house, you'll have to settle for a flat or a maisonette on a long lease. If you do choose a flat make sure it is large—the bigger the better. It should have at least three or four bedrooms. Small flats, except in the very centre of London, are difficult to resell and don't appreciate in value as fast as large flats. In general, avoid flats with leases under fifty years. You'll have trouble getting finance and reselling it later. Check the maintenance charges, ground rent, and rates (the outgoings). You may find yourself paying £10–15,000 for a lease and then paying £1500 for annual outgoings. If this is the case it may pay you to take an expensive unfurnished flat on a shortish lease and pay a small fixtures and fittings charge. You can invest the difference between the fixtures and fittings charge and the premium, and come off better.

Leasehold versus Freehold

To be your own landlord in the pure sense, you've got to buy your house or flat on a freehold basis, for you will then be the absolute owner and not just a leaseholder. Of course, holding a lease for 99 or 999 years means you'll be the owner of the property for the whole of your lifetime, which is about as far as one can plan ahead these days. Those worried about future claims imposed on one's descendants should think only of freehold property, although finding freehold property in some parts of London is nearly impossible. In areas where the majority of land is owned by the great estates you can only buy leasehold.

Leasehold houses tend to be more difficult to finance than freehold houses. Although the reverse is true with flats—freehold flats are almost impossible to finance. In fact you will not see many freehold flats on the market.

Purpose-built versus Conversion

This refers to buying a flat in a house that was originally built for flats—purpose-built—as opposed to the more recent invention of converting a single unit house into several self-contained flats. Conversions are of a mixed quality. The ones converted thirty to fifty years ago are a lot better than the ones done today. Many speculators nowadays buy large private houses and convert them as cheaply as possible into self-contained flats. Then they occupy them one at a time and sell them off on long-term leases, thereby avoiding the problems of the rent acts and capital gains tax. They avoid the tax because they can claim that the house was their sole residence, but they can't get away with this tactic too often because they might be accused of being a property dealer. One would have to be careful not to get caught out by Section 588 of the Taxes Act of 1970, which is specially designed to prevent people avoiding tax on property development. Unfortunately such flats are rarely put together with the same care as the tax avoidance scheme. Before considering a converted flat get a qualified surveyor to take a careful look at it.

Another problem with converted flats is that financing for them is more difficult than for purpose-built flats. The rooms have strange shapes and the flats have inconvenient layouts with walls that are too thin. If at all possible, buy a long lease in a long-established block of flats. They're more expensive but they're worth it. When you get ready to sell you'll realize why.

Central London versus Suburbs

To some people the definition of the centre of residential London is Mayfair. At one time Bloomsbury was the place to live. And there are some who say Hampstead or Highgate is the ultimate in residential London. Ask a trendy couple in the King's Road where's the best place to live in London and they'll probably say Chelsea, Kensington, or Notting Hill. People have as many different ideas about living areas as they do about clothes or restaurants.

There's no doubt that it's more exciting living in the heart of things. It's also noisier and a lot more expensive. The suburbs are nearer to the green belt, and recreational areas. On the financial side both houses and flats in central London tend to appreciate in value faster and hold their value better than their counterparts in the suburbs.

Many people say if you're going to live in a city live near its most vital part—the part that's throbbing with the best the city can offer: great shopping, entertainment, an infinite variety of restaurants and interesting people. Most of these delights can only be found within ten minutes of Hyde Park. But if you can't live within fifteen minutes of Hyde Park by car, tube or taxi then it's probably a lot pleasanter living in the country and really commuting than living on the fringes of central London in a boring bedroom borough. But this kind of discussion of country versus suburbs versus city could go on forever!

Old versus New

New houses, if you can find them, can be an excellent choice, as compared with older houses. Although older houses have more space and charm than new ones, they also have more inherent problems. For one thing, old houses have none of the modern conveniences that new houses have already built-in: things like central heating, modern kitchens and bathrooms, and proper insulation. The roof could be a big expense on an old house. The outside walls may need upgrading, and the wiring and plumbing may be totally inadequate. To bring an old house up to modern standards costs a lot of money. And even then it may never be as good as new. Heating costs are higher in old houses—the weather comes in and your heat goes out—so don't underestimate them. They could make a big dent in your budget.

A new house is like a new car. There's something clean and exciting about it. An old house is like an antique, plenty of character for which you pay a premium. Older houses in need of repair can often be bought fairly inexpensively in some areas. Islington, Camberwell, and Camden are good areas for rehabilitating old houses, but nearly all the old houses have been completely modernized in the very centre of London.

A Common Sense Strategy for Being your own Landlord

1) Decide where you want to live and move into the area temporarily, to get the best accessibility to houses coming on the market.
2) Determine what you can afford to spend.
3) Try to arrange your financing in advance.
4) Plan your search as thoroughly as a war campaign.
5) When you see what you want act quickly—he who hesitates is definitely lost in this game.

In this competitive house hunting market even your best friends can let you down. One couple tell a story of an incident involving the purchase of a friend's house. The price was settled and everything seemed ready for contract. Then the friends backed out at the last minute. It turned out that someone else had offered them a few hundred pounds more. When the couple said: 'Why didn't you bother to ask us if we would pay more?' the house sellers gave no answer. And that was the end of a beautiful friendship.

Yet another couple tell of the numerous bottles of champagne they drank, each to celebrate the purchase of a house. After each one of six celebrations, the prospective buyers were told the house they had agreed to buy wasn't for sale—the owners just wanted to find out the going market prices for their precious properties. But all the champagne drinking was not in vain, for the couple eventually bought a house in the beautiful Vale of Health, on Hampstead Heath.

Essential House Hunting Aids

An Introduction on how to Read the Classified Advertisements

Your first and best friend in London is certainly the newspapers' classified advertisement sections for flats and houses—no one helps you more than they do to get an accurate picture of the property market at the moment you are looking.

The Times, on Wednesday and Thursday, and the *Evening Standard*, on Friday in particular, are the best bets for London flats. The *Sunday Times* is good for every kind of property. Some flat and house hunters have also found the *London Weekly Advertiser* and *Dalton's Weekly* useful as well.

The first edition of the *Evening Standard* is available at 9.30 a.m., outside 47 Shoe Lane, E.C.4. The first edition of *The Times* is available at 10 p.m., the night before, at the back entrance of the Times Building, Printing House Square, E.C.4. *The Times* is circulated to the few newsagents who are open at night around eleven o'clock. Some people swear by their local newspapers, others find them useless. The same ambivalence applies to the flat advertisements which appear on newsagents' and stationers' notice boards.

The classifieds, useful though they are, can be misleading, so learn to read between the lines, or to question the flat or house owner thoroughly before you run to view his property. You'll save time, and face far fewer frustrations. Suspect an agent who advertises that hundreds of flats are available, for you will soon find that you're lucky if any agent—even the biggest and best— really has even a few flats to suit you at one moment in time.

The wording of an advertisement can be misleading. An advertisement for a Hampstead flat may turn out to be West Hampstead, an entirely different and separate part of the world. An Eaton Square address may turn out to be 'near Eaton Square'. Earl's Court, which is technically part of Kensington, is a far cry from the 'heart' of Kensington.

Concentrate on the postal code numbers after the addresses, for there are numerous Chesters and Gloucesters and other such names in London, often in far-flung parts. You want to be certain you're heading for the correct one!

If an advertisement mentions no specific times for telephoning, you can be fairly certain the advertisement was placed by an agency, not an individual.

A Glossary Guide

Hopefully, this glossary guide will help you through the sort of crossword puzzle which the classified advertisements can appear to be at first reading! You will quickly learn to talk the lingo of the estate agent and the property seller. You will learn about all this because you have to in this highly competitive world of the house and flat hunter.

The estate agents and property professionals have created their own little language, no doubt to confuse the rest of the world. After qualifying to add 'F.R.I.C.S., F.I.Arb, F.S.V.A., B.Sc. (Estate Management)' after one's name (letters of status in surveying, valuing, auctioneering, land, property, or estate managing) one is then expected to use words such as 'rack rents', 'assignments', and 'covenants'.

This glossary is not intended to make you an expert on property. But it may help you to sound like one. If you're not out to impress anyone, at least you'll be able to communicate with those in the business. And you'll also have a lot more fun reading the classifieds and the particulars on property, because you'll be able to understand more fully what you're reading.

All Mod. Cons—see *Modern Conveniences*.

Amenity Society—a local action group set up by the concerned residents of a district. The group attempts to preserve the area against the ever present danger of commercialism, traffic, noise, renovation and redevelopment. Amenity societies are good sources of information on what's happening in an area.

American Kitchen—the landlord thinks he has a real Hollywood set for a kitchen: lovely formica work areas, big fridges and cooker, built-in cupboards and maybe even a wall oven. Must be seen to be believed.

Assignment—a way to transfer the responsibility for a lease to someone else.
Not all leases permit assignments. The ones that do normally need the landlord's consent, but he cannot withhold this unreasonably.

Bachelor Flat—a small flat, probably just big enough or best suited for a single man. May or may not be a suitable place for seduction, and may or may not even have a bedroom! Differs from a bedsit in that it is probably located in an elegant or picturesque area, and has a higher rent!

Basement (lower ground floor)—that part of a house or block of flats that is below ground level. Sometimes called 'garden level' in advertisements. These were originally the kitchen rooms of Victorian houses. Many converted houses have self-contained flats in the basement, usually less expensive than upper level flats. They can be dark, noisy, damp and tempting to burglars; or spacious, light and secluded with private back gardens.

B/Sit (bedsitter)—a one-room flatlet where the bedroom also serves as the reception room. It usually contains a separate bathroom or W.C., and kitchen facilities which may be just a hot plate and a tiny fridge. Or a bedsitter may be just a bedroom. Most bedsits are found in Earl's Court, Gloucester Road, Bayswater, and Notting Hill.

Bijou Residence—the estate agent believes the property to be a small 'jewel' of a house.

Capital Gains Tax—the tax one would normally pay on the profit made on the sale of an asset. Not payable if you sell a house or flat which is your principal residence.

C. & C. (carpets and curtains)—see *Fixtures and Fittings*.

CH, Central Heating—still the exception in Britain. Usually found in new homes, recently built blocks of flats, or converted properties. Most older property does not have a central heating system but relies on storage heaters or wall 'fires'. There are different types of heating systems, so try to test them under working conditions. Make sure heating is not partial (only to certain rooms), but is complete throughout the house. Especially check the bathroom to see if it has a hot towel rail. Many landlords charge for central heating in their service or maintenance charge, so check up on this.

Citizens' Advice Bureau—a voluntary organization that provides advice and information on many aspects of living in London.

Closing Order—the health officer of the local council can deem under the public health acts that a flat (especially true of basement flats) is not fit for human habitation. The property must then be brought up to certain standards. Basement flats are covered by underground room regulations. Before a closing order is rescinded there will be an inspection to determine whether the premises can be used as residential accommodation. The biggest cause of closing orders in basement flats is rising damp and lack of air and light. Before buying a flat check whether a closing order exists on any part of it by getting in touch with the health officer at your local council. Many closing orders are effected after a house changes hands, and an underground room is let by the new owners. Each council has complete discretion on when to impose a closing order.

Common Areas—those areas of a building shared by all the tenants, for example, the lift, stairs, roof, landings and outside patio or garden. The service charge to the tenant is to maintain these areas.

Communal Gardens—a private garden available to those who live in a garden square. A nice extra and a lovely feature of London living. Some gardens are more attractive and better maintained than others. However, the garden is not free of charge—the local council will charge you rates which are paid into a fund to maintain it.

CHW, Constant Hot Water—in many older flats hot water is not always available. Many landlords charge for constant hot water and you'll pay for it in your service charge. Sometimes CHW is provided by immersion heater or by Ascot-type heaters, paid for separately by the tenant.

Controlled Tenant—protected under the rent acts, usually in a dwelling with a rateable value of £40 or less in 1957. Many controlled tenants pay under £3 a week rent. A controlled tenant can be brought into the 'fair rent system' if the landlord makes certain improvements. If rent is increased it must be phased in over a number of years. Upon death, a controlled tenant's flat can pass onto another family member, and still be controlled, but upon the second death in the family, it becomes regulated. A controlled tenant has complete security of tenure and cannot be evicted without a court order, which is rarely issued.

Conversion—a flat or house, the present form of which bears little resemblance to the original form. Many are slapped together solely to make a quick profit. Conversions are normally frowned upon by building societies when mortgage money is tight.

Conveyance—transfer of ownership from seller to buyer of an unregistered freehold property or property subject to a lease.

Co-ownership—Housing Society—co-ownership accommodation is a cross between owning and renting. A housing society is a non-profit-making organization made up of members who have united to create housing which they will occupy—a sort of co-operative arrangement. You pay off the cost of the accommodation on a mortgage repayment type arrangement. When you want to leave, the housing society finds a new tenant to take over your payments. If you stay for at least five years you can receive a premium based on any appreciation in the value of the property. The advantages of co-ownership housing are: low cash outlay; freedom to move at relatively short notice; no arbitrary increase in rent; same tax relief as on buying a home; and repayment of the loan over a forty-year period. Therefore you can get lower monthly payments, and a sense of belonging to a group which has your interests at heart.

For more information on co-ownership or lists of housing societies with such developments in the London area write to: The Housing Corporation (South-East Regional Office), 122 King's Road, S.W.3 or phone 589 8201.

Cottage —a small terrace house, usually with two storeys and no basement. Once poor working-men's houses with outside toilets, now very popular as converted homes for trendy couples.

Covenant —a clause in a lease or deed which binds someone to do or not to do something (restrictive). For example, in Crown Estate leases on Regent's Park, a tenant is bound to paint the outside stucco every four years.

Cul-de-Sac —a dead-end street; no through traffic and therefore very quiet. Usually a very quaint and charming place to live. In the suburbs the name has been used loosely in developments of modern 'semis'.

Dilapidations —on the expiry of a lease, when a property reverts to the land-lord, certain repairs may be necessary. If these repairs are the responsibility of the tenant, and are not carried out, the landlord has the right to recover a sum of money to cover the costs of such repairs. This charge is called dilapidations.

D/K, Dining Room and Kitchen —an accommodation where you need not eat in the kitchen. The dining room may be an alcove or a completely separate room.

Discrimination —is illegal on account of race, colour, or creed (consult the Race Relations Board). Landlords find ways of discriminating none the less. Used against long-haired or flamboyant types, young bachelors and single girls. Couples with pets or children may also be discriminated against.

Duplex —a flat with rooms on two floors; often called a maisonette.

Dutch Auction —when the owner (or the agent) of a property in heavy demand gets the prospective buyers to bid against each other, thus forcing the price skyward. Legal but not ethical.

Excellent References Essential —a device used by landlords to frighten away undesirable tenants (see discrimination). To avoid problems make sure you have friendly solicitors, bank managers and employers to write a few kind words about your respectability and liquidity.

Family Preferred —the landlord doesn't want single people.

Fixtures and Fittings (F. & F.) —permanent parts of a house or flat that can be sold along with the property—radiators, fireplaces, flooring, cup-boards, tiling. May also include carpets and curtains and anything else built into the premises, like a fitted kitchen. The price seldom bears a real relation-ship to the value of the things left behind. The F. & F. fee is often called a premium.

Flatlet —small self-contained flat. Usually found in a period house where the owner has converted the dwelling into separate two-room flats.

Freehold —the absolute ownership of property, the house and the land. The ideal form of property ownership.

Full Repairing Lease (F.R.L.) —the tenant has an obligation to keep the premises in good state of repair. At the end of the lease the tenant must leave things as he found them, or as things were when the lease was originally written. Could be an expensive undertaking. The lease may even require improving the property. The landlord has the right to enforce the dilapidation charge for work not done.

Garden Flat—may be a basement flat in disguise or a lovely flat opening on to a private garden or terrace. Garden apartments provide easy access for burglars and must be properly secured.

Gazumping—a buyer finds out from the seller that his offer, having been accepted verbally, has now been refused. He has been gazumped! Original verbal agreement is legal but unenforceable and the would-be purchaser gets stuck with survey and mortgage costs and solicitor's fees. Try to get something in writing when you make an offer. At least get the seller to agree in writing to let you meet higher bids that occur prior to exchange of final contracts. A law forbidding gazumping may soon be passed by Parliament.

Ground Rent (G.R.)—the rent paid to the landlord or the freeholder by a leaseholder or tenant who owns a leasehold property, either held on a long lease or originally let on a long lease, i.e., more than twenty-one years. Ground rent is usually under £100 per annum.

Improvement Grants—provided by the local council. The provisions are outlined in the Housing Act of 1969. The grants, standard and discretionary, provide money for installing basic amenities like basins, baths and toilets, and also for complete renovations. Grants from £15 to £1200 are available.

Integral Garage—part of the main house, not down the road or in a mews behind the house.

Inventory—official list of everything provided when you move into a furnished flat. Very important to check the list with the landlord or agent when you start your lease. When you move out you'll be liable for any damages or missing articles. Landlord can also hold you responsible for cleaning, if flat is not left as clean as you found it.

Investment Property—a house or block of flats purchased solely for investment purposes and not for personal occupation. The investment quality comes from a combination of the rental income as a yield on the capital invested, less expenses, plus the capital growth on the property itself. Should be a freehold or long lease.

KB, Kitchen and Bath—you need never be unwashed or unfed. Some flats provide only a hot plate, and toilet down the corridor, believe it or not!

Leasehold—ownership of property for a fixed period of time granted by the lease. A leaseholder may be obliged to pay rent, called ground rent, for the land on which the property stands. A tenant of a long lease (over twenty-one years) is entitled, in certain circumstances, under the Leasehold Reform Act of 1967, either to buy the freehold or extend the lease for another fifty years (does not apply to flats).

Lower Ground Floor—see Basement.

Maisonette—a flat or any other separate dwelling on more than one floor, but not taking up the entire building; sometimes called a duplex. Can be very expensive but worth it if you like spaciousness and the combination of a city flat and a multi-storey house. In some suburban areas, with new residential developments, a maisonette is any flat which has its own private entrance from the road.

Mews House—a small house converted from stables or coachmen's lodgings. Found in back streets behind large city houses. Some have been done up with flower boxes and hanging lamps. The houses are small and often devoid of direct sunlight.

Mixed Area—has some lovely houses and streets, and some dreary sections.

Also may refer to the racial composition of the area. A good example of a mixed area is North Kensington and Notting Hill.

Mxd Flt/Mixed Flat—a flat shared by boys and girls or men and women, all living happily together under one roof.

Mod. Cons, modern conveniences—don't expect a refrigerator, cooker, washer, or a drier. More likely means heating, hot water and a bathroom.

Notice to Quit—a formal way of asking you to leave. In furnished tenancies, or unfurnished where the ratable value is under £400, the landlord must give the tenant a 'notice to quit' on a date which coincides with the end of the period of the tenancy.

Outgoings—the total direct cost of living in a flat or house. Includes rent, rates, service and maintenance charges and mortgage repayments.

Part. CH, Partial Central Heating—while it's better than no heat at all, partial central heating can be a bit uncomfortable. Partial central heating may be adequate on cool days but when it gets really cold it can be totally unsatisfactory. Don't pay for central heating unless it's complete.

Patio/Roof Garden—a small garden, usually paved, where the owner has made the most of little space.

Peppercorn—used when referring to a nominal or non-existent rent. Often when someone pays a great deal for a house he's told the ground rent is a 'peppercorn', as an added incentive to close the deal.

Period House—usually refers to a house built prior to the First World War. Victorian or Georgian period houses are the most common. There's nothing modern about a period house unless the inside has been done up.

PH., Phone—if it's advertised it's probably of the pay phone or coin box variety. Good if you're sharing a flat. To get a new phone installed takes some time, depending on your area.

Pied-à-Terre—a small convenience flat in the centre of things. Useful for a rendezvous. Popular with the well-heeled country folk who keep a *pied-à-terre* in the city for shopping trips, theatre parties, and the like.

Planning Consent or Permission—prior to making a change to your property or building, or altering its use, you must, under the town and country planning act, get permission from the local authority. Consult your local council or Citizens' Advice Bureau.

Porterage—a handy service that you pay for either directly or indirectly. Includes things like litter removal, mail and newspaper delivery, minor repairs and other useful aids. It helps to have a pleasant porter who's around to perform services. Make sure you get to know him, and don't forget him at Christmas.

Premium—key money asked for a flat or the lease on a flat. Not legal under the rent control laws for London flats with a ratable value of £400 or less. Because of the scarcity of decent unfurnished flats premiums are being charged to give tenants assignments or even an introduction to the landlord. Some people disguise premiums as 'fixtures and fittings'. If the flat is rent controlled you aren't required to pay any more than a fair market price for anything left in the premises. One could use legal avenues to recover a premium illegally charged. Consult your solicitor.

Preservation House—many London houses, because of their historical or architectural distinction, are under preservation order. Houses within 'conservation areas' are similarly protected. The grades of protection vary from one to three. Alterations, either internally or externally to these houses must be approved by the local authorities. Grade one houses normally cannot be touched, either internally or externally. In grade two houses, permission is often granted for internal modifications. With grade three houses minor external alterations are normally approved. If you rent or buy a house that is under preservation order you have a built-in insurance policy against property developers. Anyone can request that a house be put on preservation status. Houses built as recently as 1939 have been so designated. For more information contact your local council or G.L.C.

Protected Tenant—a tenant whose accommodation falls within the protection of the rent acts. Normally applies to any accommodation whose rateable value is under £400 in London.

Purpose-Built Block—something built originally to be a block of flats and not converted to flats from something else. It is easier to obtain a mortgage for purpose-built blocks than for conversions.

Quarterly in Advance—the traditional way rent is paid. A good custom for the landlord.

Rack Rent—a term referring to a rent approximately equal to the full annual market value. Generally applied to rent on short leases. Has come to mean an outrageous rent.

Rates, ratable value—rates are a form of tax paid by anyone occupying a flat or house. Some landlords include the rates in the rent, especially with furnished property. The rates go to the local council and in London almost 50 per cent are passed on to the Greater London Council. Rates are used to pay for housing, education, health, roads and other essential services. The rates one pays depend on the ratable value of the property, which is assessed by the valuation officer who works for the Inland Revenue. All properties are revalued every few years. Depending on the ratable value of your house or flat it is either regulated or unregulated by the rent acts. Renovating, converting or redecorating your house or flat can have an influence on its ratable value, although size is the most common factor considered. Each council sets its own local rate which is expressed as so many pence in the pound. To determine the rates payable, simply multiply the ratable value by the local rate. Rates are not payable if buildiders are working on your house and you're not living there. If the house is ready to be lieved in but you haven't moved in, rates can be assessed. Refunds can be claimed on over-payments with a six-year statute of limitations.

Recep., Reception Room—a main room other than a bedroom or kitchen. Theoretically the room where one entertains or receives guests. Some flats or houses have two or three reception rooms.

Regulated Tenancy—unfurnished tenancy with a ratable value of not more than £400 in London. A 'fair rent' for a regulated tenancy is registered with the local council's rent officer, and cannot be increased or reviewed more frequently than every three years. A landlord cannot fix a 'fair rent' solely by getting a tenant to agree to the rent. If landlord has been overcharging, tenant has right to be reimbursed.

Rendering—the plaster or stucco work done on the outside of a house. It's used for ornamentation and in imitation of stonework. May be used to cover up bad bricks.

Rent Book—a receipt book, kept by the tenant, which the landlord uses to acknowledge rent paid.

Rent Reviews—covenant in a lease which gives the landlord the right to review the rent and increase it, in keeping with market conditions. On an unregulated flat the review can be done as often as is agreed in the lease—

normally three to five years.

S/C, Self Contained—a flat that is entirely self sufficent and separate from other flats or from the main house. Usually has its own entrance, bathroom or W.C., and kitchen facilities. Self-contained flats are normally furnished and very often are located in the basement of a converted house.

S/D, Semi Detached—a house attached on one side to another house, usually of the same design.

Service Charge —the charge levied by a landlord over and above rent and rates to cover the costs of a porter, central heating, and other conveniences and amenities.

Service Flat —a furnished, self-contained flat. The landlord provides basic. services like linen supply, front desk, mail, telephone and often daily cleaning. Excellent arrangement on a temporary basis, while you're looking for an unfurnished flat or house.

Shrg, Sharing—a convenient way to save on rent. Room or flat mates of the same sex or of opposite sex share accommodation. Very popular with the young single set.

Shower—no bath available, so you'd better like taking showers.

Sitting Tenants—controlled or regulated tenants with security of tenure granted under the rent control acts. They cannot be forced to vacate the premises.

Slot meters—mechanisms placed in furnished flats and bedsitters to regulate the use of gas and electricity. The tenant pays for units by inserting appropriate coins. By law landlord is allowed a fixed percentage on the meters.

Squatters—an ancient law protects a squatter who comes across a piece of vacant property and settles in. The landlord cannot regain possession by force. The law dates back to 1831 and states that if a squatter stays for twelve years the property is his to hold or to sell. Don't plan on being able to do this in London.

Stamp Duty—a tax paid by the purchase of property to the Inland Revenue. Only paid on houses or premiums of over £10,000: 25p per £50 up to £15,000 and 50p per £50 thereafter. Also paid on the basis of the rent payable on a lease.

Studio —one big room used as reception room, bedroom and kitchen. Bedsit is the more popular term.

Suburban —generally means bourgeois. Not usually a compliment if a house or piece of furniture is described as suburban.

Terrace House —a house attached on both sides to other houses. In a true terrace, the houses are all part of a single design.

3/4 beds or 2/3 receps —six rooms in all. You decide how you want to divide them. Either more bedrooms or more reception rooms.

To View or Viewing—giving a house or flat the once-over.

Town House—usually a modern terraced house on three or more floors. Contains a garage, kitchen and dining room on ground floor, and reception room and bedrooms on upper floors.

Vacant Possession —a house that is completely empty. No sitting tenants when it changes hands.

Water Rates—Sometimes included in the general rates or paid separately to the Water Board, to cover cost of water used in a flat or house. Usually charged as a percentage of ratable value.

Wrighton Kitchen—status symbol kitchen: formica cupboards and work surfaces.

Accommodation Agencies or Bureaux

Location	Price
FULHAM	£14.70
HOLLOWAY	£18
BAYSWATER	£6
HENDON	£17
STAMFORD HILL	£13.50
STREATHAM	£5.50
FINCHLEY	£7.50
WEMBLEY	£25
GOLDERS GREEN	£16
EALING	£21
HOLLAND PARK	£7
KENSINGTON	£24
ISLINGTON	£20
PUTNEY	£3
CENTRAL AREAS	FROM £1.50 – 18
SHEPHERDS BUSH	£9
ACTON	£14
CLAPHAM COMM.	£8.50
MAYFAIR	£16.80
WANDSWORTH	£4
WILLESDEN	£5
KEW GARDENS	£10.50
HOLBORN	£15
PUTNEY	£16.80
EARLS COURT	£6
HAMPSTEAD	£4
KENSINGTON	£12.60
BAYSWATER	£11
KENSINGTON	£15.75
HAMPSTEAD	£9.50
STOCKWELL	£11.50
NOTTING HILL GATE	£12.50
FULHAM	£5
PUTNEY	£13
EDGWARE ROAD HOUSE!	£25
BARNES	£20

If you are lucky you will find your furnished flat to let through an advert placed privately in the newspaper; or through a friend or acquaintance who is leaving his London abode for just the few months when you will be needing accommodation. Or you will come upon one of these charming houses with a sign: 'furnished residential chambers' or 'furnished service suites' and find your temporary living quarters within.

If you aren't lucky enough to find a flat in any of the above ways, then you will find yourself, of necessity, working with accommodation agencies or bureaux, the primary holders of furnished flats in London.

The accommodation bureau phenomenon is not nearly so old-established as estate agency, and you are likely to find a few more bad seeds among the former. Accommodation bureaux or agencies are not licensed by the government, nor do they have their own professional organization with any sort of 'good conduct' code.

Since the birth of accommodation bureaux, the practice of charging a fee to both the landlord and the tenant—about a week's rent from both—has been standard. Charging a tenant a 'finding' fee for finding him an unfurnished flat was considered illegal, under the Accommodation Agencies Act of 1953.

In spring 1971, however, a Court of Appeal decision brought to the public attention the fact that it is illegal for an estate agent or accommodation agency to demand a commission from a would-be tenant for any kind of accommodation. The landlord pays the accommodation agency a fee, if it finds a tenant for his flat. So the whole situation of fee paying is in a bit of a muddle at the time of writing, and you will have to tread cautiously among the various accommodation agencies.

The line between accommodation agent and estate agent is sometimes a very fine one. In some cases, it will be quite clear that you are dealing with an estate agent, for he will tell you he deals exclusively in properties for sale, and has only a few furnished flats, for his clients who are house hunters and require temporary accommodation.

On the other hand, a man who deals almost exclusively in furnished and unfurnished flats to let may call himself an estate agent, not an accommodation bureau, and completely confuse any definition which attempts to separate the two.

It is clear that accommodation agencies do not have sterling reputations. Journalists, with increasing frequency, are revealing the agencies' tactics, which are most unpleasant. For instance, the 'operations manual' for the interviewers in one accommodation agency was reported to be filled with instructions intended to deceive the client looking for a flat. The interviewer has at her fingertips a box of cards, which the client assumes to be particulars of flats available. The manual instructs her to leaf through twenty to forty cards to find two 'real' or 'live' cards. And the interviewer has instructions how to dismiss the client's curiosity in the 'other cards', which she has flipped through and ignored.

Though all accommodation agencies do not have a commendable reputation, you will none the less find yourself working with them as you go about your hunt for a furnished flat. Here are some tips regarding that relationship:
1) Do not pay anyone a 'registration fee'. Such a fee is certainly illegal. The money you pay as a registration fee is no guarantee that the agency will find a flat for you. Seldom is that registration fee refundable, nor is it applicable to the one week's rent you may be asked to pay the agency once it has found you a flat.
2) Do not attempt to get anything accomplished by phone with an accommodation agency. You must go round in person for the initial meeting, and 'register' with the agency. This is simply a matter of signing a card, not paying a fee.
3) Accustom yourself, difficult as it may be, to hearing this comment on the advertisement which prompted you to phone the agency in the first place: 'I'm sorry, that flat has just gone. But why don't you come round and we'll tell you about the other flats which are available.'
4) Accommodation bureaux go in and out of business with the same frequency as fashion boutiques. How to know if you're on to a good one? Come right out and ask for the name of a satisfied former customer who would give you a recommendation. Or ask the interviewer a bit about the history of his agency—how long it has been in business for instance. This kind of close scrutiny is really the only form of protection the consumer, in this case the flat hunter, has in dealing with accommodation bureaux. If the agency will not co-operate with you in your questions and attempts to protect yourself, then perhaps it is not the one with which to work.

Accommodation agencies fall into two distinct breeds, and you will learn to recognize them immediately:
1) Those dealing with the huge bed-sit populous of London, and the share-a-flat crowd. Up to now, the tenant has paid a 'finding fee' of a week's rent.
2) The posh agencies, which advertise in *The Times* and the *International*

Herald Tribune, and which specialize in luxury-furnished and beautifully-located flats to let. Seldom will the posh agency, charging up to £300 a week for a flat, ask the would-be tenant for a fee. The landlord pays a commission to the agency.

A Directory of Accommodation Agencies

Remember that some of these accommodation bureaux will call themselves estate agents, but the fact that a large proportion of their business is in short lets on furnished flats means they are eligible for this list. It is impossible to make any sort of complete or up-to-date list of agencies, for they open and close too frequently. Here, however, is a list of some of the best. We have personal recommendations from clients of all these agencies:

Albinella Ltd, 36 Curzon Street, W.1, 629 9803: luxury flats

The Apartment Centre, 181 Earl's Court Road, S.W.5, 370 4044

Around Town Flats, 120 Holland Park Avenue, W.11, 229 7924: run by a group of ex-Ramblers employees

T. Maskell & Co.—At Home in London Ltd, 107 Walton Street, S.W.3, 581 2216: have been known to place fresh flowers in the flats of their clients

Bloodhounds, 4 Cromwell Mews, S.W.7, 589 6658

Crouch & Lees, 45 New Bond Street, W.1, 493 9941

J. Edwards and Co., 16 Berkeley Street, W.1, 493 2556

Evelyn Keyes A.B., 32 Shaftesbury Avenue, W.C.2, 437 7364

Ferrier and Davies, 6 Beauchamp Place, S.W.3, 584 3232

F. W. Gapp and Co., 54 Lower Sloane Street, S.W.1, 730 9245

George Knight, 9 Heath Street, N.W.3, 435 2298

Harrods Estate Agency, 34 Hans Crescent, S.W.1, 589 1490

Hunter and Co., 23 Brook Street, W.1, 629 1087: luxury flats

James and Jacobs, 94 Jermyn Street, S.W.1, 930 0261

Jonathan David and Co., 12 New Bond Street, W.1, 499 9206

King, Wood and Co., 116 Ebury Street, S.W.1, 730 6191: luxury furnished

London Accommodation Bureau (incorporating Ramblers), Berketex House, 309 Oxford Street, W.1, 629 9499; branch at 15 Hogarth Place, S.W.5, 373 0668.

Organization Unlimited (Freelance Personal Assistants) (Membership only), 88 Cadogan Place, S.W.1, 235 8356: ask for Willow. This organization will find you a flat, and anything else you want—and will charge you for their efforts. Seventy-five per cent of their clients are show business people.

Place Setter, 31 Haymarket, S.W.1, 839 6958: multi-service agency for housing, travel, hotels, etc.

Raymond Kerry, 19 Seymour Place, W.1, 723 6496

Robin Hilton and Co., 24 Curzon Street, W.1, 493 8841: luxury flats

Selected Accommodation Ltd, 23 Dryden Chambers, 119 Oxford Street, W.1, 734 2231

Up-West Flat Service, 71 Oxford Street, W.1, 493 0373: open seven days a week

Wasps and Co., 40 Beauchamp Place, S.W.3, 584 6863

For Flat Sharers

Flat Sharers, 116 Brompton Road, S.W.3, 584 0395

Share-a-Flat Ltd, 175 Piccadilly, W.1, 493 2545.

Possible changes are imminent in this accommodation agency game, all because of the new publicity and attention which has been directed to the Accommodation Agency Act of 1953:

1) The law may be modified to permit agencies to charge a fixed fee to the tenant for finding a flat, in which case the agencies will have to become licensed.

2) The landlords will use advertising and try to let flats on their own, rather than pay a fee to an accommodation agency to find tenants for them.

3) Perhaps nothing will change, and the agencies will go on charging a fee, and tenants will go on paying because a) it's a sellers' market these days; and b) people are still not entirely aware of the law.

4) Agents may decide to work only for tenants who instruct them to find suitable accommodation. Then the agent may charge the R.I.C.S. scale fees of 2.5 per cent.

Estate Agents

Property is a traditional business in England. And the buying and selling of property (residential or commercial) is well settled into the hands of estate agents, as is most of the letting of high-rent unfurnished flats. The agent through whom one rents a flat is usually the manager of the entire block of flats, which means he's in charge of mending the roof as well as collecting rents. It is his duty to screen prospective tenants for the landlord.

So before you've even begun your search, you will happen upon the term, or this man—the estate agent. When reading the papers, you may actually run across a house or flat for sale that specifies 'No Agents' as its final phrase. This indeed happens now and then, but not often. So you must familiarize yourself with the estate agent, because you will inevitably have to link up with one or more as you proceed.

Most of central London is owned by vast estates such as the Crown, the Church, descendants of the Crown and the Crown's favourites—dukes, earls, and lords, and insurance companies and property companies. Most of these 'landlords' link up with an estate agent on a long-term contract, and the agent takes on the complete management of the properties, be they flats; or the sale of the properties, be they houses. Whenever you see a 'flat for sale' or long lease for sale sign in front of a building, the name and address of the estate agent is always there in big bold type.

How Do You Choose Your Agent or Agents?

Often as you go about your search for a home, you may feel that you have absolutely no choice in the matter of which estate agent to deal with, for when you see an attractive property listed in the newspaper or with a board advertisement hanging in front, you must go to the particular agent named. You also may be frustrated by the fact that there are so very many estate agents. How can you learn who is best for you?

The most professional of the estate agents belong to the Royal Institution of Chartered Surveyors, R.I.C.S. It is safe to say they are the most professional, for they must pass a series of examinations, and when these are satisfactorily completed, the chartered surveyor's qualifications are equivalent to a university degree. Some professional societies—not the R.I.C.S.—will accept as members anyone who is buying or selling property, so do not let a row of letters after a name impress you, until you've asked what they mean. Remember, agents who are chartered surveyors are the most likely to give wholehearted service, with integrity. One other professional society whose members carry with them certain prestige is the Incorporated Society of Valuers and Auctioneers.

At first sight, you will have some idea of how professional an estate agent is. When we walked into an estate office in Dulwich, saw some of the old property deeds hanging on the wall, noticed every member of the staff was over fifty years of age, we knew in a moment the kind of agent we were meeting. Traditional. Tried and true.

In the estate agent business there are now a lot of dynamic young men as well, with trendy letterheads and glossy offices. They are building their reputations quickly by taking clients round in chauffeured cars and offering red-carpet service. You may prefer the new wave estate agent to the traditional.

Seek recommendations from anyone you know who's been flat or house-hunting recently. If you are new to London and don't know any such person, then frankly, just ask the agent when you meet him about some of his accomplishments. He'll be very quick to tell you about his glories.

There is a big difference between the slick West End agent who works with itinerant millionaires or landed gentry, and the small, local agent whose office seems in a permanent state of inefficiency. You must work with the agent who handles properties which parallel your life style. The elegant estate agents will be terribly polite to you if you phone or call, telling them of your need for an unfurnished flat at £1000 a year, but you can be almost certain that they will not work their heads off for you.

Because there are no stringent qualifications for the man who wants to set up an estate agency, you are bound to run into the 'bad seed', the questionable practitioner among all the other well-intentioned firms. This would happen in any area of life, so you cannot condemn the estate agency business. You may sometimes be annoyed that the estate agent seems more interested in his seller, who will pay the commission, than he is in you, the buyer or renter. Human nature? Occasionally you will read in the press of an estate agent who is not operating in the interest of the buyer, or the seller, but in his own!

Some house hunters have reported being sent to look at a house by an estate agent, and then learning from another that the same house was sold a week ago.

Canvassing is yet another well known, but not appreciated, practice of estate agents. Estate agents do a regular canvassing job of up and coming residential areas, asking people if they are intending to sell their houses, and then persuading them that it would be a good idea to do so, because the houses are of such high value in the market place.

All you can do if you run into the bad seed is to move on. There is always another agent round the corner in this highly competitive business.

What Will You Pay?

What makes the occasional difficulties in working with estate agents bearable is the fact that you do not have to pay a penny for their services, that is unless you instruct an agent to acquire for you a certain house, or a house on a certain street, and then put these instructions into writing. In this instance, you'll have to pay a fee to the agent. In all other instances, the owner or seller pays—even in flat renting. If you rent a £3000 a year flat in a modern block, the owner of that block pays 10 per cent of that £3000 to the estate agent. If you buy a house, the seller pays the agent's commission.

There are two scales payable to the agent who follows your instructions to find a house on a particular street, or the very house you want. If he simply negotiates for the house you pick out, and brings about a sale, you will pay £150 fee on a £10,000 house; £275 fee on a £20,000 house; £375 on a £30,000 house, the actual scale being 1.5 per cent on the first £15,000 and 1 per cent on the residue.

If, rather, the estate agent finds a house to suit you within a small area which you have specified, you will pay a scale fee, set by the R.I.C.S., which is slightly higher: £200 on a £10,000 house, £325 on a £20,000 house, and £425 on a £30,000 house. The actual scale is 2.5 per cent on the first £5000, 1.5 per cent on the next £10,000, and 1 per cent on the residue.

If an estate agent, who is not properly instructed or 'retained' by you does attempt to charge you a fee, or a percentage of the annual rent of a flat that he has on his books, he is acting illegally. In 1971 a Bond Street estate agent was held to be not entitled to recover commission from a man for whom he had found a flat at £950 a year. The estate agent had acted contrary to the Accommodation Agencies Act of 1953. This 1953 act is not nearly as well known as it should be to the public, and that is why a number of estate agents do manage to continue charging clients a fee for their services.

Once You've Found Them, How to Work With Them?

To work most effectively with estate agents in order to get the quickest results, look at this list of pointers:

1) Choose agents specializing in properties in the areas in which you think you'd like to live. If you choose to work with the Big Twelve agents who hold prestige properties all over central London, then don't expect a bargain, like a Georgian house near Hyde Park for £20,000. The small agent in Islington might come up with a bargain for you, but the agent with a red carpet in St James's will not. In the beginning, work with as many estate agents as you can keep up with. And go round London to see as many properties as you can. The quicker you become familiar with the market, and the neighbourhoods, the better. Eventually, you will work only with those who offer you the best service, i.e. the best properties.

2) Don't expect to accomplish anything by phone. The agent, after all, is responsible for vetting potential tenants or buyers, and he wants to have a good look at you. You may introduce yourself to the agent by telephone, but do go round to see him.

3) Know exactly what you and your family require in terms of space: three or four bedrooms, central heating, conveniences, outlook or view, garden space. Make certain that each agent you work with knows your requirements. Of course you must be flexible about the exact area in which you want these requirements. But once you've been to St John's Wood or Battersea a couple of times, you'll know whether it's the kind of place where you'd like to live. Knowing just what you want will save you much running round. From our experience, we know how hard the agents try to sell anything that's on their books—even properties they have never seen. If you want to see nothing but mews houses, make sure the agent knows this.

4) If an estate agent tells you a property you like is 'under offer', ask if you might see it anyway, if you're really keen on it. So often these property agreements fall through, and you'll be surprised by a phone call: 'That maisonette in Brompton Square is available now.' You'll have seen it, studied it, and be ready right away to say: 'We'll take it.'

5) Do not accept *No* easily from an agent who says he doesn't have what you want. He may not, on that particular day. But your phone call a few days later may just coincide with the moment when particulars of a suitable property land on his desk. Your regular phone calls show your serious interest. Get to know the local agents on a personal basis. Visit them often, and show you're seriously interested. And one day you'll get that magic call about a particularly interesting property *before* it goes out to the public. Then you'll know you've arrived.

6) Look at flats or houses in a somewhat higher price range than your maximum price. The owner could come down, if he's in a hurry, or having difficulty ridding himself of his property. Or you might put your price up, if a property

looks to be a particularly good investment for your money.

7) When an agent hands you a six-page list of properties for rent or sale, be sure to find out the length of time the flats or houses you like have been on the market. The really good properties go quickly. And you may want to do some in-depth questioning about a flat or house that's been on the market for six months, before you run off to see it. Efficient use of time will be one of your saviours as you set about your house hunt in London. Also, ask the estate agent if he has seen the property. You'll know you're working with a good man if he can describe the property to you as he has seen it.

8) It is not part of an agent's duty to warn you of the defects of a house or flat. The agent is employed by the owner. If you find an agent who will point out certain flaws to you, you are in luck.

9) If an estate agent is the manager of a block of flats in which you are interested, tell him of your interest. One clever Londoner got his eight-room flat overlooking a Kensington garden square, for *no* premium, in just this way. He wrote to the estate agent, then went to meet him explaining his interest in the flats in a particular building. When a tenant in the neighbouring building (which was exactly the same as the building the letter-writer liked) died, the agent offered the letter-writer the flat, without even putting the flat on the market.

10) An estate agent may come in handy later on, when you've been settled in a long time, and are considering letting your flat or house. If then you instruct an estate agent to find a tenant for your furnished flat or house on a term of less than twelve months, you will be charged 10 per cent of the rent, payable over the term. For that type of fee, you may ask the agent to help in reading of utilities, determining an amount for dilapidations, and advising on drawing up a proper agreement between you and your tenant. The 10 per cent fee does not include the compiling of an inventory list; this is always a separate charge. However, many people operate by letting their flats or houses through a newspaper advertisement, and then relying on a solicitor to do most of the other work.

The Big Twelve

Listed below are twelve estate agents who continually offer flats and houses in most parts of central London. Other agents may have an equally large turnover, but over a period of a year we found that these twelve advertised more residential properties in central London than anyone else in *The Times*, although many of them only deal in fairly high priced properties. (There are also some estate agents who are very active, but specialize in certain areas of London.)

Since the Big Twelve operate in so many areas the reader will, for the sake of convenience, find them referred to in the summary pages throughout the book simply as 'the Big Twelve'. We have also shown in the summaries where some of the Big Twelve pay special attention to specific districts, usually indicated by a branch office there.

Allsop & Co.	153 Park Road, N.W.8, 722 7101
	20 Montpelier Street, S.W.7, 584 6106
Roy Brooks	Moravian Corner, 359 King's Road, S.W.3, 352 0061
Chesterton & Sons	116 Kensington High Street, W.8, 937 1234
	26 Clifton Road, W.9, 289 1001
	40 Connaught Street, W.2, 262 7202

	2 Cale Street, Chelsea Green, S.W.3, 589 5211
Druce & Co.	Druce House, 54 Baker Street, W.1, 486 4241
W. A. Ellis	174 Brompton Road, S.W.3, 589 2425
Edward Erdman & Co.	6 Grosvenor Street, W.1, 629 8191
Folkard and Hayward	115 Baker Street, W.1, 935 7799
Gross, Fine & Krieger	27 Princes Street, W.1, 493 3993
Chalfen	
Hampton & Sons	6 Arlington Street, S.W.1, 493 8222
	21 Heath Street, N.W.3, 794 8222
	4 Hill Road, Wimbledon, S.W.19, 946 6464
Keith Cardale Groves	43 North Audley Street, W.1, 629 6604
& Co.	
Knight, Frank & Rutley	20 Hanover Square, W.1, 629 8171
John D. Wood and Co.	160 Kensington Church Street, W.8, 727 0705
	9 Cale Street, S.W.3, 352 1484
	23 Berkeley Square, W.1, 629 9050.

London Landlords — Who Owns London?

The greater part of central London is owned by a variety of dukes, lords, earls, viscounts, property companies, the Church and Crown commissioners, London governing bodies, and some schools, hospitals and insurance companies. The Crown, of course, is where it all started. And the Crown Estates Commissioners administer a fair chunk of Crown estate land.

While estate duties have whittled away a part of some of the major landowners' estates, most have weathered the storm of taxation, leasehold reform, legislation and other socialist-inspired methods designed to return the land to the people. Most of the estates have been in the same family for hundreds of years. One can learn a lot of tricks in five hundred years, especially when it comes to ways of holding onto property.

If you have some genius, plenty of money or access to some, and also plenty of time, you could join the ranks of the great estate holders. Joe Levy of Stock Conversion, a property company that owns Euston Centre near Euston Station, took almost six years and £16 million, including some 315 property negotiations, to put together this thirteen-acre Euston site. So it can be done. But who cares. Most of us are content to have a long lease on a flat or the freehold on our own house. While you may have no ambitions to be a great landowner let's see who is. It may give you some ideas in reaching your goal—finding the right flat or house. Some of the 'great estate' landowners are not bad landlords.

Some of the best-known landowners:

Viscount Portman owns more than 100 acres of London, currently valued at between £10 and £20 million. His Portman Estate covers the north side of Oxford Street from Selfridges to Marble Arch, and extends over nearly half the area bounded by Edgware Road, Marylebone Road, Marylebone High Street and Wigmore Street. Some of London's most prestigious squares are located therein: Montagu, Bryanston, Portman and Manchester. The estate used to be a great deal larger. But the death of the seventh Viscount in 1948, forced the sale in the early fifties of more than a hundred acres to meet an estate duty bill of £7.5 million.

The Earl of Cadogan of the Cadogan Estates owns a good part of Knightsbridge, Chelsea, most of Sloane Street and all of Cadogan Place and Cadogan Square, as well as a large part of the King's Road. In all, the estate is about 100 acres in size.

The Duke of Westminster who heads the Grosvenor Estate is probably the best man to know if you want to live in Mayfair or Belgravia. His estate includes about a hundred acres of Mayfair and nearly all Belgravia, two of London's prestige areas. The Grosvenor Estate is said to be worth nearly £100 million—with more than 10,000 properties, and 600 flats on Eaton Square alone. The Grosvenor Estate's most famous tenant is the U.S. government, for the American Embassy sits on Grosvenor Square. This is the only place in the world where the U.S. government does not own the property on which its Embassy is located.

A trip to the offices of the Grosvenor Estates may be worth while. It's near Claridges Hotel, at 53 Davies Street, W.1, 629 5782.

Lord Howard de Walden heads the de Walden Estate, consisting of about 110 acres of choice London property. The area is above Oxford Street, between Marylebone High Street and Great Portland Street. Its most famous street is no doubt Harley Street, London's most exclusive surgery. The estate requires that the top floor or, in some cases, two floors, of Harley Street houses remain residential. The de Walden Estate Office telephone number is ex-directory, and only handles the selling of long leases. Renting of flats is handled by agents, such as Elliott Son and Boyton, 86 Wimpole Street, W.1, 935 8191.

The Duke of Bedford heads the Bedford Estate. The Duke lives in Chester Terrace, Regent's Park, when in London, but his ancestral home is Woburn Abbey. He owns most of Bloomsbury. If you like learning, education, history and Georgian houses and squares, Bloomsbury is the place to live, though every year there is less of it for residential use. The Bedford Settled Estate Office is at 29a Montague Street, W.C.1.

The Church Commissioners administer the estate of the Church of England. In addition to its concern for spiritual matters, the Church of England owns a large amount of property. In London the Church Estate covers most of Maida Vale—a good hunting ground for inexpensive mansion-block flats. The estate also owns a good part of Paddington and Bayswater, known as the 'Hyde Park Estate'. Through some ambitious joint ventures with property developers, notably Max Rayne of London Merchant Securities, the Church lands are becoming quite fashionable. An example of this joint redevelopment is the area around Sussex Gardens, off the Edgware Road. A number of luxury tower blocks have recently been built there. The most exciting are the Water Gardens and the Quadrangle.

The Church has also been selling bits and pieces of its property, either to the present tenant or the highest bidder. The Bishop's Avenue in Hampstead, long known as Millionaires' Row, was once owned by the Church.

The Crown Estate Commissioners administer the Crown Estates for the Queen. The properties administered by the Crown Commissioners are among the most desirable in London. The Crown lands cover some of London's most exclusive streets: the land surrounding Regent's Park; and Kensington Palace Gardens where Princess Margaret lives. There is also St James's Park and the land under the elegant strip of flats bordering the east side of Green Park. In all the Crown owns about 4000 to 5000 properties in London, let out on long leases, and about 50 to 100 flats on short leases. The Crown Estate Commissioners are pretty tough landlords, however. If you live in one of the Nash houses on Regent's Park you're not permitted to make any structural changes, and you must repaint the outside stucco every four years. The Crown estates are exempt from, but in practice adhere to, most of the provisions of the Rent Acts, including the Leasehold Reform Act. The Crown Estate Office is in Whitehall, S.W.1, 839 2211.

Actually, none of these estate offices welcome flat or house hunters with open arms! In fact, most estates will very quickly refer you to the estate agents who represent them. But if you approach the estate office in a polite and efficient manner, you could receive some surprising co-operation.

Property Companies

After the hereditary landowners, the Crown, and the Church, the largest London landowners are the property companies. And the remarkable thing about the property companies is that they are a fairly recent addition to the property ownership scene. Most of the property companies that are today's giants only really got going in the 1950s and 1960s. Many of the property companies were founded and guided to their success by entrepreneur property developers. Such names as Charles Clore, Max Rayne, Harold Samuel, Maxwell Joseph, Harry Hyams, many now titled, are among some of the better known wizards of the property development business. Initially the property tycoons worked with the landowners in joint ventures. And later they became great landowners in their own right. While most of the property companies today are unloading their residential portfolios in favour of commercial holdings, many companies still hold residential blocks of flats as investments.

The large property companies are an excellent source of leads for the London flat hunter. They are the landlords of tens of thousands of flats in London. They know even before the estate agent does what's available or will be available in their buildings. Working with them is one way of short-circuiting the estate agent's stranglehold on the flat hunting market, or at least pinpointing the best estate agents to work with.

The thing to do is to sign up with a number of the property companies which own blocks of flats. Tell them you'll be happy to go on their waiting lists. Make sure you specify how much you'd like to pay, where you'd like to live, and how large a flat you'd like. Also tell them a bit about yourself and your family. Then get hold of the name of a key person in the management of the estate office, and phone him every so often. By keeping in touch you'll indicate your eagerness to find something. And waiting lists are often short-circuited. Many people put their names down and then find something else or lose interest. If you're persistent you'll be given first choice.

So don't despair when you hear, 'There's really nothing available right now but if you'd like to go on the waiting list . . .' Go on it, but don't patiently sit back waiting to be called in turn.

Insurance Companies as Property Owners

Other excellent sources of leads for the flat hunter are the established insurance companies. Many got into the residential property market during the 1930s

The Main Residential Property Companies of London

Name and Address of Company	What They Own, Type, Location, Price, Lease	Procedure for Applying
Freshwater Group, 162 Shaftesbury Ave, W.C.2, 836 1555	Freshwater Group, a private company, controls two public companies, City and Country, and Daejan Holdings, and a private group of companies, The Metropolitan Property groups. With assets of more than £100 million, mostly in residential property Freshwater is probably the largest private landlord in London. Freshwater's holdings include 25,000 flats in 300 blocks. They have taken over the 'Key Flats' name from London County Freehold and Leasehold, in addition to some of their properties. In autumn 1971, the Freshwater Group quietly split into two parts. William Stern, former managing director of Freshwater's, took about 3000 of the flats under his new company, Consort Management. The remaining 22,000 flats stayed with Freshwater and are managed by the Highdorn Company. Freshwater's and Consort's properties include: Heathcroft, Hampstead Garden Suburb Brookfield, Highgate Eyre Court, South Lodge, Hyde Park Mansions, all in St John's Wood Grove Hall, Langford Court Evelyn, Carlisle, Morpeth, and Stafford Mansions, Victoria Clare Court, Bloomsbury. Flats are mostly unfurnished with rents varying from £350–2000 per annum, with an average of £550–600 per annum. Leases are for three years and renewable for five years, with a rent view after three years. Freshwater prints a monthly newsletter for tenants, and even sponsors outings, such as river cruises, for tenants. Their services and the upkeep of their buildings are excellent.	Apply to: the letting office of the area of London in which you are interested: *Highdorn Company*, W.C.2, 158 Shaftesbury Ave, 836 1555, for St John's Wood, Paddington, Maida Vale, Marylebone, Euston, Chelsea, Westminster, Notting Hill, Bayswater, Victoria. Beechworth House, 40–8 High St, Acton, W.3, 992 0113, for Chiswick, Shepherd's Bush, Ealing. Vivian House, 166 Hampstead Way, N.W.11, 455 4685, for Haringey, Brent, Barnet and Hampstead. Eagle Star House, High St, Sutton, 643 5276, for Twickenham, Richmond, Putney. 24 The High Parade, Streatham High Rd, S.W.16, 769 3344, for Clapham Common, Brixton, Lewisham. *Consort Management*, 586 3121, or go to the estate agents who handle most of Freshwater's flats: Worthington and Stewart Ltd, 162 Shaftesbury Ave, W.C.2, 240 1581

Name and Address of Company	What They Own, Type, Location, Price, Lease	Procedure for Applying
London County Freehold & Leasehold (Key Flats), 58 Albert Court, Prince Consort Rd, S.W.7, 589 7080	Was once one of the largest residential property groups in London. It was then taken over by Metropolitan Estates Property Company (MEPC) the second largest commercial property company in Britain. In 1971 MEPC sold off its residential holdings with about 75 per cent going to First National Finance Corporation and 25 per cent to Freshwater Group. First National Finance Corp. recently sold 115 blocks of flats to 22 different buyers (including Regalion Properties). Freshwater intends to continue to rent its parcel. The name 'Key Flats' will become part of the Freshwater Group. Most of the Key flats were in Maida Vale, St John's Wood, Hampstead, Hammersmith, Putney and Kensington. Usual type was a mansion block, without central heating, and let unfurnished. Inclusive rents on three-year leases were between £500 and £700 per annum—although their best quality flats went for £1000 to £1500 per annum.	Goddard and Smith, 106 Westbourne Terrace, W.2, 723 1299 Edward Erdman, 6 Grosvenor St, W.1, 629 8191 George Weston, 10 Sutherland Ave, W.9, 286 7217 Fineman Lever, 316 Uxbridge Rd, W.3, 992 2237, and 31 Brechin Place, S.W.7, 373 7804 Philip Fisher and Co., Fisher House, 379a Hendon Way, N.W.4, 202 8255. To *let* a flat, apply to: The Freshwater Group, or the 'Key Flats' office at 58 Albert Court, or to Consort Management, 586 3121 To *buy* a flat, you can apply to (amongst others): Regalion Properties, 18 Cumberland Mansions, George Street, W1, 723 8232, who will give you names of their managing agents.

Name and Address of Company	What They Own, Type, Location, Price, Lease	Procedure for Applying
Property Holding and Investment Trust, Artillery House, Artillery Row, S.W.1, 222 6650	Owns a few thousand flats in the more prestigious central London areas. Mostly unfurnished and unregulated by the rent acts. Many blocks have flats up for sale to sitting tenants or new tenants. Prices for long leases range from £5000—20,000. Some blocks include: Hanover Gate Mansions, Park Rd, N.W.1 Kingston House, Princes Gate, and Ennismore Gardens, S.W.7 Swan Court, Manor St, Chelsea, S.W.3 Abbey Lodge, Regent's Park, N.W.1	Druce and Co., Druce House, 54—6 Baker St, W.1, 486 4241 Gross, Fine & Krieger, Chalfen, 27 Princes Street, W.1, 493 3993 Apply to agents: Folkard and Hayward, 115 Baker St, W.1, 935 7799 Allsop and Co., 20 Montpelier St, S.W.7, 584 6106 Yates and Yates, 70 Brook St, W.1, 629 0501
Regional Properties Management, Wellington House, Strand, W.C.2, 836 6174	Owns a few thousand flats ranging in size from one to seven rooms. All are in modern post 1930s purpose-built blocks. Rents range from £5 per week to £3000 per year. Leases on unfurnished flats are three years. Starting to sell flats to sitting tenants. Blocks include: Arlington House, 17—20 Arlington St, S.W.1 Inver Court, Inverness Terrace, W.2 King's Court, Hammersmith, W.6 Duchess of Bedford House, Duchess of Bedford Walk, W.8 Stockleigh Hall, Prince Albert Rd, N.W.8.	Apply to: Regional Properties Management, Wellington House, Strand, W.C.2, 836 6174 Maintains waiting list which sometimes closes when demand exceeds twenty per block. Requires references.
Star Property, 16 Grosvenor St, W.1, 499 0444	A large commercial property company having some residential properties in central London. Owns a few hundred flats. Rents range from £40—150 per week on a furnished basis, to £400—2000 per annum on seven-year unfurnished flats. Mostly post 1930s centrally	Apply to: Star Property, 16 Grosvenor St, W.1, 499 0444

Name and Address of Company	What They Own, Type, Location, Price, Lease	Procedure for Applying
Peachey Property, Park West, Edgware Rd. W.2, 262 0161	heated blocks. Including: 49 Hill Street, W.1 46 Upper Grosvenor St, W.1 Portsea Hall, Portsea Place, W.2.	Apply to: Peachey Property, Park West, Edgware Rd, W.2, 262 0161
Buckingham Properties Ltd, 170 Finchley Rd, N.W.3, 435 0077	A public property company, once heavily involved with residential property but lately shifting to commercial developments. Developed the Churchill Hotel in Portman Square, W.1. Still owns blocks of flats in Hampstead, St John's Wood, and Swiss Cottage. Buckingham Properties, a subsidiary of Slater Walker Securities, is moving into residential property in a big way. They deal mainly in 'break-ups'. This technique involves buying Victorian mansion blocks and either selling the flats on long leases to current tenants or waiting until they are vacant and then refurbishing them and selling them off to new tenants. Currently they own about fifty blocks containing a few thousand flats in areas throughout London including: 35–6 Buckingham Gate, Victoria King's Court, King's Rd Hamilton House, Hamilton Place, Holborn Barkston Gardens, Earl's Court	Apply to: Buckingham Properties Ltd, 170 Finchley Rd, N.W.3, 435 0077 or managing agents: Gross, Fine and Krieger, Chalfen, 27 Princes St, W.1, 493 3993 Chesterton and Sons, 40 Connaught St, W.2, 262 7202 Buckingham Properties also deal with numerous other agents who specialize in finding suitable break-up situations. These agents then become managing agents for those blocks.
Crown Lodge Properties, 124 Old Brompton Rd, S.W.3, 373 0750	Private property company that owns about 1000 flats in Chelsea and South Kensington. Mostly of the furnished bed-sit or flat-share variety.	Apply to: agents, Johnson and Pycraft Management, 228 Fulham Rd, S.W.10, 351 0925

West London Property
Corporation,
Ashley Gardens, S.W.1,
834 5547

Owns numerous blocks of flats, some let on a furnished basis, in Mayfair, Victoria and Kensington.

Apply to:
West London Property
Corporation,
Ashley Gardens, S.W.1,
834 5547

Trafalgar House Investments,
Cleveland House,
St James's Sq., S.W.1,
930 9501

Owns six large blocks of flats in Kensington, containing 110 flats. Flats are to be sold as they become vacant.

Apply to: agents,
Hampton & Sons,
6 Arlington St, S.W.1,
493 8222

City and St James's Property
Company Limited,
56 Ennismore Gardens, S.W.7,
581 2511

Owns ten leasehold blocks at Coleherne Court, Old Brompton Rd. Blocks contain 190 flats. Flats may either be modernized and relet at higher rents, or sold off as they become vacant.

Apply to: agents,
W. A. Ellis, 174 Brompton Rd.
S.W.3, 589 2425
Knight Frank & Rutley,
20 Hanover Square,
London W.1,
629 8171

Insurance Companies with Residential Property

Name of Insurance Company	What They Own. Type. Location. Price. Lease	Procedure for Applying
The Prudential Assurance Company Ltd, Holborn Bars, E.C.1, 405 9222	Owns numerous luxury blocks of flats in central London. Park Lane, Portman Sq., Park St, Curzon St are some of the locations of Prudential's blocks. All flats are unfurnished and let on five- or seven-year leases. Most flats are expensive, in the £750—3000 per annum class. Flats are spacious, some up to five bedrooms in size, with excellent service provided by management.	Write to: Chief Surveyor, Prudential Assurance Co., Holborn Bars, E.C.1. or phone Estate Department, 405 9222. There is normally a long waiting list.
Norwich Union Insurance Group, 49 Fleet St, E.C.4, 353 7181	Owns a few hundred flats in central London, let on seven-year leases with assignment clauses. Sharing or subletting is not allowed. Rents range from £500—1700 per annum. Some of their blocks include: Queen's Court, Finchley Rd, N.W.8 Queen's Mead, St John's Wood, N.W.8 Seymour Place, Crawford St, W.1 Walpole House, Weymouth St, W.1.	Apply to: Norwich Union, London Estates Office, 41 Piccadilly, W.1, 734 2804. A waiting list is maintained.
Sun Life Assurance Society Ltd, 107 Cheapside, E.C.2, 606 7788	Owns flats in blocks 1—49 Lowndes Sq., S.W.1. Flats range from two rooms, kitchen and bath to five bedrooms. The flats are on seven-year leases, unfurnished, with the right to assign clauses. Flats are in the over £1000 per annum class.	Apply to: agents, Farebrother Ellis, 29 Fleet St, E.C.4, 353 9344
National Provident Mutual Life Assurance, 48 Gracechurch St, E.C.3, 623 4200	Owns a few hundred luxury flats in central London, let unfurnished on five- to seven-year leases. Rents £800—1800 per annum. Some of the locations of their blocks are: Queen's Gate, Sloane St, Bedford Court, W.C.1, and Prince of Wales Drive, Battersea.	Apply to: The Property Supervisor, 48 Gracechurch St, E.C.3, 623 4200

when property was the favoured form of investment. In addition to seeking property investments, insurance companies found themselves in the residential property business through the back door, so to speak. During the years of mass unemployment, many mortgage holders found they couldn't keep up their payments, and the insurance companies were forced to take over the properties. Under normal conditions they would sell the property, but if the market was weak it made more sense to rent the property and become the landlord.

With their huge cash reserves, insurance companies are also the main source of financing for property developers. While insurance companies used to lend money only on interest, they now demand a piece of the equity in the development. Some insurance companies are venturing into their own property developments. The Pearl was involved with the luxurious Portman Towers development above Portman Square.

Some of the most elegant blocks of flats in London are owned by insurance companies, and most are rented on short leases. Though the rents are often high, the blocks have excellent service and the flats are large and spacious. Many blocks have duplexes and penthouses. The locations can't be beaten —Portman Square, Grosvenor Square, Park Lane, and Lowndes Square are just a few of the choice locations where insurance companies own and manage blocks of flats. Insurance companies are very careful about tenant selection, so do a good public relations job on yourself when you write to the respective companies.

Local Authorities

Greater London Council

Whether directly or indirectly every flat or house hunter will be affected in some way by his local council or authority. To many, their ways are a big mystery. Who cares, ask some. Things will get done whether I show an interest or not. Life goes on, and London will go on. Of course there is a certain amount of apathy among many Londoners regarding the local authorities, but this is true of people in almost any big city. But the newcomer is often inquisitive about who runs things: what happens to all his tax or rate payments, for instance.

Ask a native Londoner about the workings of London and he'll shrug and mutter something about the Greater London Council or the Town Hall, but he'll probably not be able to tell you how they work. London's organization is more complicated than that of any other city in the U.K., so this section is to familiarize you with the workings of the governing bodies of London.

The London Government Act of 1963 defined the present geographic area of what is known as Greater London—roughly 620 square miles, and a population of about 7,400,000 (down from 8,000,000 in 1961). It took an Act of Parliament to make London into one of the world's largest cities. With one stroke of the administrative pen, London took a big jump up the league table of world cities.

Prior to 1963, London possessed only 3,250,000 inhabitants. To arrive at her present population London annexed 2,250,000 from the county of Middlesex, 1,000,000 from Surrey, well over 1,000,000 from Essex, about 500,000 from Kent, and nearly 60,000 from Hertfordshire. It seemed logical that they

should be included in the population of London since most of them worked there, shopped there, and used the services of the central area. Why not have them pay taxes and rates there too? In addition, the various local authorities had begun to overlap and conflict, and just couldn't handle the administrative burdens demanded by a modern city. So the Act of Parliament was designed to make things better.

The Act established new authorities and swept away many local authorities including the old London County Council (L.C.C.). In their place was created the Greater London Council (G.L.C.), the Inner London Education Authority and thirty-two separate London borough councils.

While some thought went into trying to preserve the integrity of small districts and small borough councils, much was lost in the changeover. Today a council like Camden makes decisions affecting as diverse a population as lives in Hampstead, Camden Town and Bloomsbury. To combat this problem concerned citizens in local districts have set up amenity societies to lobby the councils about things affecting their own areas. (See name and address of each society in area summaries.)

Today the administration of each of the Greater London areas ia shared between the Greater London Council and the individual borough council. The theory is to centralize, with the G.L.C., services affecting the entire London area, or those involving large amounts of money or expertise; and to de-centralize those services which are of concern only to the local areas. While this theory may be good in principle, it is often difficult to implement on a day-to-day administrative basis. Overlapping and duplication continue to occur. Decisions are taken by the G.L.C. which greatly affect local districts, who may not have been consulted for their opinion. You often will read in the papers stories of a borough like Battersea or Westminster protesting against some action of the G.L.C.

Some of the responsibilities shared between the G.L.C. and each borough council are:

General Planning—what will the London of tomorrow look like?

Roads—the bridges and trunk roads belong to the G.L.C. Each borough worries about the roads that go through its own area of responsibility.

Traffic—traffic management and control is the responsibility of the G.L.C., which seems to be doing a far better job than its counterparts in Rome or Paris. The East End and the City can be dreadful, but the West End is not bad except for Hyde Park Corner and awful Oxford Street. Responsibility for parking is shared, because a good part of the revenue produced by the boroughs goes to the G.L.C. Parking meters, off-street parking and permit parking are the coming modes of coping with the parking problem.

Housing—the G.L.C. took over those houses—338,000 of them—owned by the old London County Council. Some properties are being returned to the councils of the boroughs in which the houses are located, and some houses are being sold to the tenants. The rest will be maintained by the G.L.C. The borough councils have full powers regarding housing within their areas. Housing grants, the sale of council flats or houses, redevelopments, building permits, health standards—all are regulated by each individual council. Each council has a housing office to serve the residents of the borough. (See address of each in summary preceding each neighbourhood description.)

Parks—the G.L.C. took over the 150 parks formerly administered by the L.C.C. The Royal Parks, with some 28,000 acres, are maintained by the Department of the Environment.

Licensing—the G.L.C. is responsible for licensing, registration of motor vehicles, driving licences, and places of public entertainment, including pubs and betting establishments. The borough councils handle street traders, em-ployment agencies, and nursing agencies.

Refuse and collection—the borough councils are responsible for collecting refuse and the G.L.C. kindly disposes of it—3,000,000 tons a year! If you've got a problem with refuse collection get on to your local council.

The main services that the G.L.C. is solely responsible for are:

maintaining ancient monuments and palaces

the courts and judicial services

fire prevention and control and the fire brigade (for information phone 735 3811)

ambulance service (for help phone 928 5000)

education: Inner London Education Authority, a special committee of the G.L.C.

The main services for which the borough councils are responsible are:

housing in the borough area

administration of shops

control of infectious diseases, and public health services

sanitation

local parks

planning applications

noise and smoke abatement

elections and registration of electors

food and drugs

public libraries

registration of births, marriages and deaths

welfare services for the aged,

    infirm, deprived children, etc.

How the Greater London Council is Organized

The Greater London Council consists of 100 councillors and 16 aldermen. Each of the thirty-two London boroughs elects, according to its size, two, three or four councillors. Elections are held every third year. Only citizens of the U.K. who register are entitled to the vote. In 1973 London will be divided into ninety-two electoral areas, in line with Parliamentary constituencies.

Councillors hold office for three years. Aldermen hold office for six years (half the number retiring every third year), and are elected by the councillors. Both councillors and aldermen are referred to as members of the Council, though councillors represent the interests of their borough's populace, and aldermen are non-committed.

As in Parliament, the Council has a leader, who is selected by the majority party. And as in Parliament, there is also a leader of the opposition. Much of the work is done by committees, which elect their own chairmen.

Councillors donate their time as a community service. They may claim for expenses, and loss of earnings on their regular employment—this subsistence pay amounts to £5·90 per day.

The G.L.C. councillors may become the first of their kind in Britain to receive salaries. A Tory plan, to be submitted to Parliament, would compensate G.L.C. councillors by a sessional allowance of £500 a year, and leading committee chairmen could receive as much as £5000.

Day-to-Day Running of the G.L.C.

The full time salaried staff or administrative employees, who carry out the policies and decisions of the Council, is headed by the Director-General and Town Clerk to the Council, who is the chief executive responsible for carrying out the Council's programme. John Lindsay, Mayor of New York City, has a job that is a combination of leader of the Council and Town Clerk or Director-General of the administrative staff. You couldn't compare the Lord Mayor's job to that of any mayor abroad—he is more of a host or chief public relations officer than a government executive.

What Does the G.L.C. Spend?

During 1971–2 the G.L.C. spent £265,000,000, plus £175,000 for the Inner London Education Authority.

Where does that kind of money come from? Well, 36 per cent from income from services, rents collected from council-owned properties, etc.; 50 per cent from rates; and 14 per cent from government grants. Rates are not paid directly to the G.L.C., but come via the local borough councils.

The Borough Councils

In the London geographical area included in this book, three major boroughs are covered. These are: the Royal Borough of Kensington and Chelsea; the City of Westminster; and the London Borough of Camden. Two other boroughs have a large portion of their area discussed: the London boroughs of Islington and Hammersmith. Miscellaneous areas covered in this book are found in the boroughs of Wandsworth, Richmond-upon-Thames, Greenwich, Southwark, Lambeth, Haringey, Merton, Lewisham, Hounslow, and in the City of London.

Each borough has its own set of councillors, elected every three years by the local populace. Aldermen are elected by the councillors from among themselves, as is the mayor, who presides over the borough council. In the 1971 election, the Labour Party won control of twenty-one of the London borough councils.

What Will the Borough Council do for the House Hunter?

Now that you know something about how London is governed, you will probably want to know specifically what your council can do for you. Almost every borough has a Housing Advice Centre or Housing Office of some sort, existing primarily for the needy residents of the borough, who live in below-standard housing and want to improve their standards. But that housing office or advice centre will also be able to help the middle- or upper-income house or flat hunter, by giving him a thorough picture of the housing situation in the borough, and explaining what grants are available if a buyer wants to renovate an old house.

The government civil servant has no axe to grind, as the estate agent sometimes does (his client, the homeowner who wants to get the highest possible price when he sells his house). But the chap in the Housing Office of some chauvinistic borough like Islington will tell the truth about the housing situation. He will inform you of the locations of the council estates, what private

housing associations or property developers are doing with certain squares or streets or, just as important, what they intend to do—demolish, restore or do nothing.

Some councils, depending on whether the Labour or Conservative parties are in power, will offer houses for sale within their areas. Hammersmith's Estates Office at 233 Hammersmith Road, W.6, is well known for its policy of buying houses within the borough, and then offering them for sale to individuals.

Two of the wealthiest boroughs—Westminster, and Kensington and Chelsea—are the exception to the rule that council Housing Offices will give help only to the needy. Both mentioned boroughs have some higher rented accommodations—flats and houses to let for people with higher incomes than the average council tenant. The waiting list for these flats is long, but the rents are low in comparison to other rents in the area.

To qualify for residence in these higher rented accommodation council properties, you must have resided in the borough for at least one year, and in London for five years. Allocations of the vacant flats are normally made in order of date of application. Westminster Council owns about 300 units in four buildings, in the N.W.8, W.1 and S.W.1 postal areas, and a few terraced houses in S.W.1. Rent for these flats, most with central heating, are around £500 a year for four rooms. Service and rates are payable as well.

In Kensington and Chelsea, apply to the Chief Housing Officer, Central Library Building, Phillimore Walk, Hornton Street, W.8, for an application form. Apply for flats in one of three buildings:

Brunel House, 105 Cheyne Walk, S.W.10
Ingelow House, Holland Street, W.8
Elm Park Gardens, S.W.10.

Again, rent for these flats is around £500 a year.

Each of the borough councils publishes an official guide book to the borough—it doesn't tell you all you need to know about living in Camden or Westminster or Lambeth, but it gives useful information none the less. The books carry all the names and addresses of borough services which you might need to know.

Amenity Societies and Citizens' Advice Bureaux — Community Service Organizations

Amenity Societies are groups of interested or concerned residents who band together to preserve the essential quality of their area against the ever-present dangers of commercialism, traffic, noise, and redevelopment.

To protect the virtues and preserve the charm of the district, the amenity societies restore buildings, maintain public gardens, plan action campaigns to protest roads and motorways, and sponsor the occasional social gathering. The protest phase of the amenity society's work could take the form of published material distributed to influential persons; or direct action in govern-

Borough Councils of Districts Described in this Book

Council name, address and telephone number	Housing Office	Population	Rates (1972–3)	Average Ratable Value of Residential Property
London Borough of Camden, Town Hall, Euston Rd, N.W.1, 278 4444	Bidborough House, 38–50 Bidborough St, W.C.1, 278 4444	232,000	$86\frac{1}{2}$p in £	£171
London Borough of Greenwich, Town Hall, Wellington St, S.E.18, 854 8888	Churchill House, Greens End, S.E.18, 854 8888	230,000	$84\frac{1}{2}$p in £	£86
London Borough of Hammersmith, Town Hall, King St, W.6, 748 3020	233 Hammersmith Rd, W.6, 748 2077	187,000	79p in £	£114
London Borough of Haringey, Civic Centre, High Rd, N.22, 888 1282	Town Hall, High Rd, N.15, 808 1000	258,000	89p in £	£108
London Borough of Hounslow, Town Hall, Treaty Rd, W.4, 572 2561	Brentford and Chiswick, Town Hall, W.4, 994 4391	206,000	78p in £	£100
London Borough of Islington, Town Hall, Upper St, N.1, 226 1234	220 Upper St, N.1, 226 3300	261,000	$85\frac{1}{2}$p in £	£115
Royal Borough of Kensington and Chelsea, Town Hall, Kensington High St, W.8, 937 5464	New Library Buildings, Phillimore Walk, W.8, 937 5464	230,000	$65\frac{1}{2}$p in £	£258
London Borough of Lambeth, Town Hall, Brixton Hill, S.W.2, 274 7722	Town Hall, Brixton Hill, S.W.2, 274 7722	329,000	81p in £	£102
London Borough of Lewisham, Town Hall, Catford, S.E.6, 690 4343	Leegate House, Lee Green, S.E.12, 852 4391	280,000	86·3p in £	£91

London Borough of Merton, Town Hall, Broadway, S.W.19, 946 8070	116 Kingston Rd, S.W.19, 542 7288	188,000	$88\frac{1}{2}$p in £	£110
London Borough of Richmond-on-Thames, Town Hall, Richmond Rd, Twickenham, 892 4466	Regal House, London Rd, Twickenham, 892 4466	57,000	82p in £	£120
London Borough of Southwark, Town Hall, Peckham Rd, S.E.5, 703 6311	29 Peckham Rd, S.E.5, 703 6311	237,000	96p in £	£82
London Borough of Wandsworth, Municipal Buildings, Wandsworth High St, S.W.18, 874 0488	Welbeck House, 43 Wandsworth High St, S.W.18, 874 0488	335,000	$72\frac{1}{2}$p in £	£100
City of Westminster, City Hall, Victoria St, S.W.1, 828 8070	City Hall, Victoria Street, S.W.1, 828 8070	245,000	$69\frac{1}{2}$p in £	£242

ment, through appearances at local council meetings.

There are more than 700 amenity societies in Britain, and most have been formed in the years since the Civic Trust was established in 1957.

The residents of an area who participate in the amenity society's activities are excellent contacts for the flat or house hunter. Phone an officer of the society, or attend one of its meetings. You'll learn a lot about the area and receive some excellent tips about ways to find a place to live there. If you've already chosen your area for living, join the amenity society after you've moved in. You'll be looking after your own interests, as well as your community's!

The amenity societies and their addresses are included in the neighbourhood summaries.

Citizens' Advice Bureaux are part of a national service which developed during the Second World War. They are staffed by volunteers, usually local residents, and are politically independent of the party in power in their area. They are supported by grants from the local council.

The Citizens' Advice Bureau is a very useful place to go to get answers to questions about housing, insurance, legal aid, consumer problems, landlord and tenant disputes, taxation, education, family budgeting and the workings of the local government. It is often the only place where one can turn to avoid the red tape of the government departments, who regularly want to refer you to yet another department. The Citizens' Advice Bureaux and their addresses are to be found in the neighbourhood summaries.

A Check List for the Flat and House Hunter

Look Closely Before you Rent or Buy

If you can confidently say you've satisfied yourself on all the questions below, you should be in a position to make an objective decision on whether the house or flat is really right for you.

Flat or House

☐ Is there central heating? Full or partial?

☐ Are there many stairs to climb?

☐ Is there enough cupboard space or will you have to spend a lot of money to build them or buy wardrobes?

☐ What are the bathrooms like? Are they far from the main bedroom or suite?

☐ Is there a separate W.C.?

☐ What are the rates and what is the ratable value?

☐ How secure are the doors and windows?

☐ What direction do the windows face? Is there enough light and ventilation? What about noise from the street? Are the windows double glazed?

☐ How many electrical outlets are there in each room? Is the overall wiring adequate? Or will wiring be a major expense for the new tenant?

☐ Turn on the taps. What's the water pressure like?

☐ Are the area and street going up in status or downhill?

☐ Are there many unsightly pipes, exterior and interior? Do they bother you? Are they a hazard?

☐ Study area conditions morning, afternoon, weekday, weekend. See it at its worst time, and best. By making numerous visits to the flat or house, you will learn if there are trains or schools or very heavy traffic nearby.

Flat

☐ What will be left behind when the tenant leaves? Is there a fixtures and fittings charge? Is it fair?

☐ How would you dispose of rubbish?

☐ Is there a lift? What are the common areas of the building, such as garden, hall, stairs, like?

☐ What are the provisions of the lease. What is the term and when was it originally written? Does the lease specify a service charge?

- [ ] Is the flat furnished? If so review the inventory.
- [ ] What are the other tenants like?
- [ ] Is it a conversion, or in a purpose-built block? Check walls for sound and windows for noise level from street.
- [ ] Is there a porter? What is he like? (Ask the other tenants and talk to them on your own as well.)

House

- [ ] Is it freehold or leasehold?
- [ ] Is there a ground rent?
- [ ] What is the condition of the roof?
- [ ] Any dry rot or damp in the basement?
- [ ] Any sitting tenants, or will the house be sold with vacant possession?
- [ ] How long has the house been on the market?
- [ ] Is there a garden? What condition is it in? What do neighbours' gardens look like?
- [ ] Are the floors, walls, ceilings level?
- [ ] Can a self-contained flat be incorporated in the basement?
- [ ] What's the rendering like on the outside of the house? Is the brickwork hard or eroded and flaking? Are any outside walls bulging?
- [ ] Is there a garage?
- [ ] What are the total outgoings—mortgage payments, interest charges, insurance, heat and hot water, ground rent, and maintenance?
- [ ] Are the drains working properly?

Profiles of London Districts

Area Summaries: an Introduction

This book is a highly selective guide to London living, and therefore cannot be fully comprehensive. The districts we have chosen to describe in detail are the very central areas which rank highest in popularity among Londoners and newcomers alike; and also those places which are just off-centre, but long-established in their appeal. Kensington and Chelsea are typical examples of the former; Dulwich and Wimbledon, of the latter. A third group of London neighbourhoods we have included are some up-and-coming areas, such as Islington/Highbury, Camberwell and Kennington—long rundown but recently showing signs of taking on a new lease of life.

Each of the districts you will read about in the chapters that follow has some special quality or combination of qualities that attracts many Londoners to live within its boundaries.

Note on Area Summary Sheets

Local Estate Agents

Some new ones may exist that we have missed. And it's also possible that some we've listed have moved or even gone out of business. It's almost impossible to keep track of them all. If you've noticed any really glaring errors or omissions, please let us know.

Residential Parking Permits

This refers to those boroughs which require permits to park. Residents (only) pay a fee and then can park anywhere in the area for nothing. Apply at your local town hall. Not all areas have this system, and even those that do may not require permits for every part of the borough.

Approximate Cost of Housing

This is a really tough one. Property prices change so quickly, especially in the up-and-coming areas, it's practically impossible to be up-to-date. The price ranges given may be irritatingly vague: if so, we're sorry. The price ranges quoted for short leases do not include 'fixtures and fittings' charges: usually £1000 per year of unexpired portion of lease plus fair value of things actually left behind.

Basically, London areas can be summarized as follows:

	Price range (Houses and large flats)
Up and coming	£15,000–20,000
Almost there	£20,000–30,000
Arrived	£30,000–50,000
Super de-luxe	over £50,000

At least these were the approximate prices in spring 1972. With prices increasing at the rate of 10 to 15 per cent per year, who knows what prices will be like in five years' time.

Of course in each area there are exceptions to the general price ranges. There's always someone who will find a small gem for under £10,000. And the really luxurious properties will find buyers willing to pay £75–100,000, even in the 'arrived' areas. Use the prices given as a rough guide—and good luck!

MARYLEBONE—BAKER STREET

Local council
City of Westminster

Postal areas
W.1

Type of housing
Pre-war
Modern blocks
Mansion blocks
Georgian

Approximate number of flats and houses in district
13,000

Local estate agents
Druce & Co., Druce House,
54 Baker St, W.1, 486 4241
Folkard & Hayward, 115 Baker St,
W.1, 935 7799
Big Twelve

APPROXIMATE COST OF HOUSING

Short lease unfurnished flats
annual rent
£1200—2000

Long lease unfurnished flats
price
£15—25,000

(non commercial)
Houses freehold or leasehold
price
£35—50,000

Citizens' Advice Bureau
Westminster Council House,
Marylebone Rd, N.W.1
935 7766

TRANSPORTATION

Tube stops
Marylebone
Baker Street
Marble Arch
Bond Street

Bus service routes
2 Victoria
3 Camden Town—Piccadilly Circus
30 Hyde Park Corner—Knights-bridge—Kings Cross
53 Great Portland St—Trafalgar Sq—Westminster

Tube lines
Bakerloo
Metropolitan
Central

Travelling times
West End 5 mins
City 10—15 mins

Resident parking
Yes. Permit £18 per year. Almost off-street Parking; Chiltern St, W.1: 394 spaces; Chandos St, W.1: 380 spaces; Gloucester Place, W.1: 443 spaces; Cavendish Square: 545 spaces

Marylebone –
Baker Street

A Bit of History . . .

Edgware Road and Oxford Street were the two main Roman roads from London to the north and the west. As early as 1200, there was a hamlet at the foot of Marylebone Lane, with a little church called St John Tiburne. The church was often plundered by robbers from Tyburn Road (Oxford Street), and gallows, called Tyburn tree, were set up near the site of Marble Arch, public executions continuing there until 1768. In 1400, unhappy Marylebone villagers appealed to the Bishop of London for permission to move their church higher up the river Tyburn, away from the highway and robbers. They built a new chapel, dedicated to St Mary the Virgin, and called it St Mary by the Bourne — hence the name, Marylebone.

When the gardens surrounding the Manor House of Marylebone were at their height as a pleasure resort for Londoners, the Duke of Newcastle sold the village of Marylebone for £17,500, in 1708. His daughter and heiress, Lady Henrietta Cavendish, married Edward Harley and they decided to develop the village as a residential estate, patterned on the successful growth of squares and streets south of Oxford Street. Cavendish Square was Lady Henrietta's first project, in 1720. Between 1745 and 1795, Harley Street, Wimpole and Welbeck Streets appeared. And by 1775, Manchester and Portman Squares, and Baker Street had been built. In Portman Square, Mrs Elizabeth Montagu had her private palace, where she held salon for *literati* of the day.

The Atmosphere . . . The People . . .

Within the very large 'north of the park' area known as Marylebone are several smaller separate-identity areas, each of which is well known:
1) Harley Street: a formal atmosphere; Georgian houses; headquarters of London's doctors.
2) Baker Street: all business, shops and mansion blocks; Georgian houses on streets going off to left and right.
3) The area between Edgware Road and Gloucester Place: again, Georgian in flavour; Montagu and Bryanston Squares.
4) Area round Marylebone High Street: the most village-like part of Marylebone; Paddington and Dorset Streets are typical of the area.
5) Area just above Oxford Street (Portman Square, Manchester Square): busy with shops, hotels, office blocks, and some large blocks of flats.

Marylebone also takes in the area where the wholesale fashion and fabrics or 'rag' trade is centred—round Mortimer Street—but this area is not at all residential.

Marlebone has the special quality of appearing to be the heart of Central London, around Marble Arch, in particular. Yet just minutes' walk away is a quiet mews or square. A real city lover thrives on this contrast. Some of the peaceful streets may not survive for long in this prosperous area, however. George Street, a row of Georgian houses and shops off Baker Street, is a recent victim of the demolition crews.

The only unifying characteristic about the people of Marylebone is their affluence.

A Look at the Buildings, Outstanding Streets and Squares . . .

There are probably more mansion-block-dwellers in Marylebone than in any other part of London. Marylebone Road, and many of the streets running off Baker Street, are lined solidly with mansion blocks.

Two of the most attractive blocks of flats in London are just above Oxford Street, in Portman Square. One is *Orchard Court*, with fifty-four flats, some

Park Crescent

with as many as seventeen rooms. During the Second World War, this block served as the headquarters for the French Resistance. Orchard Court has its own private drive from Orchard Street, a doorman always on duty, and a beautiful wide entrance hall, always bedecked with an elaborate arrangement of flowers. The Prudential Insurance Company is the owner of this building, and one may direct inquiries about flats in it to the Estate Office at the Prudential. The other, *Portman Towers*, is a tall modern block just the other side of Portman Square, boasting eighty-eight flats, starting at £19,000. The building went up between 1969 and 1971, and all flats were sold on completion. Allsops is the managing agent of Portman Towers.

Just to the west of the distinctly urban Portman Square are more human-scale Georgian squares such as Bryanston Square, with attractive houses divided into equally attractive flats. North of this square, around York Street and Molyneux Street, are many fine small houses, removed from the bustle of Marble Arch, and yet very close to the superb shopping of Edgware Road.

To the east of Portman Square is the sedate De Walden Estate, which includes Welbeck Street, Queen Anne Street, Devonshire Place, Harley Street, and Wimpole and Upper Wimpole Streets. These streets, though dotted with modern buildings, manage to retain their quiet Georgian charm.

Bryanston Square

The De Walden Estate insists that the top floors of each of its buildings remain residential—but it's difficult for outsiders to land those Harley Street flats before the doctors and dentists in the offices below get their hands on the leases. One disadvantage of the buildings is that the porter goes off duty when doctors' office hours end, and so the top floor tenant must go down several flights to let in his guests in the evening. Few of these buildings have intercommunication systems or buzzers which open the front door automatically.

Amenities of the Area

Great location for bus, tube or taxi travel. Queen's College, an excellent school for girls is in Harley Street. The Wallace Collection, in Hertford House in Manchester Square. The Courtauld Institute of Art, at 20 Portman Square, in one of the houses designed by Robert Adam.

Regent's Park, with Queen Mary's Rose Garden, is nearby for residents of the Harley Street part of Marylebone. Also a couple of 'key gardens'—one in Park Crescent—for residents who will pay £15 for the key. Hyde Park is an easy walk away for people in the western sector of Marylebone. People in the 'west' have the advantage of all the colourful, low-priced street markets like Bell and Church Streets; and the very reasonably priced antique shops of Crawford Street.

The Cordon Bleu Cookery School, and restaurant, on Marylebone Lane.

For shopping: Marks and Spencer and Selfridge's food halls; a Sainsbury in Marylebone High Street; Coopers, Safeway and yet another Marks and Spencer in Edgware Road. Coopers will deliver. So will Selfridges if you have an account there.

Wigmore Street—home of the most elegant optometrists in London, the most complete open-all-night chemist, John Bell and Croydon; and a well-known concert hall.

Disadvantages?

No resident of Marylebone could ever say anything bad about this area, except that 'nothing happens here'. Which is true, except for Speakers' Corner in Hyde Park which is very busy on Sunday morning. Most shops shut at five, and you don't see many people around after office hours. In other words, the trendy night people do not inhabit the area. Does that matter to you? The bistros *et al.* are to the west in Bayswater, or to the south in Piccadilly or Kensington.

The quiet and calm of the area could attract burglars. One tenant, in a new building in Harley Street, was burgled three times during the months when the building was half full.

MAYFAIR

Local council
City of Westminster

Postal areas
W.1

Type of housing
Georgian
Mews houses
Pre-war
Modern blocks

**Approximate number of flats
and houses in district**
9000

Local estate agents
Alfred Savill, Curtis & Henson,
5 Mount St, W.1, 499 8644
Blake & Co., 103 Mount St, W.1,
499 2353
Lane Saville Mark Wilks & Co.,
10 Carlos Place, Grosvenor Sq,
W.1, 629 7061
Big Twelve

APPROXIMATE COST OF HOUSING

Short lease unfurnished flats
annual rent
£1500–2500

Long lease unfurnished flats
price
£15–30,000

**(non commercial)
Houses freehold or leasehold**
price
£50–70,000

Amenity society
Westminster Society,
25 Vincent Sq, S.W.1
834 2063

Citizens' Advice Bureau
70 Lupus St, S.W.1
834 5727

TRANSPORTATION

Tube stops
Hyde Park Corner
Green Park
Marble Arch
Bond Street

Bus service routes
Numerous

Tube lines
Piccadilly
Central

Travelling times
West End 2 mins
City 10–15 mins

Resident parking
Yes. Permit £18 per year. Also off-street Parking; Audley Square Garage,
South Audley St: 350 spaces; Park Lane Garage, Park Lane: 1100 spaces

Mayfair

A Bit of History . . .

Seventeenth-century aristocrats chose Mayfair as the site for town houses—Berkeley, Grosvenor and Hanover Squares were the first to be developed. But Mayfair had its seemy side as well as its aristocratic air in those days. The annual May Fair in Shepherd Market was so unruly, with beggars, thieves and prostitutes, that by the mid-eighteenth century, George I had called a halt to it. To this day Mayfair carries its heritage well, for it is known as that part of London where only the wealthy can afford to live. Grosvenor Square was the last London square to give up its oil lamps, because the residents considered gas to be vulgar.

An aerial view of Mayfair

(Aerofilms)

The Atmosphere ... The People ...

Within Mayfair, an almost perfect triangle of land, are many contrasts: cobble-stone mews, where one would not be at all surprised to bump into a horse-drawn carriage; pompous Park Lane, with the Hilton Hotel towering over its lawn, Hyde Park; and the American Embassy, a piece of modern architectural sculpture, right in the centre of early eighteenth-century Grosvenor Square.

The people on the streets look smart, and appear affluent. The area is now and then star-studded, with the film stars who stay at the Dorchester and lunch at Tiberio, in Queen Street. At one time Michael Caine lived in Grosvenor Square; Peter Sellers, in Clarges Street; Laurence Harvey and Margaret Leighton in a mews off Berkeley Square. Basically, there are simply not very many ordinary people living in Mayfair. Many of the people you see in the streets are not Mayfair-ers at all, but tourists, or shoppers from other parts of London, or the world.

A Look at the Buildings, Outstanding Streets and Squares ...

High-priced housing: that sums up Mayfair. For the man with a lot of money, Mayfair is indeed happy house-hunting ground. A financially-comfortable couple moved out of their flat in South Audley Street, and an Arab oil millionaire bought it for his servants' quarters. He himself lived in Park Lane.

Some people have managed to find bargains in Mayfair. One fashion designer moved into a mews house behind the Connaught Hotel, as a house sharer. He paid the owner of the house for the use of a bedroom, kitchen and reception room. This letting of part of a flat or a house happens, surprisingly, in some of the highest-priced property areas of London. We once lived in a bargain Mayfair flat—three furnished rooms plus tiny kitchen, for £22 a week in Park Lane, no less. That building, number 55, where minimum rent is now up to £31·50 a week, has more porters and service staff than a tenant could count.

If you want to find a short lease on an unfurnished flat, Chesterfield House, just off Curzon Street, is a very good block to set your sights upon. This pre-war building contains flats with as many as four bedrooms. Direct telephone inquiries or letters to the Prudential Insurance Company, the landlord.

Albany, just two minutes from Piccadilly Circus, is the *crème de la crème* of Mayfair and London flat blocks. No one in the know ever says *The* Albany. Enter the building from Piccadilly proper, or from Burlington Gardens, at the back. If you are related distantly to Lord Byron, or the Prime Minister, Edward Heath or Dame Edith Evans, all former tenants—don't be timid about telling the Secretary of Albany so when you write to him applying for a flat. For the Secretary will pass your credentials on to the Board of Trustees, who vote in a new tenant or resident whenever a flat becomes available, every six to ten years. However, most of the leases will be expiring in the 1970s, so flats may come on the market more frequently. There are 70 'chambers'

Albany Chambers

A Mayfair mews

Grosvenor Square

and current tenants include Terence Stamp, Baron Rothschild and other dignitaries.

Furnished chambers on short lets do become available frequently, owing to the globe-trotting life of the residents of Albany. Be aware of these 'rules' for residents, however. Albany was built as bachelors' chambers, and to this day, children under eleven are banned. If a tenant loses the key to the main door, he must buy a new door lock, and keys for each of the residents.

Beautiful Berkeley Square has gone commercial, though its facade appears to be just as pretty as it was in the eighteenth century. If a building has not been taken over by a motor company, then an advertising agency has invaded. Grosvenor Square, on the other hand, is highly residential. It is unlikely you'll ever see a 'flat for sale' board outside a block of flats in Grosvenor Square. These high-price flats change hands quietly, in the offices of West End estate agents. Only one building in the Square offers short, unfurnished leases, and that is number 37. The Legal and General Insurance Company is the landlord, but the building could go any day to Maxwell Joseph, as an annex for his Brittania Hotel.

Where to live while you're looking round Mayfair?

An abundant number of high-priced service flats lie behind the Dorchester Hotel, in charming little streets like Hill Street—or in Shepherd Market. One couple we know paid £37 a week for bed and breakfast at the Carla, on Hertford Street. They though had a bargain, for the same accomodation just across the street cost £60 a week. Many newspapers have advertisements like 'Service Flat off Park Lane, £25 a week and up': they refer to the little neighbourhood behind the Hilton.

If you join the English Speaking Union (headquarters at 37 Charles Street), you are eligible to lodge in that beautiful mansion for a very reasonable price. Go in person to inquire about membership.

Amenities of the Area

Hyde Park as your front garden. St George's Gardens, off Mount Street, quiet and pretty.

Lots of sophisticated nightlife. Annabels on Berkeley Square. Gaming clubs aplenty. Lovely pubs, like The Red Lion on Waverton Street, and The Guinea, Bruton Lane. The posh hotels are great places for tea, or breakfast, or a splurge meal.

Annual antiques fair at Grosvenor House.

West End theatres and restaurants practically within walking distance.

Shopping: couldn't be better, for elegant shops that is. The bath boutique in Mount Street and the china shop in South Audley Street stand unparalleled in London. With Oxford Street as its northern boundary, and Regent Street as the eastern boundary, what else need be said about the quality of Mayfair shopping. South Molton Street is the Beauchamp Place of north London!

Supermarkets? Coopers, just out of Mayfair, in the Edgware Road, will deliver. So will Selfridges food hall. Marks and Spencer food hall in Oxford Street. Alan of Mount Street is a beautiful butcher, and his neighbour the poulterer has a window like a seventeenth-century Flemish painting.

Disadvantages?

Though there is a surfeit of specialist shops in Mayfair, try to find an ordinary round-the-clock grocer when you need a pint of milk or half a pound of butter. A launderette is almost impossible to find!

The area has no sense of 'community' about it. Many a Mayfair flat stands empty for a good part of the year, because it happens to be only one of the several homes of its owner.

Mayfair is not the kind of area where you send your child round the corner to school, or to play in the garden square. Nannies take the children into Grosvenor Square, or across into Hyde Park, where they can be seen, but not heard.

Mayfair is becoming more commercial each year, as businesses take over the huge town houses which cost a small fortune to run and maintain. Upper Brook Street and Park Street are two of the best examples of the commercial takeover.

Even though Lord Mountbatten of Burma, the Queen's cousin, used to live in Park Lane (in Brook House, before it became an office block); and many of the leaders of British commerce and industry live in Grosvenor Square, Mayfair is not considered the place where 'real' English people live. The area, in fact, has a very high proportion of Americans among its populace. Some people would consider this a disadvantage.

ST JAMES'S

Local council
City of Westminster

Postal areas
S.W.1

Type of housing
Pre-war
Modern blocks
Queen Anne
Georgian
Regency

Approximate number of flats and houses in district
2000

Local estate agents
Hampton & Sons, 6 Arlington St, S.W.1, 493 8222
Mellersh & Harding, 43 St James's Place, S.W.1, 493 6141
Big Twelve

APPROXIMATE COST OF HOUSING

Short lease unfurnished flats
annual rent
£1200–2500

Long lease unfurnished flats
price
£20–35,000

(non commercial) Houses freehold or leasehold
price
£45–70,000

Amenity society
Westminster Society,
25 Vincent Sq, S.W.1
834 2063

Citizens' Advice Bureau
33 Charing Cross Rd, W.C.2
839 2825

TRANSPORTATION

Tube stops
Green Park
St James's Park

Bus service routes
Numerous

Tube lines
Victoria
Piccadilly
District
Circle

Travelling times
West End 2 mins
City 10–15 mins

St James's

A Bit of History...

St James's Square, in the heart of St James's, was the fashionable address for many of King Charles II's courtiers, including his mistresses. St James's is among the oldest of London squares, built in 1660, but none of the square's private palaces survive. St James's Palace was built for Henry VIII.

The Atmosphere... The People...

What comes to mind when you say 'St James's'? Not houses, but gentlemen in bowler hats; Christies, the fine art auctioneers in King Street; the private clubs of Pall Mall; the shops of Duke and Jermyn Streets. It is residential London, but purely gentlemen's residential—*pied à terre*, in other words. This is where the spirit of the Upper Class English Male still exists. St James's Park has a few peacocks, and lots of civil servants about at lunch hour.

A Look at the Buildings, Outstanding Streets and Squares...

This elegant area called St James's is split in two by St James's Park. So if you go by tube to St James's Park you will be nowhere near St James's Place or Pall Mall. You will, however, be near lovely St James's Park, and one of London's loveliest group of eighteenth-century houses, Queen Anne's Gate, where Windsor lanterns light the street.

On the other side of the park are St Jame's Street, and the little lanes and streets which lead off it. One of the handsomest blocks of luxury flats in London is 26 St James's Place. This eight-storey building contains four large split-level flats, two smaller flats and a penthouse. The large flats sold for £70,000 each when the building was constructed by D. Lasdun and Partners for Malvin Investment. Numbers 25, 24, 21 and 22 St James's Place are also modern blocks of flats, facing Green Park at the front. The Rothschild house is number 23, with the handsome, curved wooden door. Tiny Essex Court, at 30 St James's Place, is a perfect *pied à terre* type building.

In Arlington Street, around the corner from the Ritz Hotel, is Arlington House, the largest block of flats in the St James's area. Short unfurnished leases are available through the Regional Property Company, Wellington House, Strand, W.C.2. Some of the flats may be for sale.

Many of the handsome smaller houses in the area around St James's Place have been converted into offices, but from the outside they look as charming as they did a hundred years ago.

Behind St James's Street toward Haymarket are some of the best shopping streets in London. Art galleries in Duke Street. The best of everything in Jermyn Street. Now and then you'll come across some service chambers to

Queen Anne's Gate

let. Those at 2–10 Ryder Street are called St James's Chambers. Eighteen flats within are owned by the Crown Estate, but are managed by Cluttons, 5 College Street, S.W.1. Just across the road is another service chamber.

Amenities of the Area

St James's Park, a Royal park, which rivals Regent's Park as the prettiest in London. Green Park adjoins St James's Park.

A five-minute walk to Piccadilly Circus and all its splendours.

Madame Prunier and The Caprice, two illustrious restaurants situated in St James's.

Shopping: bespoke shirts, shoes and boots. Cigars, wines and spirits. All the pleasures a gentleman or family requires. And Fortnum and Mason, in Piccadilly, of course.

Disadvantages?

None, for the man who has money and requires the pleasures that money can buy. For an average couple needing a launderette or supermarket, well, St James's has drawbacks.

KNIGHTSBRIDGE

Local council
Royal Borough of Kensington &
Chelsea

Postal areas
S.W.3, S.W.5, S.W.1

Type of housing
Mews houses
Georgian
Victorian
Pre-war
Modern blocks
Mansion blocks

Approximate number of flats and houses in district
10,000

Local estate agents
Allsop & Co., 20 Mountpelier St,
S.W.7, 584 6106
Andrew Milton & Co., 9 Milner St,
S.W.3, 584 4501
Harrods Estate Office,
34 Hans Crescent, S.W.1, 589 1490
Lloyd Rees, 51 Beauchamp Place,
S.W.3, 584 6512
Samuel Properties, 197
Knightsbridge, S.W.7, 584 3331
Big Twelve

APPROXIMATE COST OF HOUSING
Short lease unfurnished flats
annual rent
£1200—2500

Long lease unfurnished flats
price
£15—30,000

(non commercial)
Houses freehold or leasehold
price
£40—70,000

Citizens' Advice Bureau
Chelsea Town Hall,
King's Rd, S.W.3
352 8101

TRANSPORTATION

Tub stops
Knightsbridge

Bus service routes
Numerous

Tube lines
Piccadilly

Travelling times
West End 5 mins
City 15—20 mins

Knightsbridge

A Bit of History...

Knightsbridge 'proper' is the small strip of land running from Hyde Park Corner, along Hyde Park, past Knightsbridge Barracks. This area was the one most feared by Londoners in the reign of Elizabeth I, for it had deep ruts, poor lighting, and many bands of highwaymen lurking nearby. As late as the early 1800s, Knightsbridge was an outlying suburb of London, and Apsley House at Hyde Park Corner looked down upon a village. Harrods, probably the best known landmark of the Knightsbridge area, was built between 1901 and 1905, in terracotta stone, to tone in with the fashionable area around Hans Crescent and Cadogan Square then called Hans Town, just south of it.

The Atmosphere...The People...

Knightsbridge is a luxurious little corner of London. It is side-by-side with Mayfair in terms of image—expensive shops, expensive flats and houses, and well-turned-out people. Brompton Road now rivals Bond Street with its exclusive shops, and their appeal to shoppers from all over the world. Instant access to the serenity of Hyde Park makes the heavy population and traffic of Knightsbridge bearable for residents.

A Look at the Buildings, Outstanding Streets and Squares...

'Knightsbridge Way' is the expression referring to several locations, all of which are close to that small strip of land, Knightsbridge proper, where the tube stops. You may safely call Knightsbridge the areas lying along or off Brompton Road and Sloane Street. The land along Hyde Park, as far as Ennismore Gardens, is certainly Knightsbridge as well.

Kingston House, facing the park, has flats of all sizes, at varying high prices: Allsops is the agent. Rutland Gate, facing the Park, is a great square of white-pillared, stucco, mid-nineteenth-century houses, most of which are divided into family flats. Rutland Gate has a couple of modern blocks, and one villa, which was on the market for £400,000 in 1971, and sold for £290,000. The fixtures and fittings within the house dictated the highest price ever asked for a house in central London. Rutland Mews West looks like a corner of the south of Spain.

Probably the most attractive part of residential Knightsbridge is that which you approach via the Brompton Road—Montpelier and Brompton Squares to the right, Hans Crescent to the left. The little roads around Montpelier Square—Cheval Place, Montpelier Walk—provide enchanting small family houses, with a village-like quality so different from the boom of traffic and

Harrods, Knightsbridge

Cheval Place

Montpelier Square

commerce on nearby Brompton Road. Actress Leslie Caron's house, in Montpelier Square, sold for £65,000 in 1970. One couple managed to pay considerably less for a house in the same square, because it was a run-down boarding house when they found it. Most of Montpelier Square's houses, however, are well taken care of by proud family owner-occupiers.

Heading along the Park in the opposite direction, toward Hyde Park Corner, is a small yard, which is typical of the surprises to be found in London. Old Barrack Yard is two minutes away from the unceasing traffic of Knightsbridge. But in spirit, it could be many miles away. The leases of most of the small houses in the yard are for seven years, and they are of course, difficult to get hold of. One couple in the yard are paying £20 a week for their unfurnished three-bedroom house, but they expect an eventual takeover of the entire yard by the people who have just built the Berkeley Hotel next door to them. There was a period of about a year when this couple paid a mere £6 a week for their dream cottage in Knightsbridge—when they purchased the last year of their previous landlord's lease, for a pittance, because he was leaving the country.

The departure from Knightsbridge proper via Sloane Street leads to many mansion blocks with elegant shops at street level, and the flats above. Knightsbridge Court is an example, with its short, unfurnished leases, at a cost of £80—100 a month for a six-room flat. Capital and Counties Property Co. Ltd, St Andrew's House, 40 The Broadway, S.W.1, is the landlord.

Off the bottom of Sloane Street is Cadogan Square, to the right. This Square, with its red-brick mansions built around 1880, is the prototype for all the mansion blocks which sprouted in London in the late 1800s and early 1900s. The mock Dutch gabled houses in the square are of questionable

Sloane Street

Cadogan Square

attractiveness, but they are considered very posh, and the flats inside are very large. Only a few of the houses are one-family dwellings, in this day of fewer servants and higher taxes.

Flats in these houses often become available. The best way to land one is to follow the 'boards', which are hung in front of the houses when a flat becomes available. Though the Cadogan Estate owns the long leases on all of these houses, it is the estate agents who handle the letting of the shorter leases, which various individuals or companies have purchased from the Cadogan Estate. If you are really keen on Cadogan Square, and strategically it is an excellent location, just between Chelsea and Kensington, telephone some of the Cadogan Square houses, the numbers of which are listed in the telephone book. You'll get the porter when you ring, and there's no one who knows more about which families are moving, or planning to move.

Knightsbridge, the entire area, boasts a larger than average upper-income-transient population, and for that reason it is not really difficult to find a furnished property to let. MacKay Securities have furnished flats overlooking the Park. Minimum length of let is one year, and rent is payable quarterly, in advance (not an unusual practice in the high-price service flat market). Basil Street, a sort of crescent shaped street, behind Harrods, is a solid strip of flats to let.

Amenities of the Area

Beauchamp Place, a petite street of eccentric sorts of shops—reject china, suede cleaners, handbag restoration, an oyster bar, and many small and popular restaurants.

Food? Harrods Food Hall and Coopers Supermarket across the road. Both deliver. Norway Food Centre and Searcys, side by side further up the Brompton Road from Harrods. A cluster of small shops in and near Montpelier Street.

Hyde Park. Rowing and sailing boats on the Serpentine and swimming at the Lido. Sunday morning football and softball games, and kite flying by the Round Pond. Ducks, restaurants and other delights for children.

Hole-in-the Wall: a no-longer so-secret passage which brings Brompton Road just a few minutes walk from residents living as far west as Rutland Gate and Ennismore Gardens.

Gardens of Cadogan Place, often called Cadogan Gardens, are great—private sector for adults include a tennis court; children's sector includes sandpit, swings and a shelter.

Disadvantages?

Extremely high cost of living. If things ever got rough financially in your family, you'd probably have to bus to Chelsea or elsewhere to buy your food.

A very steady stream of heavy traffic along Knightsbridge and the Brompton Road.

BELGRAVIA

Local council
Royal Borough of Kensington &
Chelsea and City of Westminster

Postal areas
S.W.1

Type of housing
Georgian
Pre-war
Modern blocks
Regency
Mews houses

**Approximate number of flats
and houses in district**
8000

Local estate agents
Broomhalls, 61 Petty France,
S.W.1, 799 1673
Harrods Estate Office, 34 Hans
Crescent, S.W.1, 589 1490
Henry & James, 1 Motcomb St,
S.W.1, 235 8861
Marler & Marler, King Wood & Co.,
6 Sloane St, S.W.1, 235 1727
Scott & Co., 162a Sloane St,
S.W.1, 730 2108
George Trollope & Sons,
7 Chesham Place, S.W.1, 235 8099
Tufnell & Partners, 28 Elizabeth St,
S.W.1, 730 9112
Big Twelve

APPROXIMATE COST OF HOUSING

Short lease unfurnished flats
annual rent
£1500–2000

Long lease unfurnished flats
price
£18–35,000

**(non commercial)
Houses freehold or leasehold**
price
£50–80,000

Citizens' Advice Bureau
70 Lupus St, S.W.1
834 5727

TRANSPORTATION

Tube stops
Hyde Park Corner
Knightsbridge
Sloane Square
Victoria

Bus service routes
Numerous

Resident parking
Yes. Permit: City of Westminster—£18 per year; Royal Borough of
Kensington & Chelsea—£26 per year. Also off-street Parking; Pan
Technicon off Motcomb St: 289 spaces

Tube lines
Piccadilly
Circle
District

Travelling times
West End 5 mins
City 15–20 mins

Belgravia

A Bit of History . . .

During the reign of Queen Victoria, the main town house of the Crown became Buckingham Palace, and thus Belgravia, the area nearby, became the site for residences of servants of the Crown, and the St James's area yielded to commerce.

Belgravia is what some call a brilliant example of nineteenth-century town planning—the mansions of Belgrave and Eaton Squares; the middle-income houses of Chester and Wilton Streets; and the artisan dwellings nearby, on the borders of Belgravia and Pimlico.

The man to take the credit for the perfection of this overall design is Thomas Cubitt, the master builder who started life as a journeyman carpenter. He is perhaps the only property developer in history who has managed to avoid criticism, and earn only praise. Cubitt set up as a carpenter in London in 1810 at the age of twenty-two; and at his death he was worth the then vast sum of over a million pounds. His solid handsome buildings of Belgravia stand remarkably uninterrupted by the passage of time. The growth of the swampy area of marsh, creek and market garden that is now Belgravia-Pimlico was the last horizontal development on such a lavish scale in inner London—until the Barbican, which is currently being completed.

The Atmosphere . . . The People . . .

Belgravia carries its aristocratic heritage well, with top diplomatic people from all over the world either working or living in and around Belgrave Square. The big-house prices are among the steepest in London, and a tiny mews house may go for the price of a spacious country estate!

In short, there is no smarter address in today's London than Belgravia. Of course people of modest means inhabit Belgravia, in the smaller flats which have been carved out of the old one-family houses. But even these middle-income Belgravians appear to be of impeccable appearance and taste. You see them shopping in Elizabeth or Ebury Streets, with their terribly smart attire, and very acceptable accents. Belgravia has all kinds of wealth—from the titled dowager to the newly rich American industrialist.

One rather young couple who own a short lease on a house in Chester Row say that when their neighbours are away, they know it's not for a fortnight in Majorca, but for a rest on a private Greek island, or business in Bombay.

A Look at the Buildings, Outstanding Streets and Squares . . .

The three well-known squares of Belgravia are Belgrave, Eaton and Chester

Squares. Whereas Belgrave Square, covering ten acres, is overrun with diplomats, Eaton and Chester Squares are what one might call overrun with Americans. Chester Square is the most charming of the three, because its houses are smaller and more life size. Eaton Square, a quarter of a mile long, is bisected by the Kings Road. Belgrave Square and its tributaries are the kinds of snow-white terraces and streets which film producers choose to shoot their prettiest mid-nineteenth-century scenes.

If you want to live among the upper-income Americans and British gentry of Eaton Square, direct your inquiries to the Grosvenor Estate, 53 Davies Street. The estate controls more than 400 flats in Eaton Square. It's possible to get a short lease on one of the flats through a local estate agent. But if you want to buy a longer lease, and make a permanent or semi-permanent home, deal directly with the Grosvenor Estate. One Londoner—not a property man, just an ordinary professional man—bought the tail end of a lease of an Eaton Square house for a tidy £8000. He took a great chance, but luck was on his side, for when his short lease expired, he acquired the freehold of the house. He completely redecorated it, built a swimming pool in the basement, and now he rents it to itinerant millionaires. His case is an exception however. It is not unusual to find price tags of £100,000 for long leases of the houses on either of the three super squares of Belgravia.

Lowndes Square, which is a sort of border square between Belgravia and Knightsbridge, is another costly area. This square is made up largely of flats, including several modern blocks.

The days when the houses in the beautiful squares of Belgravia could

Chester Square

Belgrave Square

be inhabited exclusively as single family units have almost disappeared, which makes for some reasonably priced flats to let. One couple went to see a 'top floor' flat in Chester Square, only to find that it was a private family house and the family, who were in 'reduced circumstances' had decided to let the top floor to tenants. Eaton Place is the kind of area where the houses are all subdivided into flats, and you can come upon a very spacious top-two-floors maisonette (without lift or central heating, however) for a very reasonable rental.

Yet you can also come upon a disappointing Belgravia address, because there are a lot of furnished flats to let in the area. These can be super-luxurious, or downright tatty. A friend recalls racing in the first available taxi to a furnished flat in Chesham Place. The landlady boasted that a Czechoslovak diplomat had lived in it for two years, and he had just left for home. But the flat was barely visible for the dirt, and the kitchen facilities consisted of one gas ring. What ensued was a nasty 'It's good enough for the diplomat but not for you' tirade from the landlady.

Amenities of the Area

Certainly the new restaurant Le Grand Vefour (sister to the Paris original) is an amenity; entrance in Pont Street, near Chesham Place.

Shopping: Elizabeth Street, the Beauchamp Place of Belgravia. A dream street of a country-village mix of shops, running parallel to Chester Square.

Lower Belgrave Street, and Ebury Street—two other shopping centres. Your Belgrave address will work magic with shopkeepers—the courtesy ratio is very high for Belgravia residents.

For supermarket shopping, Victoria is just next door, with a Sainsbury, and a huge food hall in Woolworth's.

The biggest advantage of living in this area is the view. Everything is so white-washed, clean and bright. It is truly a pleasure to walk the streets of Belgravia.

Annual Event: the Chester Square Fair for the Beautiful People of Belgravia. David Bailey and Lord Lichfield taking portrait photographs for £5 each.

Disadvantages?

Cost of living in this part of London is very high, and life style rather formal.

The streets used as throughways to Belgrave Square have very heavy traffic.

PIMLICO

Local council
City of Westminster

Postal areas
S.W.1

Type of housing
Victorian
Pre-war
Modern blocks

**Approximate number of flats
and houses in district**
15,000

Local estate agents
Best Gapp & Partners, 81 Elizabeth
St, S.W.1, 730 2266
John Foord & Co., 137 Victoria St,
S.W.1, 834 2002
John Haskins & Co.,
162 Tachbrook St, S.W.1,
828 2860
Tufnell & Partners, 28 Elizabeth St,
S.W.1, 730 9112
Big Twelve

APPROXIMATE COST OF HOUSING

Short lease unfurnished flats
annual rent
£1200–1800

Long lease unfurnished flats
price
£15–25,000

**(non commercial)
Houses freehold or leasehold**
price
£25–35,000

Amenity society
Westminster Society,
25 Vincent Sq, S.W.1
834 2063

Citizens' Advice Bureau
70 Lupus St, S.W.1
834 5727

TRANSPORTATION

Tube stops
Pimlico

Bus service routes
24 Victoria—Charing Cross—
Hampstead Heath

Resident parking
Yes. Permit £18 per year. Also off-street Parking; Warwick Way Garage,
Warwick Way: 290 spaces

Tube lines
Victoria

Travelling times
West End 5–10 mins
City 15–20 mins

VICTORIA

Local council
City of Westminster

Postal areas
S.W.1

Type of housing
Victorian
Mansion blocks
Tower blocks

Approximate number of flats and houses in district
2000

Local estate agents
Douglas Lyons & Lyons,
33 Kinnerton St, S.W.1, 235 7933
Bernard Thorpe & Partners,
1 Buckingham Palace Rd, S.W.1,
842 6890
George Trollope & Sons,
13 Hobart Place, S.W.1, 235 4441
Big Twelve

APPROXIMATE COST OF HOUSING

Short lease unfurnished flats
annual rent
£1000–2000

Long lease unfurnished flats
price
£15–20,000

(non commercial) Houses freehold or leasehold
price
£20–30,000

Amenity society
Westminster Society,
25 Vincent Sq, S.W.1
834 2063

Citizens' Advice Bureau
70 Lupus St, S.W.1
834 5727

TRANSPORTATION

Tube stops
Victoria

Bus service routes
Numerous

Tube lines
Victoria
District
Circle

Travelling times
West End 5 mins
City 10–15 mins

Resident parking
Yes. Permit £18 per year. Also off-street Parking; Rochester Row Garage,
Rochester Row, S.W.1: 300 spaces

Pimlico

A Bit of History...

Pimlico is the product of Thomas Cubitt, the property developer of the 1800s (see section on Belgravia). The low-lying fields of Pimlico were largely pasture, nursery garden or rubbish dump during the eighteenth century, when Mayfair and Highgate were the height of residential fashion. Pimlico's houses stand today as sturdy as when they were built: some of them are carefully kept; others, however, are derelict from lack of care.

The Atmosphere...The People...

Pimlico suffers from a high proportion of transient Londoners living in furnished accommodation. Look at the once grand and glorious houses of the three major squares of Pimlico—Warwick, Eccleston and St George's—all are now divided into flats of the bedsit or one to two bedroom variety. Though Pimlico is just a few minutes away from Belgravia, it has somehow never acquired the prestige of its neighbour.

The people of Pimlico are a mixed lot:
1) Council tenants.
2) Office workers going home to bedsits.
3) Trendy types who shop in Casa Pupo and live near or in Pimlico Road, attracted to the area by the prestige which Anthony Armstrong Jones brought to it when he lived there!

Thus Pimlico is what some Londoners might call an honest area. The middle-income trendy crowd has not yet succeeded in taking over, and an honest urban mix of people continue to live there.

Pimlico has always seemed a rather lonely corner of London, just south of Victoria with few buses and no tube stop. Perhaps it will come into its own when the Victoria Line tube extension opens its Pimlico stop.

A Look at the Buildings, Outstanding Streets and Squares...

That part of Pimlico nearest to Sloane Square and Chelsea is best, from the good shops and people point of view. The south-west corner, near the river, is best from the homebuyer's point of view. A house for sale there at £20,000 may cost £80,000–100,000 next door in Belgravia. The typical Pimlico house is three to four storeys high, solid and plain, and part of a cream-coloured terrace. The street is straight as an arrow. Ian Nairn, the tongue-in-cheek architectural commentator, says one could live in Pimlico for years, and still not be certain, at night time, whether he is ringing the correct doorbell. But even though Pimlico's houses are not serenic wonders, they are available at reasonable proces.

Pimlico has only a few mews: Warwick Square Mews, West End Mews, and St George's Square Mews. So this means charm is somewhat lacking in the area. But charm is in the eyes of the beholder.

One very creative flat hunter noticed a railway station that was not in use, and sought advice from friends as to how she could find out if it were to let. . . . Sure enough, British Rail let the old Chelsea Station to her (it is actually by the bridge which separates Pimlico and Chelsea) and she has the high ceilings she wanted in Belgrave Square, but could not afford there. And as an added bonus, she has a beautiful view of the Thames from every room, and a rather surrealistic view of the bridge from her kitchen. Where there's a will, there's a way! The rent is low, but the restructuring of walls, installation of plumbing and heating and floors, has brought her rent up to just what one would pay to live in any of London's prestige areas. And her investment was a risk, for British Rail need give her no more, or no less, than six months' notice to clear out. She has been in her railway terminal for five years now, but recently surveyors came to call, and told her they were measuring for a new hotel.

Some of the best buys in Pimlico houses are those on the small streets off Buckingham Palace Road, south of St George's Drive, which is heavy with traffic and houses converted into hotels. Alderney, Cambridge, Sussex and Hugh Streets are the special ones. Alderney Street, though, faces a huge

Aerial view of Dolphin Square　　　　　　　　　　　　　　*(Aerofilms)*

development of council flats. Westmoreland Place and Terrace, off Sutherland Street, have four-bedroom houses going from £17,000—30,000, not at all bad for central London. This southern part of Pimlico is becoming highly family-oriented, with fewer transients than the northern sector near Victoria.

Rivermill is a new development of forty-two flats, three minutes from the new Pimlico tube station. Each of the one to three bedroom flats has its own balcony overlooking the river—sold for up to £22,000 for ninety-six-year leases. Wates is the builder of this block, which looks like an office block from the road, and stands in a rather lonely spot just next to the bridge.

Dolphin Square, on Grosvenor Road (the embankment) is possibly the best block of service flats in London. So if you want to park yourself in Pimlico and look for a house or flat, you're in luck with regard to a temporary place to live. Dolphin Square has 1200 separate flats, from bedsit to two-double bedroom in size. The flats are fully furnished, offering all the conveniences of a hotel—theatre tickets agent, shops, swimming pool and squash courts—as well as home—iron and ironing board in every flat. For further information on rates, write to Dolphin Square Trust Ltd, Dolphin Square, S.W.1.

Amenities of the Area

Shopping in Pimlico Road. Many tests for the eye. Casa Pupo, antique shops, Elizabeth David's cookery headquarters around the corner. And around

Eccleston Square

Alderney Street

Pimlico Road

yet another corner, on Lower Sloane Street, are more colourful shops—
Mexican and Japanese gifts and garb, a French charcuterie.

Gardens: the Royal Hospital Gardens in Chelsea are within walking distance.
More gardens in a small park just opposite St George's Square, between
Grosvenor Road and the river.

Budget shopping? Lupus Street, where most of the council tenants shop.
Supermarket? Victoria Street, Sainsburys. Barrow Boys? A great gathering
in Denbigh and Tachbrook Street.

British United Airways and B.O.A.C. Air terminals nearby, convenient for
the Common Market commuter.

Good junk-cum-antique shopping at the top of Vauxhall Bridge Road.

Victoria

Because the residential area called Victoria is composed largely of mansion
blocks, not houses, and because this area has such a strong identity of its
own—all tied up with Victoria Station—Victoria must remain separate from
Pimlico. And yet the shopping and transport facilities for north Pimlico and
Victoria are exactly the same.

Only one part of Victoria has anything old-world about it: miniscule
Victoria Square, off Buckingham Palace Road. The small white houses seem
like dwarfs, at the foot of a mountainous building called Portland House.
Located in Stag Place, along with an office block called Portland House, is a
block of luxury flats.

Carlisle Mansions on Victoria Street

Luxury flats on Stag Place

Behind Victoria Station, in a small triangle which has Victoria Street and Vauxhall Bridge Road as its two sides, lie many streets of solid mansion blocks: all red brick, some spruced up with cream stripes of paint; all with reasonably priced rentals, very reasonable in fact. One family pays £800 a year for a nine-room maisonette in Carlisle Mansions, a Freshwater building. In the midst of this triangle of mansion blocks is Westminster Cathedral, the centre of the Roman Catholic Church in Britain.

The great convenience of living near Victoria is not worth repeating. But the inconvenience of living in an area with absolutely no green for children to play on or prams to be pushed on is something to think about. St James's Park is the nearest green, and it is quite a lengthy walk away.

The many acres that now make up Victoria Station's complex will be redeveloped within the near future. Victoria Street is seeing the handiwork of demolition crews and builders at this moment. But it is unlikely that any of these redevelopers will make way for open spaces in an area where commercial properties are so highly valuable.

KENSINGTON

Local council
Royal Borough of Kensington &
Chelsea

Postal areas
W.8

Type of housing
Victorian
Georgian
Mews houses
Pre-war
Modern blocks
Mansion blocks

**Approximate number of flats
and houses in district**
9000

Local estate agents
Robert Bruce, St James House,
13 Kensington Sq, W.8, 937 9684
Chesterton & Sons, 116
Kensington High St, W.8, 937 1234
Cluttons, 48 Pelham St, S.W.7,
584 3651
Farmer Son & Bennett, 1 Argyll Rd,
W.8, 937 2278
Arthur Pinelees & Co.,
266 Kensington High St, W.8,
602 3259
Row & Son, 35a Kensington High
St, W.8, 937 3214
Charles Saunders & Son,
40 Gloucester Rd, S.W.7, 589 0134
Big Twelve

APPROXIMATE COST OF HOUSING

Short lease unfurnished flats
annual rent
£1100–1600

Long lease unfurnished flats
price
£15–30,000

**(non commercial)
Houses freehold or leasehold**
price
£35–60,000

Amenity society
Kensington Society,
1 Durham Place, S.W.3
352 8517

Citizens' Advice Bureau
Chelsea Town Hall,
King's Rd, S.W.3
352 8101

TRANSPORTATION

Tube stops
Gloucester Road
High Street Kensington

Bus service routes
49 Crystal Palace—Shepherds
Bush
52 Victoria Station
73 King's Cross—Oxford Circus
74 Camden Town—Putney

Tube lines
Circle
District

Travelling times
West End 8–10 mins
City 23–28 mins

Resident parking
Yes. Permit £26 per year

Kensington

A Bit of History . . .

In the beginning, Kensington was a Saxon king's town, which grew to be a famous centre for market gardens and vineyards in Elizabethan times. This healthy spot attracted evacuees of the Great Plague of 1665, and thus Kensington grew by leaps and bounds. William II attracted even more people when he moved his court from Whitehall to Kensington, a place he thought much more amenable for his asthma. The King and his court inspired much building of fine houses and shops in Kensington. The Manor of Kensington remained in the DeVere family from the reign of Wiiliam I to James I, a period of more than 500 years.

The Atmosphere . . . The People . . .

Kensington is basically a very stable area of comfortable families, with some pockets of 'singles'. You will not find Kensington studded with stars, or even diplomats—but rather with some of London's most solid citizens, who shop in the High Street, send their children to traditional schools, and have a house in the country. Of course things are happening to change Kensington's stability. The building of large hotels like the Royal Garden is one movement. And the influx of pop shops like Biba, Mr Freedom, Bus Stop and the Kensington Market is yet another sign of changing times in Kensington. Pontings, a long-standing store in the High Street, is coming down to make way for a giant hotel.

The result of this invasion of the High Street by a new population is a very interesting mix of people—long-haired, long-skirted girls smelling of patchouli oil; blue-jeaned cowboy-jacketed boys; and conventional mums with prams heading for Barkers department store.

This is an area where property prices can be as high as those of Mayfair and Belgravia, but where there is also lower-priced property; and the people and the atmosphere are much more informal.

A Look at the Buildings, Outstanding Streets and Squares . . .

Kensington is a big borough, and you will find many visual changes as you go from one part to another.

The eastern end of Kensington—Prince's Gate and Exhibition Road—is made up of masses of big blocks of modern flats, a bit institutional-looking compared to the rest of cosy Kensington. The western end consists largely of the handsome houses which successful men will pay anywhere from £50,000 75,000 to acquire. Kensington has a high proportion of mansion blocks, and

Campden Hill

numerous small villages within the larger village of Kensington. The mansion blocks are located either in the High Street, or just behind it. You'll find French families gravitating to one block, Americans to another, largely because their friends were there before them, and recommended the place. Here is a short list of some of the best-known blocks of flats:

Hornton Court, Hornton Street

Iverna Mansions, just behind the old Pontings. Trafalgar House is the landlord

Ingelow House, Kensington Church Walk

Vicarage Court, near the bend in Kensington Church Street

Kensington Court Mansions, Kensington Court (many other mansion blocks in Kensington Court as well)

Queen's Gate and the High Street end of Marloes Road have numerous blocks of flats as well.

One of the most prestigious blocks of flats in London is located just behind the Albert Hall. Albert Court has a wide circular drive, and an entrance hall as large as a street. The staircases are carpeted in red, the ceilings are high and the fireplaces stately. The rents are reasonable, but the premiums requested by most departing tenants are extremely high, £2000–7000 for fixtures and fittings that some globe-trotting family cannot take to Teheran or Paris.

Old Court in Old Court Place is another attractive block: forty-five flats in a beautiful building above Woolworth's. The modernized lobby is deceptive: take the lift to the porter's flat on the top floor and you will see lovely wooden floors and decorative iron railings. Flats are for sale and sub-letting.

Hillgate Village, behind the High Street, heading towards Notting Nill, is Kensington's best example of a village within a village. The small houses that lie off Kensington Church Street, north of Peel Street, are former working-men's cottages, and can occasionally be purchased for under £25,000.

Campden Hill, which sits behind Hillgate Village, is another popular and village-like area. Its charm has attracted Lord Patrick Lichfield, the jet-setting photographer, and Lady Antonia Fraser, the writer. Aubrey Road and Walk were built originally to hold the stables and cottages of the larger houses in Campden Hill and Campden Hill Square.

To find your way round the part of Kensington which lies north of the High Street, simply follow Kensington Church Street, and take any of the roads leading off it. Be sure to see Holland Street, which is like something you'd come across in an old book of fairy-tales; and Gordon Place, a cul-de-sac of vine-covered cottages.

On the other side of the High Street, behind Barkers department store, lies a picturesque area of Kensington, much of which has been designated for conservation by the Civic Trust:

Kensington Square
Stratford Studios, off Stratford Road
Cottesmore Gardens

A period house in Kensington

Kensington Square

Scarsdale Villas
Allen Street
Launceston Place, Victoria Road.

This entire area is as quiet as a country village, with no heavy traffic roads running through it. An equally pretty area is at the western end of this 'south side' of the High Street. Edwardes Square and Pembroke Square both have a crisp well-to-do family image (Dr Roger Bannister lives on the former), and their own 'private club pub' which lies between the two squares. This is, in fact, a very artistic example of nineteenth-century town planning. When these houses, developed in 1802, went on the market for sale in 1914, the selling price was £800 each!

Highest priced Kensington? Kensington Palace Gardens is probably the most famous strip of houses in Kensington, and probably the only road in London with a liveried gatekeeper at either end! This is Crown Land, and Princess Margaret and Lord Snowdon are residents. The millionaires' Victorian mansions which line the road are inhabited to a great extent by diplomats, though some of the houses have been divided into luxury flats. Eight Kensington Palace Gardens, a new building, is made up of four flats and a penthouse.

The smaller houses on the park side of Kensington—where both Winston Churchill and John F. Kennedy once lived—come upon the market only occasionally. Number 50 Hyde Park Gate, a modern house in the Georgian style, recently sold for £170,000 on a ninety-three-year lease. Number 19 Prince's Gate went for £100,000 freehold.

Amenities of the Area

You have your choice of village-like shopping—Thackeray Street, near Kensington Square, or Abingdon Road; or High Street shopping. Many of

Kensington Palace Gardens

A Victoria Road house

London's trendiest shops are here: Biba, Feathers, Bus Stop.

For food, a Safeway and Barkers food hall.

Kensington Gardens, with the Round Pond, Kensington Palace and the London Museum.

The Royal Albert Hall, with its popular summer Promenade Concerts.

Kensington Church Street—mecca for antique hunters.

A fine selection of reasonably priced restaurants.

Disadvantages?

The borough council has been rather permissive to property developers wanting to build hotels in Kensington. As a result the borough is in some sections losing its residential purity.

SOUTH KENSINGTON

Local council
Royal Borough of Kensington & Chelsea

Postal areas
S.W.7

Type of housing
Victorian
Regency
Mews houses
Pre-war
Modern blocks

Approximate number of flats and houses in district
6000

Local estate agents
Cluttons, 48 Pelham St, S.W.7, 584 3651
W. A. Ellis, 174 Brompton Rd, S.W.3, 589 2425
Farley & Co., 46 Old Brompton Rd, S.W.7, 584 6491
Friend & Falcke, 293 Brompton Rd, S.W.3, 584 5361
Harrods Estate Office, 34 Hans Crescent, S.W.1, 589 1490
Johnson & Pycraft, 23 Cromwell Place, S.W.7, 584 6268
Knight & Co., 180 Brompton Rd, S.W.3, 589 8234
Ruck & Ruck, 17 Old Brompton Rd, S.W.7, 584 3721
Charles Saunders & Son, 40 Gloucester Rd, S.W.7, 589 0134
Big Twelve

APPROXIMATE COST OF HOUSING
Short lease unfurnished flats
annual rent
£11–1800

Long lease unfurnished flats
price
£18–35,000

(non commercial) Houses freehold or leasehold
price
£35–65,000

Amenity society
Kensington Society,
1 Durham Place, S.W.3
352 8517

Citizens' Advice Bureau
Chelsea Town Hall,
King's Rd, S.W.3
352 8101

TRANSPORTATION

Tube stops
South Kensington

Bus service routes
14 King's Cross—Piccadilly—Putney
30 Baker Street—Islington
74 The Zoo—Camden Town

Tube lines
Circle
District
Piccadilly

Travelling times
West End 5 mins
City 15–20 mins

Resident parking
Yes. Permit £26 per year

South Kensington

A Bit of History...

The profits of the Great Exhibition of 1851 were used to build the museums for which South Kensington has become world-famous: the Victoria and Albert, the Natural History, Geological and Science Museums. This spurt in the building of museums undoubtedly provided the impetus for building many of the homes which now make up the residential area called South Kensington.

The Atmosphere...The People...

The houses and blocks of flats and shops within walking distance of the tube station, plus all the museums, make up the well-known area of South Kensington. It has a very mixed bag of people. Traditional Kensingtonians live in the handsomest houses, such as those of Onslow Square, where William Thackeray used to write. There's a large population of working girls in bedsits, and singles sharing a large flat in a large house. And you'll hear a great many French accents in South Kensington shops too, for many French families live in the area, to be close to the Lycée in Cromwell Road.

Though most people consider South Ken to be limited to a small area surrounding the tube stop, in this book we are stretching South Ken's boundaries, as far west as Gloucester Road, and along Brompton Road even further west, as far as the Boltons.

A Look at the Buildings, Outstanding Streets and Squares...

Use the main roads running away from the South Ken tube station as your avenues for exploration. Once you've wandered down each of those— Harrington Road, Brompton Road, Cromwell Road, Thurloe Place, Pelham Street—you'll have seen most of South Ken. It is quite a good area for wandering and stopping in the offices of small estate agents who've been in the area since time began. That, in fact, is just the way we found our eight-room, two-bathroom flat for under £1000 a year rental.

South Ken is made up basically of three types of dwellings: the one-family house; the tall terrace house divided into small flats; or big blocks of flats, such as those right near the tube, or further along Old Brompton Road, approaching Earl's Court.

Capsule descriptions of some of the areas of South Ken:

Pelham Crescent and Place, built by an Italian architect in the 1820s: simply beautiful, and very, very expensive.

Drayton Gardens, an interesting architectural mix: cottages, large family houses, and mansion blocks with iron balconies.

Queen's Gate, heavy with traffic, but houses are stately and handsome.

Exhibition Road houses

Pelham Crescent

Queen's Gate

A mansion on The Boltons

Queen's Gate Gardens, with Queen's Gate, has some of the best examples of high ceiling, huge reception room, elegant family flats. The floor that was once a billiard room in the huge family house is now a huge flat for one family!

Thurloe Square and Place, a stone's throw from the tube, the Victoria and Albert on your doorstep, Harrods just up the road. What more could one ask of a location?

Hereford Square, and Clareville Street, off Gloucester Road: houses which sold for £1000 in 1940 go for £30,000 and upwards now.

The Boltons, a very special London address. Grand Victorian semi-detached villas, constructed with a most artistic use of iron and glass decoration—note the glass and ironwork canopies on some of the houses. A beautiful communal garden, oval-shaped, surrounding a church. Douglas Fairbanks Jr lives in the corner house, with its walled garden running along Tregunter Road. Many of the houses in the Boltons are divided into flats, but there is still an air of elegance about the place. The Little Boltons and Bolton Gardens, nearby, are nothing like the Boltons itself.

Brechin Place and Rosary Gardens, red brick houses, largely bedsits.

Brompton Road and Old Brompton Road, heavy with traffic. Turns into bed-sit land after Drayton Gardens.

Amenities of the Area

Very pretty girls at the South Ken bus stops, taking numbers 14 and 30.

The very best of the trendy Fulham Road, with its shops, restaurants and pretty people, is just a short walk away.

The area is keen on church socials and summer garden parties—nice amusements for the children in good weather. There are a large number of nursery schools as well.

The best of small-scale daily shopping is round the South Ken tube and in Bute Street. For large-scale shopping, Knightsbridge is just next door, and Chelsea King's Road is within walking distance.

The Museums, children's entertainment for all seasons.

Bousfield School, the Boltons, has the reputation of being a very fine infant school.

EARL'S COURT — GLOUCESTER ROAD

Local council
Royal Borough of Kensington &
Chelsea

Postal areas
S.W.5, S.W.7, S.W.10

Type of housing
Victorian
Mews houses
Edwardian
Mansion blocks

**Approximate number of flats
and houses in district**
7000

Local estate agents
Donaldson, 125 Gloucester Rd,
S.W.7, 370 4500
Charles Saunders & Son,
40 Gloucester Rd, S.W.7, 589 0134
William Willet, 146 Gloucester Rd,
S.W.7, 370 4066
Wilson & Co., 102 Earl's Court Rd,
W.8, 937 4321

APPROXIMATE COST OF HOUSING

Short lease unfurnished flats
annual rent
£1000—1500

Long lease unfurnished flats
price
£15—25,000

**(non commercial)
Houses freehold or leasehold**
price
£25—40,000

Amenity society
Kensington & Chelsea Rate Payers,
Residents & Tenants Association,
4 Oakfield St, S.W.10

Citizens' Advice Bureau
Chelsea Town Hall,
King's Road, S.W.3
352 8101

TRANSPORTATION

Tube stops
Gloucester Road
Earl's Court

Bus service routes
30 Baker Street—Islington
74 The Zoo—Camden Town
Marble Arch

Resident parking
Yes. Permit £26 per year

Tube lines
Circle
District
Piccadilly

Travelling times
West End 5—10 mins
City 15—20 mins

Earl's Court –
Gloucester Road

A Bit of History . . .

Earl's Court was once a rather elegant part of Kensington, as you will guess when you look at some of the big old houses there. It was the site of mineral waters called Billings Well, and fashionable Londoners flocked to those waters. Earl's Court derives its name from the original manorial court of Kensington.

The Atmosphere . . . The People . . .

Earl's Court is the epitome of London bed-sit land: though there are bed-sits all over London, it is the symbol of that way-of-life in one room. If a street is not fully made up of bed-sits, then it houses hotels. Earl's Court probably has the lowest private-ownership of property ratio of any area in London. This is a transient area—for young single people, for one-week tourists, for families on a year's sabbatical leave or business assignments. The Earl's Court area has many student hostels, and you will see the blue jeaned, rucksack-on-back young crowd all the year round, reading the room-to-let notices, or queueing up for space in a student hostel.

A Look at the Buildings, Outstanding Streets and Squares . . .

West Cromwell Road, marking the northern border of Earl's Court, consists of mansion blocks, but the fact that they are fully inhabited is a surprise, because the traffic roars by twenty-four hours a day. Warwick Road, the western boundary of Earl's Court, is dreary, with heavy traffic and dilapidated houses.

The heart of Earl's Court is around the tube station. The Neverns', Place and Square, are within walking distance of the tube. The Neverns' handsome terrace houses are made up entirely of flats, if they've not been converted into hotels. Earl's Court Square is probably the only part of Earl's Court where any of the houses have one-family occupancy. The three-storey houses on the south side of the square are single-family houses; the larger multi-tenanted houses are on the other sides.

At the junction of Old Brompton Road, Redcliffe Gardens and Earl's Court Road are some large blocks of flats—Colherne Court, with private gardens behind noisy Old Brompton Road, was recently cleared and restored to look quite handsome. Redcliffe Gardens and Square are a bit tatty, but flats in the area go for very reasonable rents. Redcliffe Gardens has abominable traffic, so you would have to look for flats in the back of the houses.

Go east of Earl's Court Road, toward Gloucester Road, and you will see

Earl's Court Gardens   Earl's Court Square

some sights that are not so grim as those in the dirtier, heavier populated area near the Earl's Court tube. Bramham Gardens and Barkston Gardens are two very attractive squares of mock-baroque buildings. Both have lovely communal gardens, and pretty mews nearby. Some mews houses sell for Belgravia prices, so the Earl's Court area can't be all bad.

Still further east, closer now to Gloucester Road tube than to Earl's Court, and now and then taking the name South Ken rather than Earl's Court—are Courtfield, Harrington and Wetherby Gardens. Harrington Gardens is going through a metamorphosis—one feels that hotels will have completely taken over the place in ten years' time. Wetherby Gardens has a small garden; and Courtfield Gardens, which is really two squares, with two separate gardens, are both very pretty, but unpredictable. Some of the houses in Courtfield Gardens west have as many as thirty doorbells, which is bed-sit land for certain. Some of the houses, in Courtfield Gardens east have huge elegant ten-and twelve-room family flats.

Both Earl's Court Road and Gloucester Road have a large number of estate agents, so you should have no trouble finding a furnished flat, if you want one in this area. It is in fact not a bad place to park yourself or your family while you do your looking about for a more permanent London address. You may find some balking or hesitation if you have children, for in bed-sit and furnished-flat London, there is some sort of horror of children, which is not difficult to understand. Landlords do not want to become ridden with tenants who are permanent and will not leave. They prefer the mobile flat-sharers in their early twenties, who move in and out of their flats very quickly.

Amenities of the Area

Great public transport. At the Cromwell Road end of Earl's Court Road, you're within walking distance of Holland Park; at the Gloucester Road end, in walking distance of Kensington Gardens and the Round Pond, where kites fly on Sunday mornings and ducks swim every day.

Excellent shopping, of department store variety, nearby in Kensington High Street. Earl's Court Road is probably best road in London for late night, or even all night, food shops. Excellent shopping on Gloucester Road as well, a step above Earl's Court Road in price and tone.

International restaurants abound: Sinhalese, Yugoslav, Italian, Indian, Chinese to name a few.

Earl's Court Exhibition Hall, site of many annual events like the Boat Show and the Motor Show. This is the site where the Wild West Shows of Buffalo Bill were held in 1887!

Disadvantages?

The Dirt—dreadful fumes to inhale around Earl's Court and Warwick Roads. Earl's Court Road itself seems perpetually dirty with papers and litter.

In this area of frequent turnover among tenants, one never knows what

A Victorian house on Harrington Gardens

Laverton Mews

house or square will disappear next to make way for a luxury hotel. There really is no security for tenants here.

Suspicious characters gravitate to an all-night area like this. Many policemen on patrol, and plain-clothes police also in evidence. Almost any single girl who lives in the area can tell you some stories of her sordid experiences as a resident in Earl's Court.

CHELSEA

Local council
Royal Borough of Kensington &
Chelsea

Postal areas
S.W.3

Type of housing
Cottages
Mews houses
Georgian
Pre-war
Mansion block
Queen Anne

Approximate number of flats and houses in district
10,000

Local estate agents
Aylesford & Co., 440 King's Rd,
S.W.10, 351 0121
Cowley & Andersen, 13 Langton
St, S.W.10, 352 0201
Friend & Falcke, 293 Brompton Rd,
S.W.3, 584 5361
Jackson Rose & Co., 296a King's
Rd, S.W.3, 352 1066
D. Pinto & Co., 15 Dover St, W.1,
493 2242
Tufnell & Partners, 28 Elizabeth St,
S.W.1, 730 9112
William Willett, 146 Gloucester Rd,
S.W.7, 370 4066
John D. Wood, 9 Cale St, S.W.3,
352 1484
Big Twelve

APPROXIMATE COST OF HOUSING

Short lease unfurnished flats
annual rent
£1000–1800

Long lease unfurnished flats
price
£15–30,000

(non commercial)
Houses freehold or leasehold
price
£35–50,000

Amenity society
Chelsea Society,
1 Durham Place, S.W.3
352 8517

Citizens' Advice Bureau
Chelsea Town Hall,
King's Rd, S.W.3
352 8101

TRANSPORTATION

Tube stops
Sloane Square

Bus service routes
11 Victoria—Bank
19 Piccadilly Circus—Islington
22 Hyde Park Corner—Bank
39 Victoria—Oxford Circus
137 Oxford Circus

Tube lines
Circle
District

Travelling times
West End 5–10 mins
City 15–20 mins

Resident parking
Yes. Permit £26 per year

Chelsea

A Bit of History...

Chelsea was once just a small village by the river, surrounded by fields and woods—a good distance from the City of London. Quiet, pretty, not much more. Early in the 1520s Sir Thomas More built a Palace there, and nobles and courtiers, and even King Henry VIII began to visit him at his country retreat. Holbein painted Sir Thomas More with his family, and Erasmus discoursed on the advantages of living by the river.

Thus Chelsea became fashionable, and even more so in 1682 when Charles the II built the Royal Hospital there. King Charles can take the credit for the start of the fame of the King's Road, for it was he who discovered it as a short cut from Whitehall to Hampton Court. It was during the eighteenth and nineteenth centuries that Chelsea acquired its reputation as a focal point for London's artists. The list of painters associated with Chelsea is long: Whistler, J. M. W. Turner and D. G. Rossetti, high priest of the Pre-Raphaelite school, who kept a private zoo in Chelsea. Chelsea has just as many literary names in its list of famous citizens: George Eliot, Henry James, Oscar Wilde, Thomas Carlyle.

The Atmosphere... The People...

Chelsea still has its share of artists and writers—the successful ones, however, and Chelsea has more than its accredited share of models, playboys, bachelors and trendy types. It is almost superfluous to go into the 'swinging Chelsea' phenomenon of the sixties, when the Beatles and the mini-skirted birds of the King's Road became world famous. Chelsea will bask for a long time in its former glory, and though Chelsea is not now the focal point for swingers of the world that it was in the 1960s, it still has enough interesting characters to make it lively. Many divorced Londoners choose Chelsea as their new home. No area has yet replaced Chelsea as a swinging centre of London.

Chelsea is simply a great place to live. It has not been overrated in any of the magazines or movies. But the househunter will probably come to believe that Chelsea is overpriced. There simply is not enough room, at price levels low enough, for all the people who would like to live in Chelsea—£20,000 and up for a two-storey four-small-room workman's cottage with window-box gardens and a brass knocker on the door! And these cottages went for £900 before the war.

A Look at the Buildings, Outstanding Streets and Squares...

Ian Nairn, that light-hearted observer of architecture, says Chelsea hasn't enough eccentric buildings to match its eccentric citizens. He is so right. Row after row of two-, three- and four-storey terrace houses seem to make up the

St Leonard's Terrace

Just Looking on King's Road

Queen's Elm Square

Cheyne Walk

Albert Bridge

bulk of Chelsea. An occasional picturesque square is added for good measure —Paulton's Square, Carlyle and Chelsea Squares.

But even with its lack of 'landmark architecture' Chelsea still works—it is a fine place to live, particularly fine south of the King's Road, heading toward the river. This southern area is best for open spaces, and for overall charm. Burton's Court is the big square-open space with St Leonard's Terrace and Durham Place facing it. Both the latter have lovely old houses with front and back gardens, some heavily planted with delicious flowers like jasmine.

Cheyne Walk and the Embankment, with some Queen Anne houses, have some of the most attractive red brick mansions in London. If you're interested in living in a houseboat on the river, rather than in a house by the river, then this is the best area for looking. One complaint from residents of Chelsea's houseboat colony is that the refuse is dumped very near their mooring, and the summer smell can be revolting. Between Cheyne Walk and the King's Road, in the area of the Cross Keys Pub, is probably the prettiest, quietest part of Chelsea. Note Glebe Place.

Oakley Street, leading south from the King's Road to the river, is heavy with traffic, but off Oakley Street are quiet, pretty pockets such as Margaretta Terrace. This terrace is church-owned property.

Radnor Walk, where Ossie Clark started his fashion empire in a little cottage, is typical of the streets of cottages found throughout Chelsea. Tite Street has some studio houses specially built in the 1870s for artists.

Lower Sloane Street and Sloane Gardens are the only areas south of the King's Road which would not qualify for a description as 'Chelsea Charming'.

World's End, an area of narrow streets at the bottom of the King's Road, will soon be the site of a ten-and-a-half acre council scheme, one of the largest council housing projects in London. Stay away from that end if you're seeking Chelsea Charm.

North of the King's Road, as far as Fulham Road, is the second half of Chelsea for the house hunter to explore. Carlyle Square, with handsome houses for over £65,000, is where author Edna O'Brien lived for a long time. Equally prestigious is Chelsea Square, just behind Carlyle Square.

The Vale, and Old Church Street, both wind through Chelsea like country lanes. Both have the ivy-covered cottages and large houses that make picture postcards, and that were never intended to be fronted by traffic-filled roads. Markham Square is a lovely 'north Chelsea' location.

Most of the big blocks of flats in Chelsea are located in or near Sloane Avenue. Cranmer Court, Chelsea Cloisters and Nell Gwynne House are good examples of flat-life in Chelsea.

Number 1 Sloane Square is an exciting example of a new block of flats: note the group of studios around a paved courtyard. The Cadogan Estate, which owns most of this Sloane Square area, has been criticized for letting the modern-block builders into Chelsea, and for being far too profit-conscious. Note the abundance of modern landscape in Sloane Street, going north from Sloane Square.

Amenities of the Area

Almost too numerous to mention!

Shopping: the King's Road has just about everything, but is a bit heavy on dress boutiques filled with mass-produced goods, and a bit over loaded with traffic. Peter Jones, with its 1930s glass-curved facade, is a popular shop—they guarantee that their prices will be just a bit lower than any other department store. World's End, the western end of Chelsea, has a cluster of bargain shops. Between those two points are butchers, bakers, supermarkets, restaurants, the works.

Lower Sloane Street, heading toward Pimlico, is a very unusual street for shops. So is Elystan Street, north of the King's Road. Walton Street, very accessible for north Chelsea, is small-shop land at its best—restaurants, decorating shops, a stationer, gift shops, florist—intimate, yet complete.

Special events going on in Chelsea all the year round: the Chelsea Flower Show, in the gardens of the Royal Hospital; the Chelsea Village Fair, in the grounds of the Rectory in Old Church Street. All sorts of shopping bazaars and fairs in the Town Hall, the Antique Fair being the best known.

The Royal Court Theatre, scene of the debut of John Osborne's *Look Back in Anger*, and site of many productions which end up in the West End or on Broadway.

The Royal Hospital, designed and built by Sir Christopher Wren: 'For the succour and relief of aged veterans and men broken by war'.

Home of Thomas Carlyle, 24 Cheyne Row.

Chelsea Open Air Nursery, Glebe Place.

Disadvantages?

Perhaps Chelsea is too crowded with tourists and other transients to please the home-maker. There is little peace in the King's Road area. The tourists are even invading the once private flat blocks of Chelsea. Tenants of Chelsea Cloisters in Sloane Avenue took their landlord to court two years ago, when he was letting some of the smaller flats in the building on a daily basis, as hotel rooms.

Chelsea has many furnished flats on short leases, but it's short on long leases or freeholds at believable prices.

The Good Pubs: the Cross Keys, off Cheyne Walk; the Queen's Elm, near Fulham Road and Old Church Street; and the Chelsea Potter, in the King's Road.

BATTERSEA

Local council
London Borough of Wandsworth

Postal areas
S.W.11

Type of housing
Victorian
Mansion blocks
Cottages

**Approximate number of flats
and houses in district**
12,000

Local estate agents
Aylesford & Co., 440 King's Rd,
S.W.10, 352 6744
Bell, Son & Co., 73 Battersea Rise,
S.W.11, 228 0935
Edward Evans & Sons,
251–3 Lavender Hill, S.W.11,
228 0051
Lofts & Partners, 123 Sydney St,
S.W.3, 351 0077

APPROXIMATE COST OF HOUSING

Long lease unfurnished flats
price
£10–15,000

**(non commercial)
Houses freehold or leasehold**
price
£15–20,000

Amenity society
Battersea Society,
197 Elseley Rd, S.W.11

Citizens' Advice Bureau
Katherine Low Settlement,
108 Battersea High St, S.W.11
228 0272

TRANSPORTATION

Bus service routes
19 Sloane Square—Piccadilly
Circus
44 London Bridge Station
49 Kensington—Shepherd's Bush
137 Sloane Square—Oxford Circus

Train services
British Rail, Southern Region

Travelling times
Battersea Park—Victoria
4 mins
Clapham Junction—Victoria
5–7 mins
Clapham Junction—Waterloo
10 mins

Frequency
Battersea Park—Victoria
Every 10 mins
Clapham Junction—Victoria
Every 4 mins
Clapham Junction—Waterloo
Every 5 mins

Travelling times
West End 15–20 mins
City 15–20 mins
(via 'train' from Waterloo to Bank)

Resident parking
No permit required

Battersea

A Bit of History . . .

The old riverside village of Battersea is still faintly recognizable today, but won't be for much longer. Remains of the Church, Church Road, High Street Inn, market place and Manor House, common to almost every village 200 years ago, can still be seen in Battersea, and there is a maritime air to the old part of Battersea to this day.

The Nine Elms ward of Battersea, which is the new home of Covent Garden, is of interest historically. It began as a market garden, organized by Flemish immigrants. Nine elms actually did grow on the river bank. The orchard owners used to throw open their gates to children who, for three old pence a head, could eat as much fruit as they could manage. Battersea asparagus was famous at the time.

In 1828, the road from Vauxhall to Battersea began to be dotted with houses. Battersea flourished, as did most of south London, with the coming of the industrial revolution, and the concurrent building boom.

The Atmosphere . . . The People . . .

The atmosphere round old Battersea Village, the southernmost part of Battersea, is one of demolition with dust in the air and construction crews everywhere. This is an area with a heavy concentration of council flats, and there is actually no part of Battersea which you could call handsome. One writer of old lamented: 'In the whole circuit of this borough of Battersea it is noteworthy that there is hardly a single feature of real architectural excellence apart from the stern beauty of a power house and a handful of relics of the time of Wren'. (The Wren relics he speaks of are Devonshire House and Old Battersea House on Vicarage Road—he was a very accurate observer!)

Battersea is far from beautiful, but it is convenient in terms of location, just across the river from Chelsea. And the Chelsea overflow has to settle somewhere. This area of Victorian houses and mansion blocks, almost all in red brick, is filled with young families doing up flats and houses they simply could not afford just the other side of the river.

There is a rather pessimistic feeling among many Battersea residents, of long and recent standing alike, that their area will become amalgamated into the borough of Wandsworth, and will lose its old village identity. The Battersea Society is at present opposing the acquisition of Battersea Square by the G.L.C. for it wishes the square to be developed so as to retain the characteristics of the old village. Battersea was once administered by the former Metropolitan Borough of Battersea.

A Look at the Buildings, Outstanding Streets and Squares . . .

The best of Battersea—that which is attracting the crowds for whom there is no room in Chelsea, is along and behind Prince of Wales Drive. Prince of Wales Drive is a long solid line of mansion blocks, all of the same interest visually, but some are better tended than others. These flats are attractive because they are just across the bridge from Chelsea, and because they face Battersea Park. All these blocks of flats have the name of the owner and/or the location of the porter clearly displayed for the benefit of the flat hunter!

Battersea's houses are not great, but they are bigger than those of Fulham, which has seen an incredible increase in property values when you consider the minimal inherent qualities of the properties there.

Between Prince of Wales Drive and Battersea Park Road (the latter a real traffic-jammed eyesore) are Battersea's most popular roads: Brynmaer Road, Kersley Street, Lurline Gardens. Kersley Road, with the largest houses, has a mews which is also popular. More mews are located off Albert Bridge Road and Petworth Street. Cambridge Road also has some large houses, but there is very heavy traffic along it.

The trouble with Battersea is not its questionable aesthetic quality, but the council, which seems to have bought up half of the borough. If redevelopment is not obvious at present, as it is round Battersea Church Road, Surrey Lane and Battersea High Street, then talk to the council before you buy. Motorways threaten Battersea just as much as large towers of council flats.

Prince of Wales Drive

Lurline Gardens

Cambridge Road

Battersea does not hold much for rent-a-flat families, except for the big blocks on Prince of Wales Drive, and many of these may soon be for sale, rather than for rent. One exception: at Vicarage Crescent near old Battersea Village, will be a private development of ten flats, some facing the river with private mooring facilities. Prices will be about £16,000 for two-bedroom flats.

Battersea is best for the person with a limited budget to spend on a Victorian house. In general, a Battersea house is not a bad buy, for the houses have tended to stay solid one-family places, and have not had the wear and tear of many tenants.

Leave Battersea proper by Latchmere Road, where one would never choose to live because it is so dreary. When you reach Lavender Hill, which is not as picturesque as it sounds, you'll find some Victorian terraces as attractive, if not more so, than those of Battersea—Lavender Gardens and Marjorie Grove are examples. These roads are closer to Clapham Common than to Battersea Park, and thus have a different set of shops, transport and other amenities.

Amenities of the Area

Not many.

Battersea Park, Battersea Fun Fair.

Old Battersea House, a seventeenth-century house reputedly designed by Wren, and sold last year for a 'peppercorn' to an American who is going to restore the house, and use part of it as his London home. The other part will be a museum, open to the public.

Proximity to Chelsea and the Swinging Centre of London.

129

Disadvantages?

The council housing projects are many, and the motorway threats are many as well. Battersea Village is a bit of a ghost-town. Heavy industry hovers all around the place. No tube stop. Transportation is poor, except near Clapham Junction, where British Rail trains whisk you to Victoria and Waterloo in a couple of minutes.

HOLLAND PARK — NOTTING HILL

Local council
Royal Borough of Kensington &
Chelsea

Postal areas
W.11, W.14

Type of housing
Victorian
Pre-war
Regency
Cottages
Mansion blocks
Edwardian
Modern blocks

**Approximate number of flats
and houses in district**
14,000

Local estate agents
Beale & Capps Willmott,
126 Ladbroke Grove, W.10,
727 5671
Harley Munt & Co., 7 Wellington
Terrace, Notting Hill Gate, W.2,
229 6227
Anthony Hill & Co., 16 Needham
Rd, W.11, 229 0072
Lofts & Partners, 141 Westbourne
Grove, W.11, 229 4344
Marsh & Parsons, 5 Kensington
Church St, W.8, 937 6091
J. A. Sinclair, 116b Holland Park
Ave, W.11, 727 1283
Sladden Stuart & Powell,
44 Royal Crescent, W.11, 602 0117
Frank Swain, 26 Notting Hill Gate,
W.11, 727 4433

Resident parking
Yes. Permit £26 per year

APPROXIMATE COST OF HOUSING

Short lease unfurnished flats
annual rent
£900—1300

Long lease unfurnished flats
price
£15—20,000

**(non commercial)
Houses freehold or leasehold**
price
£25—35,000

Amenity society
The Ladbroke Association,
25 Ladbroke Grove, W.11

Citizens' Advice Bureau
85 Ladbroke Grove, W.11
727 8170

TRANSPORTATION

Tube stops
Holland Park
Notting Hill Gate

Bus service routes
12 Oxford Circus—Trafalgar Sq
15 Bank—Piccadilly Circus
49 Kensington—Clapham
52 Victoria
88 Oxford Circus—Tate Gallery

Tube lines
Central
Circle
District

Travelling times
West End 10—14 mins
City 20—25 mins

Holland Park

A Bit of History . . .

In 1605, Sir Walter Cope began to build the great mansion which was to become Holland House, but for a time it was called Cope Castle, and then Kensington House, until 1661. The property descended to Cope's daughter, whose husband was the Earl of Holland. Four Lord Hollands in all lived in Holland House, the last owner being Lord Ilchester.

Holland House was a country house in London, right up to the nineteenth century; and it was one of the first social centres where the middle classes mixed with the wealthy upper classes. Holland House was destroyed, except for one wing, by bombs in the Second World War; and the London County Council acquired the property, and opened the grounds to Londoners in 1952.

Holland Park grew to be the residential area it is today in the mid-nineteenth century, when property development was booming next door in Notting Hill, with the building of grand houses demanded by a growing wealthy bourgeoisie.

The Atmosphere . . . The People . . .

There seems to be no unity or all-pervading aura about the Holland Park area until you go into the Park, and there it seems that everyone belongs to a big happy family. Holland Park is almost entirely a residential area, with clusters of two or three small shops here and there. The area, when it is good, is very very good; and when it is bad, it is horrid. It is more often good than bad, however. In the past five years, some property prices have doubled!

A Look at the Buildings, Outstanding Streets and Squares . . .

Some of the best of Holland Park is the area near Kensington High Street. Turn into Melbury Road, and there is Melbury Court, a huge and handsome block of flats, part of what was the Freshwater Group of properties (see p. 49). Melbury Road illustrates how the wealthy late-Victorian painters lived, for these houses were at one time their homes. Addison Road is lined with the same type of huge Victorian houses, and a few Regency-type buildings of cream stucco.

This part of Holland Park, the western sector, is full of big blocks of flats. Park Close, a nine-storey tower at the eastern end of Melbury Road, overlooks Holland Park. Farley Court, a six-storey block, is at the western end of Melbury Road, where it joins Addison Road.

One of the best-known blocks of flats in London is Oakwood Court, which is so big that it doesn't even have a street address. Simply W.14. About 200 huge flats, on five- to seven-year leases, make up the complex. One couple pay £80–100 a month, plus rates, for eight rooms and a private garden. Oakwood Court has many Americans as tenants; and some of the most spacious short-lease unfurnished flats in London. Again, it was part of the Freshwater Group. Usually one must pay a high fixtures and fittings premium to acquire a lease in Oakwood Court.

Two of the smart roads near the park are Abbotsbury Road (all fairly new, neo-Georgian houses facing the park but criticized as 'too small' by some of their owners) and Ilchester Place. Ilchester Place is often stated as an 'ideal location' by London house hunters, which also contains neo-Georgian houses, but they are double-fronted and thus more stately than the variety in Abbotsbury Road. Woodsford Square, off Addison Road, consists of brand new small family houses, built on the site where large, hard-to-manage mansions used to be. The old trees still remain, however. Chesterton is the agent.

Holland Road is the through route from Kensington High Street to Holland Park Avenue. This heavily travelled road is probably the worst part of the Holland Park residential area. Holland Park Avenue is also heavy with traffic, but the yellow stucco Regency houses are set far back from the road, often behind brick walls, and seem protected from the noise and dirt.

Addison Gardens, and Upper Addison Gardens, running east and west of Holland Park Road, are mostly multiple-tenanted, as is the road called simply, Holland Park. Houses, in their prime, were inhabited by a single family, and run by six or seven servants. Just across Holland Park Avenue is the Royal Crescent, another group of very handsome houses which seem to be on an upswing from dilapidated multiple tenant occupancy to private ownership.

The area north of Holland Park Avenue, on the same side of the road as the Holland Park tube stop, has a different, more village-like flavour than the area south of the Avenue. The houses are smaller to begin with, and the roads are less wide and traffic clogged. Yet the homes this side of the Avenue have almost doubled in market price over the past five to eight years. There is almost nothing left under £20,000 in formerly humble roads like Portland Road and Princedale Road. High prices are the order, even though the Victorian terrace houses are very shabby, and have sitting tenants in the basement or attic. Clarendon Road, the border road between Holland Park and Notting Hill, has always been on the high price side.

St James's Gardens is a lovely oasis on the western edge of the Holland Park area. Houses in this lovely green square start at £30,000. Norland Square is another handsome spot, which has been designated as a conservation area under the Civic Amenities Act of 1967.

The very north-east corner of Holland Park has problems. The council seems to be tearing down and putting up, and you sense the dramatic change in the neighbourhood when you come to the top of Princedale Road. A vast acreage of land under 'redevelopment' then appears before your eyes.

Amenities of the Area

Holland Park itself, with peacocks, pieces of sculpture, adventure playgrounds, and a cosy Dutch Garden. It is a personal park, and in that sense is unique among London parks. A great sand pit for toddlers.

Holland Park Comprehensive, and a very good selection of private schools.

Shopping: not so good within the boundaries of the Holland Park area, but Notting Hill, Shepherd's Bush and Kensington High Street all are nearby. The top of Portland Road features the best small cluster of local shops. Two trendy restaurants have opened there within the past two years.

Portobello Road, with its street stalls and antique shops, is within walking distance of the northern sector of Holland Park.

Leighton House, 12 Holland Park Road, houses the British Theatre Museum.

Holland Park Road

Notting Hill

A Bit of History . . .

The Manor of Nuttyngbarnes, with the name evolving to Knotting Barnes and Knottynghull, dates back to the sixteenth century. The area called Notting Hill remained rural until 1830s, when a race course called the Hippodrome Park was built for Queen Victoria, on the ground called Ladbroke Grove. The attractive communal gardens which remain to this day are a legacy of the racecourse.

After 1840 the whole of the northern division of Kensington Parish was known as Notting Hill. The Kensington Wells, located at the top of Notting Hill, were attracting many health-conscious Londoners to summer holidays in the area. At about the same time, property developers like Messrs John and Joseph Radford began to build double row houses and mansions, such as those in Pembridge Gardens and Pembridge Square. These buildings attracted prosperous Londoners as residents.

In 1886 Portobello Farm, which had always been separate from Notting Hill, disappeared and its lands became built up as well, so that by 1870, Notting Hill had grown up to be what it is today, in terms of architecture.

The Atmosphere . . . The People . . .

Is Notting Hill an urban jungle, or an up and coming residential area? It is both. While prospecting for a family house in the heart of Notting Hill, we have had to depart, simply to work off the depression brought about by the surroundings. To come upon a London neighbourhood which nobody seems to care about is a shock. Notting Hill has recently been cleared of racketeer landlords who were profiteering in rentals from immigrants. So it will take a while for all those big white houses to stand tall and proud again.

The Observer said, in August 1970: 'The district has a higher concentration of sociologists, community organizers, welfare workers, political activists, middle-class philanthropists, church missionaries and journalists than any other 1·4 square miles in the U.K. It's really difficult to find anyone who hasn't appeared on T.V. or figured in a social survey or doctoral thesis'. That's Notting Hill in a nutshell. If you're comfortable seeing your neighbours buy *New Society* instead of the *Daily Mirror*, then you'll like Notting Hill. As one student from Sheffield said when she took a flat there: 'I mean this is where things happen. David Hockney lives here! This is why I came to London'.

A Look at the Buildings, Outstanding Streets and Squares . . .

Many of the white monsters which were once called slums are now being converted to decent family flats, because property developers know that Notting Hill is an up-and-coming area—though if you walk along Talbot

Road or Powis Terrace today, you might well question that fact. The five- and six-storey houses there look as if they're beyond repair. Notting Hill is really not the place for a small or even a large family to take a house. The houses are simply too large, making renovation costly, and day-to-day management most difficult.

One man may say: 'I don't want to pay £900 a year rental for a super flat, when next door to me is someone who has never even heard of £900 a year'. This is just the sort of situation you might face if you choose one of the North Kensington addresses like Aldridge Road Villas as your address. Many North Kensington houses are inhabited largely by immigrants.

The Portobello area is a step above the far reaches of North Kensington, in that more middle-income families have come into the neighbourhood.

137

Elgin and Blenheim Crescents are marked by most estate agents as places likely to improve. The Powis Square and Colville Square areas seem to have far to go, in that their decline has been taking place for almost a hundred years!

Kensington Park Road, at the Notting Hill end, is a very safe area, consisting of large, modern purpose-built blocks of flats; the road changes at its Portobello end, however. Off Kensington Park Road, near the top, is Chepstow Villas, a tree-lined road of Victorian houses which always has been an elegant little pocket of Notting Hill.

Chepstow Road, leading from Westbourne Grove to Westbourne Park Road and North Kensington, is lined with small attractive houses, but the traffic is dreadful. The house prices have zoomed up in the streets behind Chepstow Road. It all started when one tenant on Artesian Road painted a psychedelic serpent on his front door: the neighbourhood has never been the same since. Courtnell Street, Northumberland Place and Sutherland Place are the key streets.

Portobello Road

138

Kensington Park Road   Ladbroke Grove

The western end of Westbourne Park Road appears beyond repair, quite frankly, but the eastern or Paddington end is very handsome. Detached houses with front gardens line one side of the road; Victorian terrace house line the other.

Surely the most elegant areas of Notting Hill are those which lie in the Kensington Park Estate, which was built from 1845 onwards—Ladbroke Grove, with its own tennis courts in the centre gardens; Lansdowne Road, and Clarendon Road, the semi-official border between Notting Hill and Holland Park, were part of the same estate. The villas of Lansdowne Crescent and Lansdowne Road are much like those of the Eyre Estate in St John's Wood, which was developed at about the same time as the Kensington Park Estate.

Pembridge Road, Villas and Square fall into the elegant Notting Hill area category. Off Pembridge Road is Bulmer Place, a row of country-like cottages.

Amenities of the Area

Green space: Holland Park on one side; Hyde Park on the other.

Portobello Road: quite cheap shopping at the top; trendy, pricey shopping at the bottom. Throbbing, alive and interesting at both ends! Mangrove Restaurant, headquarters for Black Power Movement. Plenty of health food shops.

Shopping along Notting Hill Gate itself is alive and even exciting. Pizza, fish'n chips, delicatessen, W. H. Smith, Boots, boutiques, an all-purpose shop filled with interesting imported household and decorative items.

Disadvantages?

Ten to fourteen thousand of Notting Hill's population are immigrants, from Africa and the Caribbean. Part of Notting Hill's reputation is its rough element. That element is bound to remain in Notting Hill for a while, for where else in central London is there to go? Central London has very few slums, and have you ever seen the centre of a city without a slum of some sort? Even the most liberal of our acquaintances have expressed concern at feeling like strangers in a foreign land, living in some parts of North Kensington.

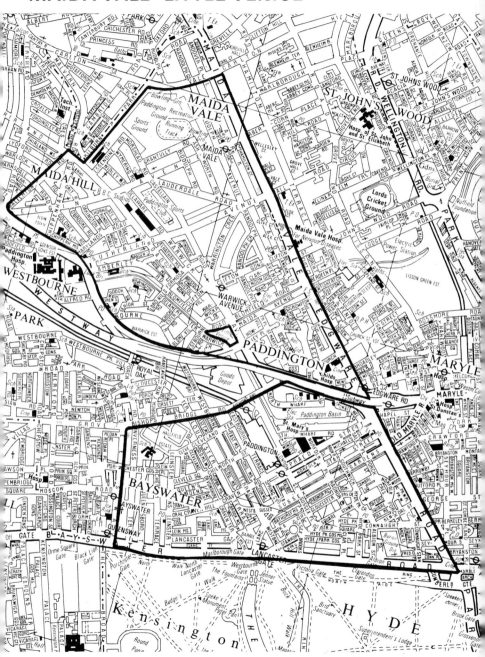

BAYSWATER — PADDINGTON

Local council
City of Westminster

Postal areas
W.2

Type of housing
Victorian
Mews houses
Tower blocks
Pre-war
Edwardian
Modern blocks

Approximate number of flats and houses in district
15,000

Local estate agents
Bourdas & Co., 1 Craven Terrace, W.2, 723 6612
T. H. Cartwright & Co., 23 Leinster Terrace, W.2, 262 1085
Chesterton, 40 Connaught St, W.2, 262 7202
Cowan & Partners, 123 Queensway, W.2, 229 1414
Andrew Milton, 8 Portland Rd, W.11, 229 8874
Frank Swain, 26 Notting Hill Gate, W.11, 727 4433
Tipping & Co., 45 Queensway, W.2, 229 6686
Big Twelve

APPROXIMATE COST OF HOUSING

Short lease unfurnished flats
annual rent
£1200–2000

Long lease unfurnished flats
price
£15–20,000

(non commercial)
Houses freehold or leasehold
price
£35–50,000

Amenity society
Paddington Society,
30 Westbourne Park Villas, W.2
229 3281

Citizens' Advice Bureau
313 Harrow Rd, W.9
286 4815

TRANSPORTATION

Tube stops
Bayswater
Queensway
Lancaster Gate
Paddington

Bus service routes
12 Oxford Circus—Piccadilly—Trafalgar Sq
15 Piccadilly—Bank
27 Marylebone Road—Camden Town
88 Westminster—Stockwell

Tube lines
Circle
District
Central

Travelling times
West End 5–10 mins
City 15–25 mins

Resident parking
Yes. Permit £18 per year

Bayswater – Paddington
A Bit of History . . .

When the village of Paddington's first census was taken in 1801, it consisted of 357 houses and 1881 people. At the same time Bayswater was a tiny hamlet on the road to Uxbridge. Both were about a mile from London. By 1850, Paddington was a sizeable suburb of London. The boom in Paddington building began when the Paddington arm of the Grand Junction Canal system opened, in 1801. After the canal boom, short lived indeed, came the railway boom. In 1863 the steam-hauled Metropolitan railway was opened from Paddington to Farringdon Street. Paddington Station, covering 70 acres, was completed in 1854.

The fields of Paddington and Bayswater slowly disappeared as much of the church-owned land was sold to private developers, who built terraces and squares of tall houses for the rising middle classes, attracted to Paddington because of the transport boom.

In the days when it was a great area—the mid and late nineteenth century, for instance, the established Londoners who lived south of the park are reputed, to have been a bit suspicious of those who lived north, on Bayswater Road.

The Atmosphere . . . The People . . .

Sadly, the elegance of Bayswater-Paddington has succumbed to seediness in many parts, and Bayswater bedsits and Paddington second-class hotels are well known all over London.

The best place to get the flavour of the people of Bayswater and Paddington is along Queensway, the round-the-clock shopping street, and Westbourne Grove, another road of shops. Loads of young people, itinerant students and immigrants, so the area is very much alive.

Bayswater-Paddington is a short-term place of residence for many people, who choose it as their first place to live, while they look around for just the right place. It is difficult to build up any great enthusiasm for living in most of Bayswater-Paddington, with the exception of beautiful Bayswater Road; and the occasional jewel of a road such as Bridstow Place, a strip of small cottages just behind Hereford Road.

A Look at the Buildings, Outstanding Streets and Squares . . .

The element of elegance that remains in Bayswater is along Hyde Park. The small roads leading from Bayswater Road to Moscow Road are quite pretty, and just a stone's throw from Hyde Park. (Bark Place is one of the prettiest.) The south-eastern corner of Paddington-Bayswater, near Marble Arch, is probably the only part of the area that still bears any of its previous glory . . . Connaught Street and Square, Hyde Park Square and Hyde Park Gardens.

The largest part of Bayswater and Paddington consists of big houses with

Hyde Park Gardens

peeling paint, and multiple-tenant occupancy. Inverness Terrace is a good example of a once very handsome road, now solely occupied by flats and hotels.

It is difficult to differentiate between Bayswater and Paddington for they sit so closely together. You could say Paddington is east of Bayswater. Gloucester and Westbourne Terraces actually make a fine arbitrary boundary. Both those terraces of six-storey Victorian houses have been given new life, in the form of restoration, during the past decade. The houses are occupied by several tenants, some by single families, and many are beautifully kept. The Greater London Council is giving a similar facelift to Porchester Square, which has some of Paddington's most beautiful nineteenth-century buildings, with cast iron balconies and high windows looking onto a garden square. Some 130 houses will be modernized to contain 471 flats.

Around Paddington Station is heavily commercial property, with a few attractive mews still remaining. Eastbourne Terrace Mews seems a dreadful location, nestled behind the imposing office blocks of Eastbourne Terrace. But during non-working hours, the mews takes on a quiet-as-the-country feeling.

As you leave the Paddington Station-Bishops Bridge Road area and get nearer to Edgware Road, you'll find brand new properties. Numbers 10–72 Sussex Square is a modern block of flats, and there are modern town houses round there as well. A brand new tower block is The Quadrangle in Cambridge

Connaught Square

Eastbourne Mews

Square. Chesterton and Sons are the agents for this block of two to five-room flats, letting from £1000 a year for two rooms, up to £2500 for four rooms. The building was constructed by Wates Ltd, a name you'll see and hear often if you're looking for new property in London or Greater London.

The Hyde Park Estate has been in the hands of the church since the Middle Ages. This estate is the triangle formed by Bayswater and Edgware Roads and Sussex Gardens. The Water Gardens, a huge development of modern flats, is located in this estate. Not so long ago, the Water Gardens' Tenants Association was formed to protest against the 60 to 70 per cent rent increases presented to them by the landlord. (£2200 a year for a three-bedroom flat is a typical Water Gardens price.) One tenant of the Water Gardens says that it is not the place for the person who wants to know the real London, for Edgware Road, on which The Water Gardens site, has a 'nowhere' feeling about it: tall uninteresting buildings; efficient shops and restaurants with very little charm. Yet other tenants prize the magnificient views from their Water Gardens tower.

Amenities of the Area—

An indoor ice-skating rink on Queensway.

Convenience is likely to be the very best feature of life in Bayswater-Paddington. Convenience for transport to anywhere, and for Hyde Park with its lakes and horses and wide open spaces.

Shopping is excellent: Whiteleys department store in Queensway, antique shops in Westbourne Grove, speciality food shops and cheap restaurants in and near Queensway. Great area for Greek restaurants, taverna, and grocery shops.

Disadvantages?—

A tendency to tattiness throughout the area. And a feeling of transience, which bother some people when they want to establish a feeling of 'home'.

MAIDA VALE — LITTLE VENICE

Local council
City of Westminster

Postal areas
W.9

Type of housing
Victorian
Mansion blocks
Pre-war
Modern

Approximate number of flats and houses in district
11,000

Local estate agents
Chesterton, 26 Clifton Rd, W.9, 289 1001
Match & Co., 15 College Crescent, N.W.3, 722 8907
Snell & Co., 47 Maida Vale, W.9, 286 6181
George Weston, 10 Sutherland Ave, W.9, 286 7217

APPROXIMATE COST OF HOUSING

Short lease unfurnished flats
annual rent
£800–1200

Long lease unfurnished flats
price
£12–20,000

(non commercial)
Houses freehold or leasehold
price
£20–35,000

Amenity society
Paddington Waterways Society,
29a Maida Ave, W.2
723 6490

Citizens' Advice Bureau
313 Harrow Road, W.9
286 4815

TRANSPORTATION

Tube stops
Maida Vale
Warwick Avenue

Bus service routes
6 Marble Arch—Piccadilly—City
8 Bank—Oxford Circus
16 Victoria

Resident parking
Yes. Permit £18 per year

Tube lines
Bakerloo

Travelling times
West End 5–10 mins
City 15–20 mins

Maida Vale – Little Venice

A Bit of History...

The name 'Little Venice' was coined by the poet Robert Browning, who once lived in a house overlooking Paddington Basin, where the Regent's Canal, Paddington Arm and Paddington Basin meet to form what someone else termed 'Browning's Pool'.

Maida Vale or Little Venice grew up at the same time as Paddington, its growth spurred on by the canal transport system. In the 1840s, Little Venice was the starting point for daily packet boat pleasure cruises to Uxbridge.

To safeguard the character of Little Venice, the City of Westminster designated it as a conservation area, under the Civic Amenities Act of 1967.

The Atmosphere...The People...

When you see that several-mile stretch of red brick buildings, the continuation of Edgware Road which is called Maida Vale, then you are apt to think Maida Vale has no atmosphere at all. It is personality-less. You will feel the same if the only part of Maida Vale you see is the council estates, or the road called Maida Vale.

But when you come across Little Venice, to the left of Maida Vale, the road, that's another story. The roads off Maida Vale along the canal form a separate little world—of pristine white houses, lots of space and gardens, canals and boats, peace and quiet. This is a mecca for the successful film, artist and writer set. Some writers have called Little Venice a backwater from the rest of London, a surprisingly remote corner. It certainly is, and is well worth a good look from the house hunter.

A Look at the Buildings, Outstanding Streets and Squares...

The buildings in Maida Vale go from high—the elegant Victorian houses along the canal—to low—the multi-tenanted decaying Victorian monsters of Sutherland Avenue, or the miles of red brick mansion blocks on Castellain Road.

Without question, the most attractive parts of Little Venice are the two roads which face the main canal—Blomfield Road and Maida Avenue. Go left from there into Park Place Villas, or right into Warwick Avenue, and the houses fade a degree in perfection, not because of design but because of upkeep. The houses nearby in Blomfield Villas and Delamere Terrace are built on a smaller scale, but are still an attractive part of this canal-side community.

Maida Vale is either all white houses, or all red blocks, and the roads with

A Maida Vale mansion block

all-white houses, like Randolph Avenue and Crescent, and Clifton Gardens, come out ahead. This is not to say that all the red brick buildings are bad. St Mary's Mansions in Park Place Villas is attractive, as are some of the red brick blocks which overlook the canal. Even the roads of bland architecture however, are wide. Some are tree-lined; and there is ample parking space! This was once 'Key Flat' area, a famous name in reasonably-priced unfurnished flats to-let. However, many of the one-time key flats are now up for sale.

Then there is canal-boat living to consider. Often you'll find 'houseboat-for-sale' adverts in the papers. Or you can scout the canal at any time and talk to the owners whose boats are moored there. The boats you see here are much more colourful and charming than those 'houseboats' you find on the Thames in Chelsea.

In almost any part of Maida Vale you look, you'll find lots of council flats. The Warwick Estate of more than 1200 flats, maisonettes and houses and houses supposedly went up because so many mid-Victorian houses had deteriorated. The Romans would turn in their graves if they could see the Maida Vale Estate of three eighteen-storey blocks of flats, built on the line of Watling Street, the old Roman Road.

Amenities of the Area

The canals: from the canal basin you may catch a boat to the Zoo; or take Jason's Trip, the best-known of London's canal boat rides, led by John James for the past twenty-two years. Beauchamp Lodge Settlement runs a boat club for young people in Little Venice. A canal information centre, with historical exhibits, is planned for Beauchamp Lodge, the large Victorian building at the entrance to Paddington Basin. The towpath walk along the canal, up to Regent's Park, is open to the public. The London Anglers Association stocks part of the canal with fish, and fishing permits are obtained through the Association.

An increasingly artistic atmosphere is invading Little Venice. Didiers, a book shop on one side and a restaurant on the other, has opened in Warwick Way. Every summer, a festival of fireworks, folkdance and art exhibits takes place in the boat basin. The Canal Boat opposite 60 Blomfield Road is an art gallery.

Shopping: Clifton Road is rather good for the basics. Edgware Road shopping is close enough to be considered the neighbourhood, and Safeway, Coopers and Marks and Spencer are there.

Little Venice canal   A house on the canal

Disadvantages?

Not enough of handsome Victorian Little Venice to go round for the seekers; far too much council stuff.

REGENT'S PARK — PRIMROSE HILL

Local council
London Borough of Camden

Postal areas
N.W.1

Type of housing
Regency
Modern
Victorian
Pre-war
Modern blocks

**Approximate number of flats
and houses in district**
4000

Local estate agents
Alan de Maid & Co., 51a St John's
Wood High St, N.W.8, 586 3088
H. E. Foster & Cranfield,
21 Soho Square, W.1, 437 6977
Match & Co., 15 College Crescent,
N.W.3, 722 8907
Big Twelve

Long lease unfurnished flats
price
£15–25,000
Nash House £20–30,000

**(non commercial)
Houses freehold or leasehold**
price
£20–35,000
Nash House £40–100,000

Amenity society
Regent's Park Tenants Association,
Community Hall,
Red Hill St, N.W.1
387 5987

Citizens' Advice Bureau
25 Euston Rd, N.W.1
837 2793

TRANSPORTATION

Tube stops
Baker Street
Gt Portland Street
Regent's Park
Chalk Farm

Bus service routes
3 Oxford Circus—Trafalgar Sq
53 Oxford Circus—Westminster
74 Hyde Park Corner—Earls
Court—Putney

Resident parking
No permit required

Tube lines
Metropolitan
Circle
Bakerloo
Northern

Travelling times
West End 5–7 mins
City 12–17 mins

Regent's Park

A Bit of History . . .

Henry VIII used Regent's Park for deer hunting in the late 1530s—when the circular green area was known as Marylebone Park. The King's surveyor assessed the park's value at £70 15s 2d.

The Regent's Park which is in use today was the creation of three men.

1) John Fordyce, a civil servant who objected to the Duke of Portland's request to run a turnpike road through Marylebone Park, and asked for a competition for the best plan for the park's development.

2) The Prince Regent, later George IV.

3) John Nash, the architect.

Regent's Park entered the twentieth century much as Nash had left it, but its terraces and houses suffered a great deal of damage in the Second World War. By 1945, two-thirds of the houses stood empty. The Royal Fine Art Commission recommended then that the layout of the terraces should be retained and houses behind the facades reconstructed in the best possible way. So, Chester Terrace has been restored in almost its original form. Park Crescent has been completely rebuilt. Cumberland Terrace was restored, and converted to flats and smaller houses. The work goes on.

The Atmosphere . . . The People . . .

The Regent's Park area is a large plot of country in the middle of a city. Even the air is rural, compared to the air just two minutes away in Marylebone Road.

The people in the park come from everywhere. The people who inhabit the Nash houses surrounding the park are obviously comfortably endowed. Residents around the park are known to be very property-proud, as they should be, when you consider that a short lease on a terrace house costs about £55,000; a long lease close to £100,000. One resident of Chester Terrace, in fact, can attest to the fact that he received a telegram from his neighbour, to inform him that his rubbish bin was showing!

Regent's Park is a real life painting of miles of cream-coloured stucco. Serene parkland is the only thing in sight from the front windows of these terrace houses which glisten in the sun, or the rain. The Crown Estate owns the land on which these houses stand, and requires that the stucco exterior be painted every four years. The Crown Lease also requires that each dwelling remain a single family residence—no commercial properties can intrude.

A Look at the Buildings, Outstanding Streets and Squares . . .

The houses that surround Regent's Park are almost entirely the work of John Nash, the architect who gained the favour of the Prince Regent. And this is the only area of London where the name refers as much to the houses as to the park. One cannot think of Regent's Park without thinking of its handsome houses. The Nash Terraces are one of London's unofficial architectural landmarks.

Cambridge Gate is the Victorian intrusion into this Regency colony. Cambridge Terrace, made up mostly of flats, was half-blitzed during the war, and has not been restored as yet. Chester Terrace has been completely restored to its original forty-four terrace houses, with illustrious residents like the Duke of Bedford, when he's in town, and lots of Americans. Chester Close, an area of modern mews houses, has been built behind the Terrace.

Cumberland Terrace, with its giant columns and pediment, is probably the most beautiful of the terraces. The centre block is made up entirely of flats, and houses sit on either side. Flats are on thirty-year leases; houses on sixty.

York Terrace is mainly flats. Those in York Terrace west, near the southern entrance to the park, range from £35–75,000 for ninety-nine-year leases, plus ground rents of up to £250 and service charges up to £700. Nottingham Terrace is a brand new block of flats, with no hint of Nash influence about it. James Lang Wootton are the agents, 103 Mount Street, W.1., 4931 6040.

The east side of York Terrace is the ultimate in luxury. Each 'shell' floor of 3360 square feet of space was offered to a tenant, who could build his six- or seven-bedroom flat just as he wanted, within that shell. The price? A ninety-seven-year lease for £120,000. So you see that the price of being near the park is indeed at the top of London's property price list. Clarence Terrace, near the Baker Street entrance to the park, consists of luxury flats as well. But this Terrace is actually a reproduction of the original Nash building,

Cumberland Terrace

Chester Terrace

which fell into complete disrepair.

Near Regent's Park, but not on or in it, is another cluster of Nash houses. Park Village East, and Park Village West, both approached via Albany Street, contain houses which are smaller and more individual than the terrace houses, but they do not come on the market very often. Nash properties in general come on the market through estate agents. The Crown Estate has nothing to do with letting them.

At the top of Regent's Park is Prince Albert Road, lined with blocks of flats that Nash never even dreamed of. The newest of the blocks are the most expensive in which to live. At 2 Avenue Road, for instance, just off Prince Albert Road near the North Gate entrance to the Park, three- and four-bedroom flats go for £30--40,000. North Gate itself is a very popular block

Prince Albert Road

of flats. If you would like to live in a block in Prince Albert Road, simply go into the buildings to your liking. You are sure to find somewhere on the premises a plaque with the name of the building's managing agent, or landlord. Or you may speak to the porter or tenants going in and out.

Harley House, a huge sand-coloured block of flats, is situated at the southernmost entrance to the park. It is well known for its large number of American tenants, and the flats are very expensive to rent. A ten-room flat is about £130 a month. One couple paid a £4500 premium to get the two-and-a-half year lease on a ten-room flat.

Amenities of the Area

Posh shopping for Regent's Park residents is in the West End. Wigmore Street and Oxford Circus are quite nearby. But two more humble shopping streets, both leading up to Camden Town, are where you'll find the bargains — Parkway and Albany Street, full of street markets and thrifty shops.

In Regent's Park: Bedford College for Girls; Queen Mary's Rose Gardens; the London Zoo; Shakespeare in the park on summer evenings; an annual parade of horses and wagons every Easter Monday; the London Graduate School of Business.

The White House is a very good place to call headquarters while you house hunt in the Regent's Park area. It's been converted into a hotel (The White House, Albany Street, Regent's Park, N.W.1, 387 1200.) You may rent rooms on a *per diem* hotel basis, or weekly or monthly on a residential basis.

Disadvantages?

The high cost of living! Would you believe there's one house in the park that goes for £5 a year?. It's Winfield House, the home of the American Ambassador. Winston Churchill somehow negotiated a Crown Lease which insisted that the house could be used only as an ambassador's residence, and that it must be maintained. Walter Annenberg, the current tenant, has spent half a million pounds to 'maintain it accordingly'. The house was once owned by Barbara Hutton.

Primrose Hill

Primrose Hill is an exclusively residential area just above Regent's Park, and beyond the zoo. The area borders Camden Town, Hampstead and St John's Wood as well. For this reason it is a great place in which to live. But for the same reason, Primrose Hill does not have a strong identity of its own.

When the railway headed north it went right through the Primrose Hill area, and the dirt sent the prosperous residents of the handsome homes further away to Hampstead or other clean air areas. Since the 1950s, however, the area has returned to some fraction of its former glory. The houses of St Mark's Crescent, built about 1840, are in very high demand, because they have spacious gardens which back onto the Regent's Canal.

Regents Park Canal house   Chalcot Park

Gloucester Avenue is heavy with traffic, but some of the large hpuses have been handsomely restored. Some of the Chalcot Road houses are being restored by the borough council, and flats within the houses will be offered to tenants on the council housing waiting lists.

Small houses are being built on sites which once contained small factories. Run down mews houses are being restored, and other things are happening in this once slum-like area, as a glance at the shopping centre in Regent's Park Road, will show. Three or four antique shops, a new health food store and a couple of restaurants mean that people with money are moving into the neighbourhood. David Bailey is one of the better-known 'locals'. What most Primrose Hill residents remark about as the best advantage of the area, is the sense of neighbourhood—the villageness of the place.

The new houses in Primrose Hill—those on Primrose Hill Road and in Chalcot Park—have very handsome prices—less charm, but more 'mod cons'. Waterside Place is a group of freehold town houses, each twelve feet in width. They face Princess Road, and back onto the canal. These houses sold during 1971 for more than £22,000 each.

ST JOHN'S WOOD

Local council
City of Westminster

Postal areas
N.W.8

Type of housing
Pre-war
Tower blocks
Mansion blocks
Regency
Victorian
Georgian
Modern blocks

Approximate number of flats and houses in district
16,000

Local estate agents
Alan de Maid, 51a St John's Wood High St, 586 3088
Allsop & Co., 153 Park Road, N.W.8, 722 7101
Anscombe & Ringland, 8 Wellington Rd, N.W.8, 722 7116
Britton Poole & Burns, 2 Wellington Rd, N.W.8, 722 1166
Folkard & Hayward, 58 Acacia Rd, N.W.8, 935 8181
Match & Co., 15 College Crescent, N.W.3, 722 8907
Big Twelve

APPROXIMATE COST OF HOUSING

Short lease unfurnished flats
annual rent
£900–1500

Long lease unfurnished flats
price
£15–25,000

(non commercial) Houses freehold or leasehold
price
£35–55,000

Amenity society
St John's Wood Protection Society, 62 Carlton Hill, N.W.8
624 4970

Citizens' Advice Bureau
98a Avenue Rd, N.W.3
722 3228

TRANSPORTATION

Tube stops
St John's Wood

Bus service routes
2 Marble Arch—Victoria
13 Oxford Circus—Trafalgar Sq
26 Baker Street—Victoria
74 Albert Road—Knightsbridge—Putney
113 Oxford Circus

Tube lines
Bakerloo

Travelling times
West End 7–10 mins
City 15–20 mins

Resident parking
Yes. Permit £18 per year

St John's Wood

A Bit of History . . .

In the Domesday Book of 1086, two Anglo Saxon manors were described: Tyburn, which was on the land which is now most of Marylebone, and Lilestone. For many years the Manor of Lilestone was held by the Order of the Knights of St John, and the Manor contained lands which are now the Eyre and Harrow School Estates. The Knights of St John gave their name to the area.

In 1800 the Eyre Estate and the Harrow School Estate were still fields, with St John's Wood farm flourishing on the site of present-day Acacia Road. As late as 1850, in fact, St John's Wood stood as fields and farms. The development of the Eyre Estate in the mid and late nineteenth century is of special interest to Londoners, for it was the first part of London to abandon the terrace house and take up the semi-detached villa, which was a revolution in housing. In its heyday, St John's Wood was the home of artists, musicians, and literary figures, and a pleasant Bohemian atmosphere pervaded.

The Atmosphere . . . The People . . .

St John's Wood has been a good place to live ever since it was developed as a residential area in the late nineteenth century. But it got a great boost when one of the Beatles—Paul McCartney—settled in Cavendish Avenue. And of course the illustrious Beatles sang about St John's Wood's Abbey Road, the location of one of their first recording studios.

St John's Wood is not all as alive and show-businessy as the Beatles might have led a lot of people to believe. Basically, St John's Wood is a bedroom area, for beyond the shops on the high street, there is no commercial life whatever. On its best roads, it is a very peaceful place to live, within ten minutes of Marble Arch. On its noisy roads, it is no bargain.

The atmosphere of St John's Wood is affluence—handsome houses and blocks of flats, everything from Regency villas to modern towers; well-dressed people entering chauffeur-driven cars. The area also has a lot of Jewish people, attracted by the new synagogue. The street life is almost non-existent—in this area life goes on in drawing rooms and private gardens.

A Look at the Buildings, Outstanding Streets and Squares . . .

In this solid upper-middle-income area you will find little if any tattiness. But certainly some of the blocks of flats have been built by men of much better taste than others. Abbey Road is a good place to take a broad look at the types of blocks from which you could choose to live in St John's Wood:

Old Manor Court, small block of about twenty flats.

Flats in Abbey Road

Langford Court, a block of sixty flats, owned by Freshwater. Flashy entrance hall and helpful porter.

Abbey Court, large and pretentious. Flats being sold to the tenants, or as they become vacated, to the public.

20 Abbey Road, 170 flats let as furnished service flats. Studios and two-room flats start at £30 a week, including electricity and five-day servicing. Bright, newly decorated flats. Leases are three months, and renewable.

Grove End Gardens, a huge 1930s block of 309 flats. Many controlled tenants in building. Fifteen of the flats are let furnished on six month leases. £26 for two rooms, service or electricity not included. The building has squash courts, hairdresser, grocer, a bar. Interiors a bit gloomy.

A modern house in St John's Wood

Hamilton Terrace

Neville Court, a big red brick mansion block. Flats being sold to tenants, or as vacated, to the public.

South Lodge, at corner of Abbey and Grove End Roads, is austere and monumental. Eighty-five flats on eight floors. A Freshwater block of 1930s vintage.

So you can see in one road alone the wide range of blocks of flats you'll find in St John's Wood: turn-of-the-century mansion blocks; 1930s blocks with boxy uninteresting rooms; brand-new blocks, some flashy, some subdued. What is interesting in this area is that the rents in the older blocks— with all their charming extras like wood panelling, marble fireplaces, high ceilings—often are lower priced than the rents of those flats in new blocks. One family pays £1500 a year for a two-bedroom flat in a new building in Wellington Road. A larger family pays £1200 a year for more rooms in a handsome 1920s block, with more space and more decorative detail. Grove End, Abbey Road, Circus Road and Wellington Road are the best stamping ground for flat-hunting. Just park your car, walk up and down both sides of the road, and linger in those blocks which appeal to you. A porter or resident is bound to offer you assistance. Want an unimpeded view of Lord's Cricket Ground? Then have a look at Lord's View, 108 St John's Wood Road.

What about those roads of semi-detached villas which made St John's Wood famous? Clifton Hill is a leafy street of Victorian villas. Hamilton Terrace is another. The freeholds of the latter are in the possession of Harrow School. Queen's Road, Norfolk Road and Acacia Road have some delightful Regency villas. Avenue Road has a bit of everything, but ostentation above all—show-off houses with pillars, and circular driveways, and new town houses, such as those that can be seen in Avenue Close. A clinic has taken over yet another. This sort of takeover often occurs in London areas where the homes are simply too large for one family to manage. House hunters in St John's Wood will have to have a 'price is no real problem' attitude.

Amenities of the Area

Rather good but pricey: shopping in St John's Wood High Street. An occasional car or taxi ride to the supermarket in Edgware Road can solve the food-budget problem.

Lord's Cricket Ground, located in the heart of St John's Wood, is an amenity for some, but a headache for crowd-haters and noise and traffic-jam objectors!

Proximity to Regent's Park. There is no park or green space known as St John's Wood.

St John's Wood Protection Society—an active community organization which fights to save St John's Wood from destruction by the builders of new property. Two meetings a year, with smaller social gatherings in between.

The new American School off Loudoun Road.

Disadvantages?

Very heavy traffic noise and fumes on some roads. Not much personality or vitality to the street life.

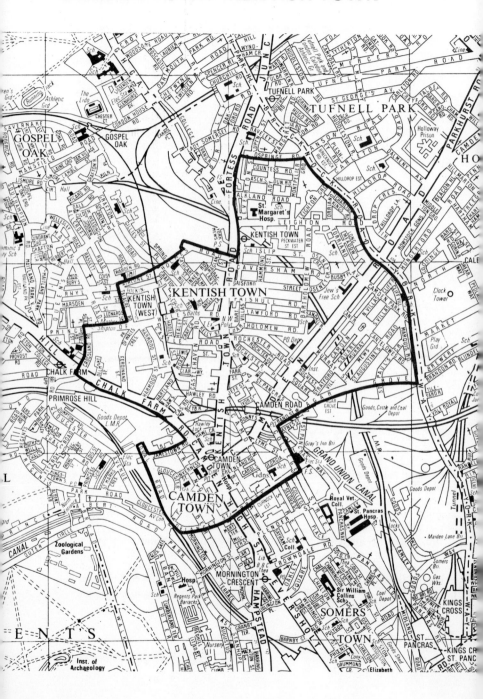

Local council
London Borough of Camden

Postal areas
N.W.1, N.W.5

Type of housing
Victorian
Mews houses
Cottages

**Approximate number of flats
and houses in district**
17,000

Local estate agents
Prebble & Co., 82 Parkway, N.W.1,
485 6767
Salter Rex & Co., 311 Kentish
Town Rd, N.W.5, 485 1085
Scott Ford & Co., 40 Camden Rd,
N.W.1, 485 3324
Spyer Brooke & Brown,
250 Finchley Rd, N.W.3, 435 5562
Stickley & Kent, 99 Parkway,
N.W.1, 485 3311

APPROXIMATE COST OF HOUSING

Long lease unfurnished flats
Camden
price
£9—13,000

Kentish Town
price
£7—10,000

**(non commercial)
Houses freehold or leasehold**
Camden
price
£18—25,000

Kentish Town
price
£12—16,000

Amenity society
St Pancras Civic Society,
10 Manley St, N.W.1

Citizens' Advice Bureau
255 Kentish Town Rd,
255 Kentish Town Rd, N.W.5
485 7034

TRANSPORTATION

Tube stops
Kentish Town
Camden Town

Bus service routes
27 Marylebone Rd—Paddington—
Kew
134 Warren Street Station
214 King's Cross—Moorgate

Tube lines
Northern

Travelling times
West End 10—15 mins
City 10—15 mins

Resident parking
Yes (small area). Permit £12 per year

Camden Town – Kentish Town

A Bit of History . . .

The history of Kentish Town goes back to the thirteenth century, when the first Lord of the Manor of Cantlowes took possession of the land on which today's Kentish Town stands. Until late in the seventeenth century there were only a few farmhouses and a couple of mansions in the area. The two well-known mansions were Kentish Town Lodge, which stood at the foot of Highgate Hill; and the Kentish Town Manor House, which stood where Caversham Road is now. By 1795 the first streets had appeared. All of the original Kentish Town has now disappeared.

Charles Pratt, the first earl of Camden, built a house in the area and gave his name to it. In 1791, the earl of Camden granted leases for the building of 1400 houses, and that is how the Camden Town of today began. Some of the first houses to be built in Camden Town were its most attractive: the

Camden Square

166

houses off Camden Road and Camden Square, and the mews behind the two long sides of the square.

The Camden Town Group of artists established some of the cultural and educational traditions in the area. Members of that group included Augustus John and Wyndham Lewis.

The Atmosphere . . . The People . . .

There's something honest and good about Camden Town. If the Irish and Greek immigrants were to move out to make way for the middle-income group, then the area would surely lose its charm. An interesting mix of people is what gives Camden Town its personality. And yet, many 'workers' are moving elsewhere, and their run-down houses are being converted by ambitious middle-class couples, who appreciate the amenities of the area— good cheap shopping, proximity to Regent's Park, and 'taxi fare distance' to the West End.

Kentish Town has two of the same amenities, but does not border the park. Kentish Town Road is more grey and glum in appearance than Camden High Street.

Both Camden Town and Kentish Town are coming up in terms of the number of middle-income residents taking over houses and restoring them to their original handsomeness. But neither area faces the threat of complete takeover by the young professionals.

Both are lively areas, where it can be fun to shop or stop at a Greek taverna for kebabs.

A Look at the Buildings, Outstanding Streets and Squares . . .

Camden Square, made up of semi-detached villas, could be Regent's Park if it were spruced up. At the moment a beautiful pink and white house has as its neighbour a house that is falling down. And in the middle of the square there is no garden, but a concrete playground, which someone has made the most of by painting Mickey Mouse cartoons on the tree house wall.

Camden Road also contains huge detached and semi-detached houses. But the road is heavy with traffic, and most of the houses have fallen into bed-sit state.

The best of Camden Town? Go and look at: Albert Street, Greenland Road, Delancey Street, Arlington Road, Mornington Terrace—three-storey Victorian houses, still shabby. The basic look of all these roads is good, but the houses have fallen into disrepair and need the kind of love and affection which has been bestowed upon the Chalcots (Chalcot Square and Road are on the border of Camden Town and Primrose Hill) where houses are already over £20,000.

In general, Kentish Town properties are lower in price than those of Camden Town. But now that two M.P.s have moved into Islip Street, one of the terrace-house streets off Kentish Town Road, that statement may not hold good for long. Caversham, Patshull and Lawford Roads are other improving parts of Kentish Town.

Two streets of smaller houses have already moved up. Jeffreys Street, which links Kentish Town Road and Royal College Street, is one. Kelly Street, a perky Chelsea-like row of workmen's cottages off Kentish Town Road, is the other. A BBC personality bought a house on Torriano Avenue in Kentish Town.

Just above Kentish Town, not far from Tufnell Park tube, is an area known by many names. . . North Kentish Town, Dartmouth Park or South Highgate. (Any area that is not a full fledged 'Up' area is bound to take on the assuredly acceptable names of the areas around it). This area known by many names is off Swains Lane, close to Parliament Hill Fields. Brookfield Park, Laurier Road, Croftdown Road and Dartmouth Park Hill are some of the streets where young professional families have formed a sort of ghetto within the working man's area. They all spent under £10,000 on their homes, and then spent another £5000 to do them up. They have made their investments partly because of the superb 'model' schools (Brookfield School and Gospel Oak) in the area.

Amenities of the Area

A large Greek-Cypriot Community adds interest to the area.

Camden School for Girls in Camden Road. North London Collegiate School for Girls in Regent's Park.

Very good public transportation—within taxi-distance of the West End.

Proximity to Regent's Park, the Zoo, canal boat rides—all good entertainment for children.

Excellent shopping, a sight better in Camden Town than Kentish Town. Good for the 'continental grocery' shops with Greek cheeses and olives, baklavas and pistachios.

The *Which?* Advice Centre: everything a clever consumer needs to know, at your fingertips—242 Kentish Town Road, N.W.5, 485 9939.

English Folk Dance and Song Society—2 Regent's Park Road, N.W.1, 485 2206.

The large amount of light industry in the area means that you can find just about any small service shop you need—glass cutter, electrician, etc.

Disadvantages?

The uncared for, sometimes seedy environment can be depressing, particularly in Kentish Town. But one could turn a disadvantage into an advantage, as an Islingtonian once did about The Angel, by saying: 'After a while you don't even notice it'. Meaning you don't even notice the dirt and scruffiness, you just appreciate the good things of your area.

Though there are two good schools north of Kentish Town, and Camden town has its excellent private Camden School for Girls, the state school atmosphere can be a bit rough, with as many as 85 per cent working-class children. Many professional parents prefer a more even balance: the families off Swains Lane are pleased with — mix of 60 per cent working-class children, and 40 per cent, from professional families. If you want a higher proportion of professionals, you will have to send your children to private schools.

Kelly Street cottages

Camden Town market

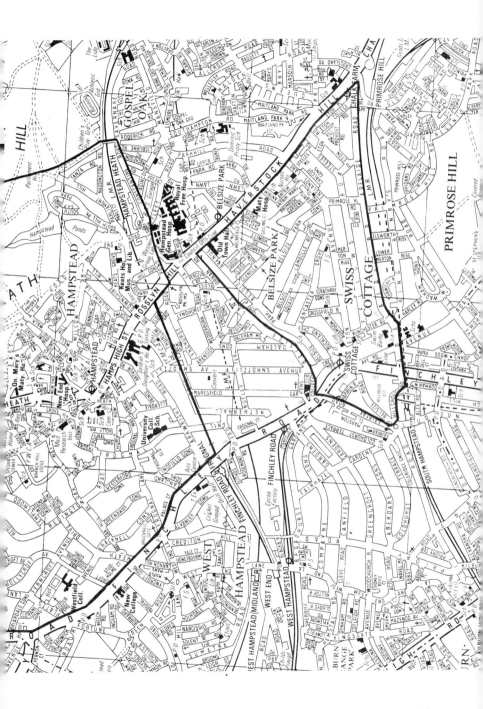

HAMPSTEAD

Local council
London Borough of Camden

Postal areas
N.W.3

Type of housing
Victorian
Georgian
Modern houses
Cottages
Pre-war
Modern blocks

Approximate number of flats and houses in district
16,000

Local estate agents
Benham & Reeves, 56 Heath St, N.W.3, 435 9822
Druce & Co., 1 Heath St, N.W.3, 435 9851
Goldschmidt & Howland, 15 Heath St, N.W.3, 435 4404
Hampton & Sons, 21 Heath St, N.W.3, 794 8222
George Knight & Partners, 9 Heath St, N.W.3, 435 2298
Match & Co., 15 College Crescent, N.W.3, 722 8907
Big Twelve

APPROXIMATE COST OF HOUSING

Short lease unfurnished flats
annual rent
£900−1400

Long lease unfurnished flats
price
£15−25,000

**(non commercial)
Houses freehold or leasehold**
price
£25−50,000

Amenity society
New Hampstead Society, 17 Redington Rd, N.W.3

Hampstead Heath & Old Hampstead Society, 1 Halsbury Close, Stanmore

Hampstead Consumer Group, 52 Solent Rd, N.W.6, 435 1743

Citizens' Advice Bureau
Swiss Cottage Centre, N.W.3
722 3228

TRANSPORTATION

Tube stops
Hampstead

Bus service routes
13 Golders Green Station—Oxford Circus—Trafalgar Sq
24 Camden Town—Victoria
268 Swiss Cottage—Finchley Rd

Resident parking
No permit required

Tube lines
Northern

Travelling times
West End 20−25 mins
City 25−35 mins

Hampstead

A Bit of History . . .

Hampstead's history is tied up with its clean air. The fresh country air and open space served as a spa for seventeenth-century Londoners, who flocked to the fashionable local for races on the heath, concerts in the Long Rooms, and other such pleasures.

To this day, Londoners flock to the heath for its fresh air, and the surrounding charms of Hampstead Village. The spa waters are gone now, but Flask Walk and Well Walk are reminders of the day when Hampstead rivalled Tunbridge Wells and Bath. The Vale of Health, now a group of houses nestled by the heath, was once a place of refuge from the plagues which ravaged central London. The heath was not always a vale of peace, however, for highwaymen haunted the countryside in the early nineteenth century.

Artists have always made their way to Hampstead, Constable and Keats being the best known picture and word artists.

Two hundred and forty acres of Hampstead Heath were sold to the Metropolitan Board of Works in 1870 for £45,000. It's easy to pay that price for a house in Hampstead today!

The Atmosphere . . . The People . . .

There are really two Hampstead villages, and the atmosphere in each is totally different. The best known is the village proper, where the tube stops, and the great circle around that village is the best known and most sought after part of Hampstead. It goes as far south as Swiss Cottage, up Fitzjohn's Avenue to Heath Street and the heath, along West Heath Road and down Finchley Road.

The 'other half' of Hampstead is east of Rosslyn and Haverstock Hills around South End Green, and it is considerably smaller, more 'kinky', and property is cheaper. It is no less pretty than the other, larger half of Hampstead, but it has not caught on in quite the same way. Its village has not become nearly as commercial as the village that surrounds Hampstead tube, and the rents are not nearly as high. So this is the area where you'll find students sharing flats, and young working West-enders taking the 24 bus home to their shared flats. This 'eastern half' of Hampstead bumps into Parliament Hill, the green area contingent to Hampstead Heath.

In between these two halves of Hampstead is Belsize Park, a separate little village known for its shops with late opening hours. Belsize Park is mostly white Victorian houses, heavily inhabited by the bedsit crowd. This is an area greatly threatened by motorways and not really worth exploring if you seek a permanent or even semi-permanent home.

South Hampstead is not really a place at all, but simply a train stop, located in Swiss Cottage, which is capitalizing more and more these days on its proximity to Hampstead. West Hampstead, however, is a real living area, but completely removed from the real Hampstead in atmosphere. West Hampstead is all red brick mansion blocks, and Victorian terraces, which lie west of Finchley Road, the unofficial western boundary for Hampstead. Many

Church Row

Holly Hill

Streatley Place

Lyndhurst Road

Grove Place

of the adverts which read 'Hampstead' often turn out to be West Hampstead, so be forewarned. West Hampstead is heavily populated by eastern European immigrants and their descendants.

Hampstead Garden Suburb is yet another London area which gains good will and some degree of prestige from the borrowing of that glorious name. Hampstead Garden Suburb is a town planning experiment of the early twentieth century. Houses there, many very handsome, especially along Hampstead Way, are now for sale on long leases, through Bernard Thorpe and Partners. This area has a very large number of Jewish residents.

Put the two earlier-mentioned halves of Hampstead together and you get one of the most popular and expensive living areas of London. An amalgam of boutiques, antiques, poetry readings, the occasional craft or pottery or book shop, theatre workshops, low and high priced restaurants . . .

In a way, Hampstead can be considered a retreat from the rest of London: tiny lanes for strolling and discovering; wide open spaces for roaming; Greenwich Village or the Left Bank set high on a hilltop.

There are a fair share of young hippies and perpetual students; another group of slightly older but still young professors and poets in tweeds; and yet another group of middle-class, middle-aged residents, who've been in Hampstead ever since they were part of groups one or two. Londoners know that if they live in Hampstead, they take on a label which means liberal, intellectual, or artistic, or some combination of all three. No wonder so many people want to call Hampstead home!

A Look at the Buildings, Outstanding Streets and Squares . . .

Hampstead has some of the best Georgian buildings in London, and some of the worst red brick of Victorian London. But all properties are attractive, it seems, in this highly popular north London village. It is safe to say that people are attracted to Hampstead because of its ambiance, not just because of its architecture, though some may question how the two can be separated.

Basically, Hampstead is an eighteenth-century village, living way beyond its years, happily, into the twentieth century. Downshire Hill and Church Row are among the best survivors of Georgian London: Fitzjohns Avenue, of Victorian London. The best of quaint and cosy Hampstead must be the Hollys, which lie above Heath Street, but are not visible from it. Holly Hill, Holly Mount, Holly Walk: tiny winding lanes—intimate Hampstead.

Then there is vast wide open Hampstead. The Millionaires' Rows— Winnington Road and The Bishops Avenue. The Bishops Avenue has more modern blocks of flats intruding upon the mansions than does Winnington Road. Reddington Road and Templewood Avenue are big roads of beautiful houses, now divided into large, beautiful flats.

A very rural section of Hampstead is the eastern area, round South End Road, Pond Street, Willow Road and East Heath Road. Here South End Road is the subdued shopping area, everyone lives just a short walk from the heath, and because there is no tube stop near, not as many people from 'outside' seem to have invaded.

To this day, Hampstead Village is one of houses, not blocks of flats. Heath

Mansions in Heath Street, and Green Hill, the huge block of flats in Prince Arthur Road, are the two exceptions. Finchley Road, the western border of Hampstead is lined with many mansion blocks, but there is too much traffic to call Finchley Road an appealing place to live.

Many houses which once suited wealthy families have been sub-divided and converted so as to suit several wealthy families in several flats. Even the more modestly built Victorian houses, such as those of Arkwright Road and Langland Gardens, have been converted into flats.

No, the modern way of life does not seem to have reached Hampstead, except for some contemporary developments like Cenacle, where four-bedroom houses facing the heath sold for £56,000 and more in 1971. The first 'modern' house in the whole of England was built in Hampstead, in Frognal Way in 1935. Frognal Way is an interesting lane, running from Finchley Road right up to the heath, containing every description of architecture. The red brick Victoriana at the bottom is the least interesting.

Hampstead Heath

Amenities of the Area

Almost too numerous to mention! A great sense of community, probably unequalled in any other area of London—and also a lot of community action. Get 'What's On in Camden', a monthly diary of local events, printed by the Libraries and Arts Department of the London Borough of Camden, 100 Euston Road, N.W.1. The people who live here somehow feel akin, and there is little of that disease called urban alienation.

Probably one of the best selections of state and public schools in all London. The Hampstead Consumer Group, 52 Solent Road, N.W.6, has made a study of them.

Hampstead has almost as many good pubs as it does schools. The two most famous are the hilltop pubs, Jack Straw's Castle and The Spaniards Inn.

Eight hundred acres of heath should fulfill any family's requirements for open spaces! Kenwood House, which lies between Hampstead and Highgate, has more intimate grounds, and open air concerts in the summertime. The house itself has a lovely collection of paintings, and is open to the public for viewing.

Beautiful views of London from the heath. The streets as well as the Heath of Hampstead afford interesting quiet walks. Set out to find the Admiral's House in Hampstead Grove, behind Heath Street. You'll see Hampstead at its most charming here . . . the admiral's quarter-deck and telescope are still intact.

Shopping: perfect for the person who likes the village-type shop. Not so good for the supermarket *afficianado*. Super-store shopping nearby however in Finchley Road or Golders Green. Finchley Road has the first full scale wholemeal bakery; and all sorts of carry out food shops. Macrobiotic food shop on Heath Street.

Disadvantages?

High prices in some of the village shops.

People on the rural or far-out roads like Winnington Road have complained of the difficulties in finding daily help and au pair girls, who like to live right on top of a tube stop.

Unless you live in the village proper, you will have to have a car.

SWISS COTTAGE—CHALK FARM

Local council
London Borough of Camden

Postal areas
N.W.3

Type of housing
Mansion blocks
Neo-Georgian
Victorian

Approximate number of flats and houses in district
2000

Local estate agents
Bourdas & Co., 1 Craven Terrace,
W.2, 723 6611
Ellis & Co., 2 Northways Parade,
Finchley Rd, N.W.3, 722 0011
Herman & Co., 309 West End Lane,
N.W.6, 794 4545
Match & Co., 15 College Crescent,
N.W.3, 722 8907
Worthington & Stewart,
162 Shaftesbury Ave, W.C.2,
240 1581

APPROXIMATE COST OF HOUSING

Long lease unfurnished flats
price
£12–18,000

**(non commercial)
Houses freehold or leasehold**
price
£25–35,000

Citizens' Advice Bureau
Swiss Cottage Centre, N.W.3
722 3228

TRANSPORTATION

Tube stops
Swiss Cottage

Bus service routes
2 Baker St—Victoria
113 Oxford Circus

Resident parking
No permit required

Tube lines
Bakerloo

Travelling times
West End 15–20 mins
City 25–35 mins

Swiss Cottage – Chalk Farm

Swiss Cottage is a sort of non-neighbourhood, for it consists of a very few roads around a tube stop, with a big restaurant called The Swiss Cottage.

Yet many Londoners will say: 'I live in Swiss Cottage'. They refer to streets like Adamson Road, College Crescent, Winchester Road, and Fairfax and Belsize Roads (two rows of neo-Georgian town houses). These roads, within a five-minute walk of Swiss Cottage tube, make up the residential area. Shopping for Swiss Cottage is Finchley Road, one of the best shopping streets in London. Another landmark in Swiss Cottage is the Camden Central Library, with its swimming pool, and the Hampstead Theatre Centre. The Tavistock Clinic is also nearby. So all in all, Swiss Cottage is a well-known area of London, but known for reasons other than its residential qualities.

Chalk Farm is another area much like Swiss Cottage—well known for a landmark or two, but not a particularly thriving or large residential area. Chalk

Finchley Road

180

Buckland Crescent

Farm Road starts in Camden Town, and ends at the junction of Adelaide Road and Haverstock Hill, almost in Hampstead. Most people in Chalk Farm—the name of the tube stop, and the site of an old farm which once occupied that land—prefer to call their address Hampstead. Most Chalk Farm flat living is in Eton College Road.

Chalk Farm does not take on the strong identity which Swiss Cottage does, because its shopping centre is almost nonexistent. An antique shop in a beautiful old farmhouse, a pub, an Italian restaurant and an ice cream bar: that's about it. The Round House is the landmark of Chalk Farm. It is a theatre housed in a big round building which was once the turntable house for railway locomotives.

These two areas, with those discussed in *The Atmosphere* section of Hampstead are important to anyone who's house hunting in Hampstead, for you are very likely to be sent to one or all of these areas by an estate agent. All three capitalize on their proximity to Hampstead, and bask in its popularity.

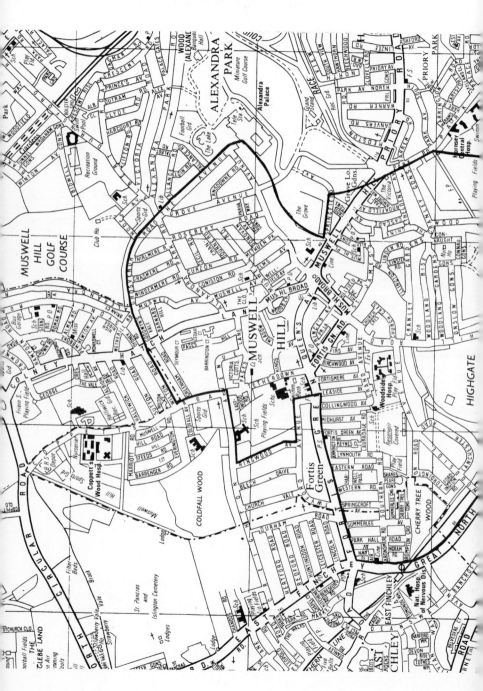

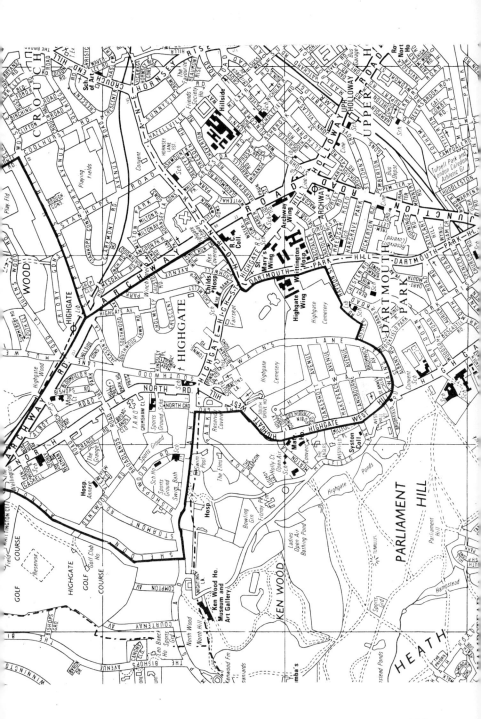

HIGHGATE — MUSWELL HILL

Local council
London Borough of Haringey

Postal areas
N.6

Type of housing
Highgate
Georgian
Modern
Tower blocks
Pre-war
Modern blocks

Muswell Hill
Victorian

**Approximate number of flats
and houses in district**
7000

Local estate agents
George Knight & Partners,
9 Heath St, N.W.3, 435 2298
Hector Littler & Partner, 2 South
Grove, N.6, 340 6229
Prickett & Ellis, 27 Highgate High
St, N.6, 340 2934
Sturt & Tivendale, 61 Highgate
High St, N.6, 348 0104

TRANSPORTATION

Tube stops
Highgate

Bus service routes
43 Islington—London Bridge
134 Warren Street Station
172 Islington—Holborn—
Westminster

Resident parking
No permit required

APPROXIMATE COST OF HOUSING

Long lease unfurnished flats
price
£10—18,000

**(non commercial)
Houses freehold or leasehold**
price
£20—35,000

Amenity society
Highgate Society,
2 Shepherds Close, N.6
348 4082

Citizens' Advice Bureau
Hornsey Town Hall,
The Broadway, N.8
340 3220

Tube lines
Northern

Travelling times
West End 20—25 mins
City 20—25 mins

Highgate

A Bit of History . . .

The name Highgate is an indication of the existence of an early tollgate at the summit of a hill. Ye Olde Gatehouse, at the top of the hill in Highgate, is famed for its eighteenth-century 'ordinaries' dinner—a bullock, roasted ribs of beef, a large goose or gander, two plum puddings, an apple pudding and a hot damson pie. The cost? One shilling!

Highgate's history is dotted with famous names:

Karl Marx is buried in Highgate Cemetery.
Samuel Taylor Coleridge lived and wrote at 3 The Grove.
The Flask, one of the best-known pubs in London, was frequented by Hogarth.

A Highgate pub

Modern history was made in Highgate as well, with the building of High Point in the 1930s. This tower-like block of flats on the North Road was a revolution in living style when it was built.

The Atmosphere...The People...

If you want a bit of country in your daily life, then Highgate, built on a series of hills overlooking London, is a choice place. Highgate is a fair way by tube from central London, but once you're there the air is healthy, and the way of life, relaxed and pleasant, if not a bit suburban in parts. Highgate is a prosperous, quiet community.

One Highgate resident says that 75 per cent of Highgate residents are architects. That statement is questionable; but Highgate has numbers of young and middle-aged professional families. Two thousand of them belong to the Highgate Society, and participate in community activities. Highgate, yes, is the kind of London neighbourhood where you can put down roots, and feel you belong—even if your family has never even heard of The Grove, which is where some of Highgate's original citizens lived, and their descendants still do.

Some house hunters, real city people, have considered Highgate too suburban, and have decided against it. The area does have a large number of new town houses, built side by side in the neo-classical style. The mixture of architecture is indicative of the mix of people who make up Highgate: some citizens of long standing, whose ancestors went to Highgate School; and others who are putting the name of their first child on the entry list for Highgate School.

It is safe to say that Highgate is a solid middle-class area. People lump it in the same breath as Hampstead although the two villages do not have much in common. Hampstead has a trendy high-powered image; Highgate does not. Both areas have large amounts of open green space, numbers of chauvinistic residents, and some untouched eighteenth-century houses. But their populations are very unlike.

A Look at the Buildings, Outstanding Streets and Squares...

The heart of the Georgian village—Pond Square, South Grove, and The Grove, which is a bit cut off from the village—form the oldest, prettiest parts of Highgate. From the houses on The Grove, one can look down over the whole of London. Pond Square actually has no pond—only trees, growing where there was once a pond.

These beautiful Georgian areas of Highgate are nowhere near the tube, however. In fact most of the areas of Highgate which you will explore will turn out not to be on a bus route or tube line! Priory Gardens and Jacksons Lane are the two roads for people who depend on public transport. At the top of Jacksons Lane are some attractive modern town houses.

You will not see all Highgate in one Saturday! Just to explore the North Road and its tributaries is a day's work. But if Highgate pleases you on your

Pond Square

The Grove

High Point

first visit, you are certain to enjoy your return visits to this refreshing part of London.

Highgate is full of surprises: lovely cottages; small houses with spectacular views of London. One couple found a small house set in its own gardens, with a swimming pool and tennis courts. Their rent? £22 per week. (Their pool house is actually part of the Highpoint complex, and the pool is for all the flat-dwellers, though it is used so seldom that it seems private.)

Some of the best of modern Highgate:

Southwood Park, a three-acre site with swimming pool.

Highgate Close and Shepherds Close. Examples of new town houses built in a quiet cul-de-sac off the main road. These new houses have appreciated in value, almost to the point of doubling the purchase price.

Holly Lodge Estate, in the southern most part of Highgate, was built between the two World Wars. It is stockbrocker tudor, quiet, spacious, with great views of London.

Near Holly Lodge, but separate from it, is Holly Village, a group of mock-gothic cottages built in 1865 as homes for retired servants. These cottages were built around a lawn, located in the angle between Swains Lane and Chester Road.

The Archway area is worlds away from Highgate, for it is filled with traffic and dirt. Some London buses are marked Highgate, with Archway in parenthesis, which means in fact that the buses simply do not go as far Highgate. There are, however, many connecting buses to Highgate, from Archway.

Amenities of the Area

A very active and thriving Amenity Society, with its own 'house' in Highgate village. The Society sponsors everything from cordon bleu cookery lessons and theatre parties to childrens' playgroups.

An interesting group of shops in the village: antique books and prints; an antique-cum-Polish folk craft shop in a one-time slaughter house in Highgate high street; childrens' clothing shops.

Some great pubs, like The Flask.

Highgate School (T. S. Eliot taught here).

Lots of wide open spaces, like Highgate Wood.

Disadvantages?

Village shopping is not as good as it could be. Very low on restaurants. Super-market style shopping just up the hill, in Muswell Hill.

Public transport very poor. Highgate tube is fifteen or twenty minutes walk to the village.

Muswell Hill

A Bit of History . . .

In Stuart times, Sir Julius Caesar, Master of the Rolls to James I, kept a splendid mansion, 'Mattysons', at Muswell Hill. Other wealthy Londoners kept their country estates in this area of wooded land. Muswell Hill takes its name from the Mus or Moss Well, an ancient spring or well which existed in Muswell Road until 1898. The well had curative properties and was a place of pilgrimage.

A Look at the Buildings, Outstanding Streets and Squares . . .

Muswell Hill looks like a large decorated birthday cake set on a hill. The area is entirely Victorian in architectural style: all red-brick houses trimmed with pink, white or blue wood or plaster work.

Muswell Hill has a few Georgian and Regency houses, which you'll find when you wander from the centre of the area to Fortis Green Road or Southern Road. In these areas you'll find more green and more privacy than in the centre of the village. These houses are higher priced than the Victorian dwellings, but lower in price than the same kind of house in Highgate or Hampstead.

Muswell Hill is not really very good ground for the furnished-flat hunter, when for just a little more money, he could buy a flat or house. Muswell Hill is no place for a commuter without a car either for there is no tube stop, though bus services connect Muswell Hill to Highgate tube.

The two best things about Muswell Hill are its views of London (which can be a disadvantage in that there are so many steep hills to climb); and its shopping centre, which includes a Sainsbury's and a Marks and Spencer.

ISLINGTON–HIGHBURY–CANONBURY–BLOOMSBURY

ISLINGTON — HIGHBURY — CANONBURY

Local council
London Borough of Islington

Postal areas
N.1, N.5

Type of housing
Victorian
Georgian
Regency

Approximate number of flats and houses in district
30,000

Local estate agents
Brown & Brown, 27 Islington
High St, N.1, 837 7338
E. Copping Joyce & Son,
284 St Paul's Rd, N.1, 226 4221
Debenham Tewson & Chinnocks,
28 Grosvenor St, W.1, 499 9152
D. Pinto & Co., 15 Dover St, W.1,
493 2242
Prebble & Co., 109 Upper St, N.1,
226 9531
Scott Ford & Co., 40 Camden Rd,
N.W.1, 485 3324
Ward Saunders & Co., 298 Upper
St, N.1, 226 2487

APPROXIMATE COST OF HOUSING

Long lease unfurnished flats
price
£12–18,000

(non commercial)
Houses freehold or leasehold
price
£20–35,000

Amenity society
Angel Association,
24 Burgh St, N.1

Barnsbury Association,
47 Thornhill Rd, N.1

Islington Society,
63 Theberton St, N.1
226 7906

Citizens' Advice Bureau
166 Upper St, N.1
226 8642

TRANSPORTATION

Tube stops
Highbury—Islington
Angel

Bus service routes
19 Piccadilly—Hyde Park Corner
30 Baker St—Marble Arch—
Hyde Park Corner
104 Moorgate
172 Holborn—Westminster

Resident parking
Yes. Permit £26 per year

Tube lines
Northern
Victoria

West End 8–12 mins
City 5–10 mins

Islington – Highbury – Canonbury

A Bit of History...

As you look at the run-down area round the Angel tube in Islington, it's difficult to believe that Islington was a pleasure place for well-to-do Londoners of the 1700s. On a Sunday, they would take their families to the tea gardens of Islington. In the 1800s, Islington gained fame as the site of the Caledonian Market, a remarkable market dealing in everything from cattle to antiques.

Somewhere along the way, as industry began to invade, elegant Islington took a downhill turn. But its been on an upward road for the past ten years. While there still is a waiting list of 10,000 people who need government-sponsored housing in the Islington area, mobs of middle-income professional people have poured into Islington to take over the strong shells of Georgian houses—houses built originally for successful city men who wanted to live near their work!

The Atmosphere... The People...

Islington's identity is wrapped up in its mix of people—factory workers, immigrants, young stockbrokers and scriptwriters and their families. This is a lively mix, but not all the sugar and spice of a good Sunday morning at the Chapel Street Market.

There is some resentment among the factory workers who were born in Islington, or whose parents were born in Islington, toward the monied-outsiders who've come into Islington and are taking it over, in a sense. In present day Islington, you can dine at Robert Carrier's emporium of fine food, or at the local fish 'n chips cafe. That sums up Islington in a nutshell. Many new Islingtonians are somewhat left of centre in attitudes political. So Islington by no means has the making of a traditional middle-class community.

Islington looks dreary in some parts, round the Angel, Upper Street and Pentonville Road, but like a picture postcards in parts of Canonbury. You may turn a corner and find a slum, or a magnificently restored row of Georgian houses backing onto a canal.

A Look at the Buildings, Outstanding Streets and Squares...

The bulk of Islington is authentic Georgian; or modern council blocks, also authentic. The pity is that in some of those beautiful Georgian races people are living four or five to a room, with inadequate plumbing and other problems. Conservation moves by the council have brought property developers in to save the houses. Barnsbury, the most run-down section of Islington, has

Lonsdale Square   Cardozo Road

been called 'a ripe chicken ready for plucking' by one property developer. He means of course that the houses are ready for restoration and upper-income rentals; or for aspiring home owners to take over.

The best way to get a good picture of Georgian Islington is to start walking up Upper Street, starting near the Angel. Colebrook Row, Duncan Terrace and Noel Road, just behind the Angel, make up one of the prettiest parts, which has the advantage of being close to the shops of Camden Passage, and the canal. As recently as a year ago, a young couple bought a house backing onto the canal for £8000. The house had twenty-three tenants in it, one bath and no kitchen. The couple earned a maximum improvement grant from the Islington council. The council is most co-operative, not only with individuals but also with associations of people who want to restore run-down properties.

Further up Upper Street, on the right, is Canonbury (reach it via Canonbury Lane), the most definitely secure section of Islington. Whereas Barnsbury and Highbury are still being saved from deterioration, Canonbury has been almost completely restored. There are very few run-down properties to buy in handsome Canonbury Square. If you venture off the square, you may still find something within a reasonable price range.

Canonbury is another world from the sooty, crowded part of Islington you glimpse around the Angel or Liverpool Road. Alwyne Villas and Alwyne Place are rich in trees. Alwyne Road and Canonbury Place face the New River, and both reap the benefits of New River Walk, a charming public garden and footpath along the river.

A large part of Canonbury is owned by the British Petroleum Pension Fund, and some of the property is in the hands of the Northampton Estate.

The estate agency which handles most of this property is not a local Islington agent, but a Mayfair one—Debenham, Tewson and Chinnocks, 28 Grosvenor Street, W.1

Canonbury Road is very busy with traffic, and thus the houses there are probably the lowest priced in the whole of Canonbury. Compton Terrace, which faces Upper Street, is also plagued with a steady flow of traffic, but a merciful strip of green stands between the houses and Upper Street.

By far the prettiest and most peaceful part of Canonbury is the Square itself, and some of the streets running to the north of it. Sir Basil Spence, the architect of Coventry Cathedral and other monuments in Britain, has chosen this area as his home, so that speaks for its merits.

Continue to the very top of Upper Street, to Highbury Corner. With the new Victoria line tube stop at this corner, Highbury is bound to soar in residential popularity. Highbury has the wide open spaces so foreign to other parts of Islington. And its Georgian terraces are superbly situated, as if on a pedestal. Life in general is quieter at the top of Upper Street, and much pleasanter than at the lower end.

Liverpool Road runs parallel to Upper Street, right through the heart of

Highbury Crescent

Barnsbury. Barnsbury Street is the star example of the saving of Islington's original houses. Barnsbury Road, on the other hand, is the star example of run-down Islington. Some Islingtonians fear it will take much toiling to bring Barnsbury back to its former glory.

A surprising jewel in Islington is not Georgian at all, but Victorian Gothic—Lonsdale Square. Nearby Ripplevale Grove is yet another jewel—this one of double-fronted Georgian houses.

Amenities of the Area

The great co-operation you can get from the council when you want to restore a house. The Housing Advice Centre at 220 Upper Street is the place to go for help.

Shopping is excellent. Camden Passage, a small maze of streets of restaurants and antique shops, which has never become what Portobello Road has—therein lies its charm. You still might find a bargain! The barrow boys of Chapel Street offer the food bargains. Sainsbury's and Marks and Spencer are on Chapel Street as well. One couple who moved from Kensington

Canonbury Square, Islington

to a flat in a restored house in Liverpool Road remarked that their food bill was cut by half after the move. Shopping in the upper part of Upper Street getting better every month: a health food store and restaurant, and a Marine Ices ice cream parlour are the latest additions.

Best location in all London for a quick journey to the City.

Tower Theatre in Canonbury Tower houses the Tavistock Repertory Company, which stages productions all year round. The King's Head Theatre Club is located in a pub in Upper Street. The Little Angel Marionette Theatre, 14 Dagmar Passage, Cross Street, is great for the children. Saturday art shows on Islington Green.

The canal: British Waterways will be establishing moorings on the length of canal by the wooded cutting in Vincent Terrace. The Islington Boat Club in City Road Basin is a converted Thames Barge—canoes, rowing boats and sailing dinghies available at the club for children aged nine to fifteen. Most of Islington's canal-side area is within or next to conservation areas, so there is great recreation potential in the canal.

Disadvantages?

Islington has the lowest ratio of open space to population of any of London's boroughs.

Animosity from some native Islingtonians to the affluent newcomers.

The air isn't fresh because so much small industry remains in the area.

Schools are a tough mixture. Islington Association for the Advancement of State Education will provide you with someone to talk to about schools. Telephone 226 1152, or seek information from the education office of Islington Borough Council.

BLOOMSBURY

Local council
London Borough of Camden

Postal areas
W.C.1

Type of housing
Georgian
Mansion blocks
Mews
Pre-war
Residential student
accommodation
Modern blocks

**Approximate number of flats
and houses in district**
7000

Local estate agents
Bailey & Woodbridge, 9 Gt Russell
St, W.C.1, 636 2624
Beard Son & Graves, 109 Gt
Russell St, W.C.1, 636 3404
Bedford Settled Estates,
29a Montague St, W.C.1,
636 2713
University of London Lodgings
Bureau, Malet St, W.C.1, 636 2818
Big Twelve

Long lease unfurnished flats
price
£15—20,000

**(non commercial)
Houses freehold or leasehold**
price
£40—75,000

Amenity society
Holborn Society,
20 Rugby Chambers, 2 Rugby St,
W.C.1

Citizens' Advice Bureau
26 Bedford Sq., W.C.1
636 4066

TRANSPORTATION

Tube stops
Russell Square

Bus service routes
14 Piccadilly Circus—Hyde Park
Corner—Putney
19 Hyde Park Corner—Sloane Sq.
29 Victoria
68 Waterloo

Resident parking
No. Meters

Tube lines
Piccadilly

Travelling times
West End 5—8 mins
City 10—12 mins

Bloomsbury

A Bit of History . . .

Bloomsbury, most of which is the Duke of Bedford's estate, boasts Bedford Square, widely accepted as the best of Georgian London. It looks today just as it did in 1774, from the exterior that is. The interiors of the houses have been converted to offices.

A builder named Burton dominated Bloomsbury until 1817; and then Thomas Cubitt came along in 1820, to complete Tavistock Square, Woburn Place and part of Gordon Square. Cubitt takes credit for a beautifully built little lane called Woburn Walk—three-storied stucco houses, with shop fronts on the ground floor.

Charles Dickens, Virginia Woolf, and E. M. Forster—all have links with Bloomsbury. In the days of Thackeray's *Vanity Fair*, many prosperous Londoners inhabited Russell Square.

Russell Square

The Atmosphere...The People...

The character of olde England permeates Bloomsbury, even though the old is fast disappearing. Bloomsbury Square, for instance, retains none of its original houses. London University has taken over much of the land. Just look at the University's Senate House, and the way it sprawls like the Roman Coliseum in comparison to its petite Georgian neighbours. Much of Georgian Gower Street is also London University.

Soon the British Museum, in its projected seventeen-acre expansion programme for the National Library, may encroach upon even more of old Bloomsbury. In 1970 a hotel took twenty of the three-storey houses on Bedford Way, just north of Russell Square. The Bedford Estate is just as much a culprit as the Camden Borough Council in this selling off of old Bloomsbury: the Duke of Bedford and the Bedford Settled Estates were recently prohibited from demolishing the row of Georgian houses at 2—14 Tavistock Place, for the Department of the Environment ordered that the houses should be preserved!

For those who are willing to take the 'demolition' risk, and seek a home in Bloomsbury, there is still a somewhat academic, quiet residential atmosphere in many parts.

Students live in many of the houses which are rent-controlled, one-room flats, or university-owned. Most of London's publishers have their head-

Tavistock Square

quarters in Bloomsbury houses. Books and students everywhere; professors, writers, and classrooms. This is unlike any other residential area of London in that it is thoroughly scholastic.

Bloomsbury is a bit like the British Museum. Once it gets into your system you find yourself gravitating back there. Just for a stroll, a look through the shops, a look at the people and the books and the antiquities.

A Look at the Buildings, Outstanding Streets and Squares . . .

Residential pockets remain in bookish Bloomsbury. And those pockets are worth seeking, if you like the pleasures of well-planned terraces and squares, the legacy of Georgian London. The scholastic half of Bloomsbury is centred north of Southampton Row. The more domestic part is to the south of Southampton Row.

Mansion Blocks? There are a few: Ridgmount Gardens and Bedford Court Mansions, near Bedford Square, are two. Tavistock Court in Tavistock Square is a privately owned, very attractive large block. Knight and Company, 180 Brompton Road, S.W.3, is the agent for the seven-year lease flats which come

Doughty Street

Hotel Russell

vacant in March, June, September and December.

Lincoln's Inn, technically a Holborn address but bordering on Bloomsbury, offers very moderate rentals to members of the Bar. If you qualify, and want to live in the Inn, address inquiries to Lincoln's Inn, W.C.2.

The mews of Bloomsbury have not reached their zenith as yet. The mews houses do come on the market at very reasonable prices. One couple managed to rent a mews house for £5 a week—the asking price had been £8 but they sought a reduction from the rent officer, because the roof was leaking. The couple's neighbour pays £1·55 a week for her mews house: it's rent-controlled of course. The mews is dreadfully unattractive by day, full of racing car motors and armies of garage mechanics. But in the evening, it's peaceful and quiet, an entirely different scene.

Amenities of the Area

Shopping: Lamb's Conduit Street and Marchmont Street are the best areas for food and household shopping. One Bloomsbury resident says she doesn't think there's another place in central London where she can phone the butcher, tell him she's ill, and find that he'll send round her order by hand, and say 'Pay me later'. Lamb's Conduit Street has two boutiques now, which says that something strange is happening to stodgy Bloomsbury. Actually, Museum Street has always been a very with-it area of interesting shops. The shopping facilities of Tottenham Court Road, with some of the best furniture shops in London, are near. And just behind Tottenham Court Road is north Soho, with many small food shops and restaurants. Shops of New Oxford Street and Oxford Street are also nearby.

The Book Bang. An annual event? The first Book Bang in London's history took place in Bedford Square at the start of the summer of 1971. The two-week-long Book Bang featured everything from poetry readings to a vast tent of childrens' books.

The British Museum.

Courtauld Institute Galleries, Woburn Square: collection of Old Masters and Impressionists.

Disadvantages?

The only real disadvantage of living in Bloomsbury is that there's less of it every year. You never know when your dream flat in a Georgian Square might be scheduled to serve as someone else's office. Look at the incredible concrete monster constructed near Russell Square tube. It's called O'Donnell Court, and is meant to be a block of council flats, not a concrete sculpture.

One advantage in taking a flat in a building destined for demolition is that the council must rehouse you, provided you've lived in that same building for three years. One Bloomsbury girl, who lived in a Georgian house near Red Lion Square for three years, was rehoused, eventually, in another Georgian house in Mecklenburgh Street. She lived through some horror stories before the good fortune of a new council flat fell to her, however. The roof of the Red Lion Square flat actually fell in on her!

Russell Square

BLACKHEATH–GREENWICH

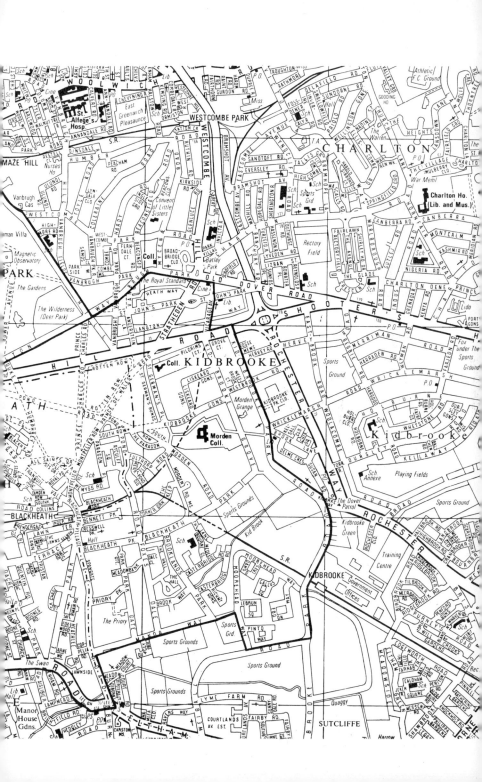

BLACKHEATH

Local council
London Borough of Lewisham and London Borough of Greenwich

Postal areas
S.E.3

Type of housing
Georgian
Victorian
Modern houses

Approximate number of flats and houses in district
6000

Local estate agents
Dyer, Son & Creasey, 22 Tranquil Vale, S.E.3, 852 0975
Victor W. Hindwood & Co., 5 Blackheath Village, S.E.3, 852 0999
Stocker & Roberts, 46 Tranquil Vale, S.E.3, 852 2983
E. Wookey & Co., 25 Montpelier Vale, S.E.3, 852 4353

APPROXIMATE COST OF HOUSING
Long lease unfurnished flats
price
£10–15,000

(non commercial) Houses freehold or leasehold
price
£20–35,000

Amenity society
Blackheath Society,
10 Pond Rd, S.E.3
852 7484

Citizens' Advice Bureau
141 Greenwich High Rd, S.E.10
858 4981

TRANSPORTATION

Bus service routes
701 Victoria (Greenline coach)
53 Westminster—Oxford Circus
54 East Croydon

Resident parking
No permit required

Train services
British Rail, Southern Region
Travelling times
Blackheath—London Bridge
20 mins
Blackheath—Holborn Viaduct
20 mins
Blackheath—Charing Cross
20 mins

Frequency
Blackheath—London Bridge
Every 3–5 mins
Blackheath—Holborn Viaduct
Every 3–5 mins
Blackheath—Charing Cross
Every 3–5 mins

GREENWICH

Local council
London Borough of Greenwich

Postal areas
S.E.10

Type of housing
Georgian
Victorian
Modern houses

Approximate number of flats and houses in district
6000

Local estate agents
Norman Hirshfield, Ryde Browne, 18 Nelson Rd, S.E.10, 858 0161

APPROXIMATE COST OF HOUSING

Long lease unfurnished flats
price
£9–14,000

(non commercial)
Houses freehold or leasehold
price
£15–22,000

Amenity society
Greenwich Society,
45a Devonshire Drive, S.E.10

Citizens' Advice Bureau
141 Greenwich High Rd, S.E.10
858 4981

TRANSPORTATION

Bus service routes
1A Charing Cross
188 Waterloo

Resident parking
No permit required

Train services
British Rail, Southern Region
Travelling times
Greenwich—Charing Cross
13–15 mins
Greenwich—Cannon Street
13–15 mins

Frequency
Greenwich—Charing Cross
Every 20–30 mins
Greenwich—Canon Street
Every 20–30 mins

Blackheath – Greenwich

A Bit of History . . .

From the tenth century to the Second World War, Blackheath Common was probably the site of a greater range of activities—battles, religious meetings, encampments, pageants, organized sports, games, fairs, circuses and demonstrations of loyalty and treason—than any other plot of green in London. Blackheath Common is a treeless plateau, 125 feet above sea level. its highest point, Point Hill, has always been strategically important to attackers and defenders alike, for from there they could keep an eye on the Thames. Blackheath Common is situated on the main roads from Canterbury and Dover, and undoubtedly that is the reason Blackheath Village came into being.

In 1871, the Lords of the Manors, who owned the freehold of Blackheath Common, bequeathed it free for the use of the people of London, and the Common was thus preserved as an open place forever.

Greenwich, once the home of Tudor Kings who built their Palace by the waterside, is now the home of the Royal Naval College, and the Cutty Sark, an elegant clipper ship which carried tea to the western world. No wonder tourists flock down the river by boat from Westminster Pier to Greenwich.

Greenwich Park was first walled with brick by King James I; then Charles

Blackheath Common

The Paragon, Blackheath

Modern flats in Blackheath

Blackheath Village

II enlarged and planted it further. The park was designed by LeNotre from Paris, and was at one time stocked with deer. Observatory Hill, the high part of Greenwich Park, adjoins Blackheath. The Observatory itself was built by Charles II in 1675. Henry VIII and Elizabeth both loved Greenwich.

The Atmosphere...The People...

People lump Blackheath and Greenwich together in name, and mind, because they are the two only really decent areas of south-east London in which to live. You must travel through miles of East End slums to reach both. But the similarity between the two villages ends there.

Greenwich is all nautical. You never lose sight of the fact that you're in a riverside village. Blackheath feels more like a rural village, and is perhaps more like Hampstead than Greenwich, for it has the heath as the centre of the life of the villagers, and more than its share of the artistic, theatrical sort of people. Glenda Jackson gave the area's status a boost when she won the Academy Award and got the name of Blackheath in all the papers.

Both Blackheath and Greenwich have a lovely independent flavour, which is not at all suburban. Greenwich is a riverside village, but if a man who commutes to London wants to make it his home, he may. Almost the same may be said for Blackheath, but Blackheath does have a few wide roads with big houses similar to those in Wimbledon or some other more suburban setting.

King William Walk, Greenwich

Crooms Hill, Greenwich

210

A view down King William Walk and the *Cutty Sark*

A Look at the Buildings, Outstanding Streets and Squares . . .

The best part of Greenwich is Crooms Hill, where Georgian houses overlook Greenwich Park. The houses here have already been picked over and restored. But note the roads behind Crooms Hill, like The Grove, Hyde Vale and Gloucester Circus, still within walking distance of the park, and the river. A price of under £15,000 for a Victorian terrace house in such an interesting area of London is certainly good going.

Blackheath offers more variety in life style than does Greenwich, where Victorian houses predominate. Take a look at The Paragon, a Regency crescent which has been restored and converted into flats; Langton Way, new mews-style cottages; Blackheath Park, a wide tree-lined private road with two- and three-storey Georgian houses; the Cator Estate, a private estate of detached Georgian mansions, £25,000 and up.

Period houses around the heath go for £30,000 and more, and these houses are the stronghold of Blackheath's professional population— Shooters Hill Road, for instance.

Blackheath has a sizeable amount of new town house property. And the amount of 'new stuff' is likely to increase, for some of the big grey brick houses have had their day and are beyond repair.

Amenities of the Area

Very good shopping in Tranquil Vale, the 'High Street' of Blackheath.

Two very active amenity societies. The Greenwich Society successfully opposed the G.L.C.'s plan to build a six-lane road right through the complex of buildings around the Naval College and the Queen's House, thereby setting a precedent among the many amenity groups fighting insensitive planning.

Greenwich Park, and all the tourist and children's attractions arround it: the *Cutty Sark*, the Maritime Museum, the boat rides on the Thames.

Blackheath Common has twenty-eight football pitches and five cricket fields; an annual May Fayre, held on the Washerwoman's Bottom part of the Heath! The Blackheath Golf Club dates from the 1700s.

Morden College, built in 1694 to a design attributed to Sir Christopher Wren, is the most famous of the fine buildings facing Blackheath Common.

Greenwich Theatre—try-out spot for some West End plays.

Blackheath has a Saturday morning flea market with antiques.

Disadvantages?

Shopping in Greenwich: once you leave the tourist-crowded riverside, you feel there's a ghost-town-like quality about the heart of Greenwich. One must go over to Blackheath or Lewisham to shop. However, the council has proposed to bar traffic from the central tourist area, and link it by pedestrian crossings with Greenwich Park. This plan, which includes provisions for a car park, may help build up life in the town centre.

The only black cloud over Blackheath is its traffic—it roars all round the heath and along Tranquil Vale, the village's main street. But the Hampstead has a similar problem, which hasn't seemed to alter its popularity. . . .

The dreary drive through miles of south-east London slums has already been mentioned as a disadvantage. Mention the glories of Blackheath and Greenwich to some sceptical friends who may say: 'Yes, but have you ever tried getting there?'

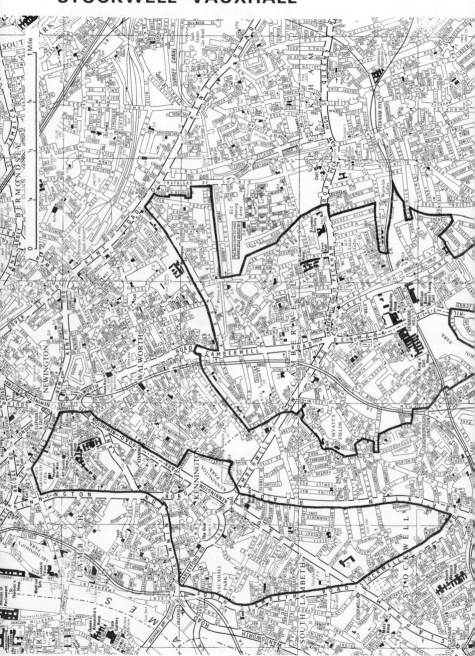

CAMBERWELL — DULWICH

Local council
London Borough of Lambeth and London Borough of Southwark

Postal areas
Camberwell S.E.5
Dulwich S.E.21

Type of housing
Camberwell
Georgian
Victorian
Regency

Dulwich
Georgian
Edwardian
Victorian
Modern houses

Approximate number of flats and houses in district
Camberwell 8000
Dulwich 5000

Local estate agents
Camberwell

Andrews & Robertson,
27 Camberwell Green, S.E.5,
703 2662 and 75 Camberwell
Church St, S.E.5, 703 4401

Dulwich
J. W. Kennedy & Co., 1c Calton
Ave, S.E.21, 693 7835
Mann & Co., 1455 London Rd,
S.W.16, 764 2282
Marten & Carnaby, 119 Dulwich
Village, S.E.21, 693 1515
Spencer & Kent, 19 Croxted Rd,
West Dulwich, S.E.21, 670 2204

APPROXIMATE COST OF HOUSING
Long lease unfurnished flats
Camberwell
price
£8–12,000

Dulwich
price
£9–15,000

(non commercial)
Houses freehold or leasehold
Camberwell
price
£14–20,000

Dulwich
price
£18–30,000

Amenity society
Camberwell
York Mansions,
Browning St, S.E.17
703 4198

Dulwich
384 Streatham High Rd, S.W.16
769 1055

Citizens' Advice Bureau
Dulwich Society,
8 Gilkes Crescent, Dulwich, S.E.21
693 2618
Camberwell Grove & District
Association,
182 Camberwell Grove, S.E.5
274 7576

TRANSPORTATION

Bus service routes

3 West Dulwich—Westminster—
Oxford Circus
12 Dulwich—Trafalgar Sq.—
Oxford Circus
68 Camberwell—Waterloo—
Euston
185 Dulwich—Camberwell—
Victoria

Train services
British Rail, Southern Region
Travelling times

W. Dulwich to Victoria
10 mins
N. Dulwich to London Bridge
13 mins
Camberwell to Victoria
12 mins
Camberwell to Holborn Viaduct
12 mins

Frequency

W. Dulwich to Victoria
Every 10–15 mins
N. Dulwich to London Bridge
Every 10 mins
Camberwell to Victoria
2 per hour
Camberwell to Holborn Viaduct
2 per hour

Camberwell Grove

Camberwell – Dulwich

A Bit of History . . .

In the thirteenth century, corn was grown at Camberwell. Two windmills at Camberwell, and one at Dulwich, ground the corn for Londoners.

Camberwell was considered a country beauty spot well into the eighteenth century. Woods, farms and meadows alternated with the large residences of wealthy people. The name Camberwell is derived from a well of healing medicinal water, situated on the site of the present Grove.

By the end of the eighteenth century, Camberwell Green was becoming an urban centre, and in the last half of the nineteenth century, Camberwell assumed its present look. Housing grew when the railways came through, in the 1890s, when Tower Bridge was built (1886–94), and when industry came to the area. Camberwell is actually a classic example of the suburb which grew up to house the working man in the time of the industrial revolution.

Camberwell is not without its luminaries: Robert Browning was born in 1812 of a Camberwell family; Ruskin and Mendelssohn lived on Denmark Hill; Sir Christopher Wren is said to have lived in Camberwell Green while St Paul's was being built.

The name Dulwich is derived from old English, and means a meadow where dill grew. The first known mention of Dilwys was in 967, when King Edgar granted the Manor to one of his thanes.

Dulwich Forest is where Charles I and his court went hunting. Part of that forest survives as Dulwich Wood.

Edward Alleyn, a famous proprietor of the Fortune Theatre and personal friend of Shakespeare, amassed a fortune and bought estates in Dulwich. In Dulwich in 1619, he founded the College of God's Gift, the ancestor of the present Dulwich College. Much later, Dulwich became a mecca for the artistic personalities of Victorian London.

The Atmosphere . . . The People . . .

Dulwich has been a nice place to live ever since people began to live there! Camberwell, however, has had its ups and downs. But Oliver Marriott, the man who wrote *The Property Boom*, lives in a Victorian house in Camberwell, so that portends something for the future of the area.

You might say Camberwell Green is a bit like Camden Town or the area round the Angel, Islington: cheap shopping, heavy traffic of cars and people on main roads, some handsome but run-down properties nearby. The Green is full of busy mums with prams and toddlers, dodging the traffic of the five major roads which lead into the Green. But Camberwell carries with it a 'south of the river' stigma which Camden Town does not.

Dulwich, on the other hand, is serenity itself, still a bit like a country village, in its heart. That village is surrounded by handsome houses, of the new, middle and old age vintage. Dulwich is a residential centre for a solid professional corps of lawyers, doctors, and professors. But Camberwell is also attracting more and more of these people.

Champion Hill

Dulwich modern

A Look at the Buildings, Outstanding Streets and Squares...

Of the 40,000-odd dwellings which existed in Camberwell in 1939, only 403 were unscathed by air attacks during the war. It is for this reason that so much of present day Camberwell is brand-new council flats.

The high spots of Camberwell are the remaining old houses south of Camberwell Church Street. That area forms an oasis of sorts, with Camberwell Grove and Lane and Champion Hill the most popular parts. Camberwell Grove is higher priced near the crescent at the top; cheaper, the closer you are to the noisy shopping area at the bottom. Champion Grove is a very pretty mix of Regency, Georgian and Victorian houses, which would surely be popular in no matter what part of London they appeared.

The new town houses sprouting around Champion Hill are a good sign of

A house in Dulwich Village

the future of Camberwell. These houses, in an area called The Hamlet, come on the market for over £15,000.

Continue south from Camberwell, pass through Peckham, and you're in Dulwich. If you go by train, go to West Dulwich, or North Dulwich. East Dulwich is 'not so nice', as the residents in Dulwich Village will tell you. Actually the best part of Dulwich, the village and environs, has no tag of West or North. These refer simply to the British Rail stations where you catch trains in or out of Dulwich. Both North and West Dulwich are within walking distance of the village.

Dulwich Village is a lovely lane, with handsome houses, and a cluster of small shops and cottages at the top. Most of Dulwich is owned by Dulwich College, whose estate governors can take credit for the maintenance fo the leafy-rural atmosphere. There are few freeholds in Dulwich, but many leaseholds for sale, and some rentals. This is an area where many people sell their own homes through a newspaper advert, rather than an estate agent, probably because their houses are so easy to sell.

The woman who runs the small antique shop in a village cottage moved there only last year, having lived for a long time in East Dulwich. She and her husband noticed that the village bookshop, located in a lovely cottage, had closed. So they wrote to the owner, asking him if he wanted to move. Sure enough the owner was contemplating a move, and the couple got his twenty-year lease, in the heart of Dulwich Village—yet another example of the advisability of living in or near the area where you really want to find your home. One couple paid £20,000 for a Regency house in Parkhall Road. They insist the house would have cost £40,000 north of the river.

The village side streets, such as Pickwick Road, have three-bedroom houses going for reasonable prices. College Road has many town house properties, expensive of course.

Amenities of the Area

Dulwich Park, across College Road from the College, is seventy acres of green, including a lake, waterfall and stream.

The Dulwich College Picture Gallery, built by Sir John Soane in 1814, claims to be London's first public picture gallery. It was bombed in the Second World War but has been rebuilt. Beautiful collection of Gainsborough, Rembrandt, Reubens, Watteau and Murillo, among others!

Disadvantages?

Dulwich is a lengthy journey from central London; but no lengthier than Hampstead or Highgate, say Dulwich advocates.

Camberwell, in some parts, borders Brixton, which is a ghetto of immigrants living in not-so-well-kept furnished flats. Brixton, even with the new Victoria line stopping at Stockwell and Brixton, is unlikely ever to rise in stature. This may well inhibit the growth in value of Camberwell properties.

No book shop in Camberwell. No interesting food shops either. Very interesting exotic food shopping in Brixton, however, if you dig the highly populated, open-air market scene.

Camberwell state schools not so good. Excellent selection of private schools in Dulwich. Many choose Dulwich solely because of its schools.

KENNINGTON — STOCKWELL — VAUXHALL

Local council
London Borough of Lambeth

Postal areas
S.E.11 Kennington
S.W.9 Stockwell

Type of housing
Victorian
Cottages
Georgian

Approximate number of flats and houses in district
20,000

Number of residential flats and houses in district
20,000

Local estate agents
P. J. Broomhalls & Partners,
61 Petty France, S.W.1, 799 1673
Briant Chambers & Done Hunter,
157 Kennington Lane, S.E.11,
735 2292
Inwood & Son, 230 Stockwell Rd,
S.W.9, 274 1736

APPROXIMATE COST OF HOUSING

Long lease unfurnished flats
Kennington
price
£8–12,000

Stockwell
price
£7–10,000

(non commercial)
Houses freehold or leasehold
Kennington
price
£15–25,000

Stockwell
price
£12–15,000

Amenity society
Hanover Gardens Association,
46 Hanover Gardens, S.E.11
Vauxhall Society,
20 Albert Sq., S.W.8

Citizens' Advice Bureau
384 Streatham High Rd, S.W.16
769 1055

TRANSPORTATION

Tube stops
Kennington
Stockwell
Vauxhall

Bus service routes
2 Victoria—Baker St
36 Victoria
185 Victoria

Tube lines
Northern
Victoria

Travelling times
West End 10–15 mins
City 8–13 mins

Resident parking
Yes. Permit £6 per year

222

Kennington – Stockwell – Vauxhall

A Bit of History . . .

At the time of the Domesday Book, the Manor of Kennington and Vauxhall was worth £3. At the start of the fourteenth century, wine from Kennington vineyards was sold in London. At the same time, King Edward III had his Palace at Kennington, and Geoffrey Chaucer was clerk there for salary of two shillings a day. Henry VIII demolished the building in order to re-use the materials at his Whitehall Palace.

Before Westminster Bridge was opened, Kennington Road was a bridle way! The bridge and commercialization of the riverside resulted in the building of many fine houses on both sides of the road.

Kennington's real claim to fame is that it is the birthplace and childhood home of Charlie Chaplin.

Looking at Vauxhall and Stockwell today, who could believe that less than 150 years ago, Londoners were flocking to the Royal Vauxhall Gardens to hear the nightingales sing; and to see some of England's finest musicians perform. The gardens had to be approached by boat, or by carriage across London Bridge, and they were a beautiful sight indeed, with their fireworks and waterworks. Hogarth presented a picture of Henry VIII and Ann Boleyn to the Gardens, and he received from Jonathan Tyers, his friend and the owner of the garden, a Gold Pass, which admitted a coachful to the gardens in perpetuity. The pleasure gardens eventually attracted many rogues and thieves and closed down in 1859, after some years of decline.

The Atmosphere . . . The People . . .

This is working man's London, south of the river. It is the kind of area where the family with high standards for education, environmental beauty and the fine things of life must have some courage to settle. Because a working man's community can be rough, the shops sterile, neighbours and prospective friends not exactly inspiring. But the houses here go for prices as much as half of those north of the river, so some families will want to consider living here.

The areas are alive with people going about the essential tasks of daily life. One can easily picture the days when Charlie Chaplin played on the doorstep in Pownall Terrace.

A Look at the Buildings, Outstanding Streets and Squares . . .

These south London residential areas grew up during the industrial revolution, and the building standards then were not high, by any means. Industries such as Doulton Pottery created business which had much to do with the swift growth of the formerly quiet marshy lands of the borough of Lambeth. The area is still better known for its commerce than its housing.

Anyone who goes to Kennington will certainly be directed first to its showpiece—Cleaver Square. It is what one self-styled witticist calls the Angor Wat of south London. It is a beautifully restored Georgian square, surrounded by a sea of dilapidation. Albert Square in Vauxhall may be handsomer, but it is still in a run-down condition, because it houses many controlled tenants. Cleaver Square is absolutely perfect. But the rise of Cleaver Square has not played any profound influence on neighbouring streets, which are still run-down.

If you are keen on Kennington, because of its proximity to Westminster or whatever, then stick to the area within the triangle formed by Kennington Park Road, Kennington Road and Kennings Way. Cleaver Square is right in the middle of this triangle. Some of the most attractive streets within this triangle, however, like Denny Crescent and Courtenay Square, belong to the Duchy of Cornwall and are not for sale. They are primarily for retired crown servants, who must wait their turn on a very long waiting list.

Kennington Road has a number of handsome Georgian houses with delicate iron balconies. They are under a government preservation order, and they stand today just as they did when the Prince Regent and his Court passed them on their way to Brighton.

Kennington Park Road has some big blocks of flats, but if you're going to put up with the rough spots of living in Kennington, you might as well have a house.

Cleaver Square

Stockwell block of flats   A house on Stockwell Park Crescent

Hanover Gardens, the first turning past Kennington Oval Station; and Lansdowne Gardens, off South Lambeth Road, are both coming up, according to Lambeth residents who are watching the trends.

Stockwell, neighbour to Kennington, is on the way to Brixton. Stockwell has more family-size houses and fewer giants than Kennington, yet it is not moving up as quickly as Kennington, which is to say it isn't moving much! The potential is there, however. Stockwell Park Crescent has some Victorian villas which look quite like those of St John's Wood, if you look quickly! These villas are run-down, and divided into flats filled with immigrant families. The houses of nearby Durand Gardens are smaller; they sport a very pretty oval-shaped central garden. Just off Durand Gardens are some roads of two-storey workmen's cottages, yet to be restored.

Vauxhall may be named in the same breath as Stockwell, for they lie adjacent, and have similar properties and qualities. Albert Square, with its Victorian giants, could be a showpiece, but instead it borders on being a slum. The reason? Most of the houses are rent controlled, and tenants cannot be ousted by interested parties who would like to spruce up the buildings. Behind Albert Square are terraces of very small two-storey cottages, varying in their state of up-keep.

Amenities of the Area

Excellent underground transportation: Northern Line at Kennington and Stockwell, Victoria Line at Stockwell and Vauxhall. Excellent location for those who work in Westminster.

Lambeth Palace, the official London residence of the Archbishop of Canterbury. The Vauxhall Society sponsors a Lambeth Palace Garden Party every now and then.

Some good sturdy properties, still available at low prices.

Interesting West Indian shopping in Brixton, on Brixton Road, from the town hall to the police station. Busy street markets along Electric Avenue and Brixton Station Road.

The Oval cricket ground for sports fans.

Plenty of music and theatre nearby at the Old Vic or the Royal Festival Hall, South Bank. The Hayward Gallery for exhibits of the Arts Council of Great Britain.

Disadvantages?

Shopping is uninspiring, except for the ethnic area in Brixton.

This area is loaded with immigrants, living many families to a house. The area will not be transformed as if by a fairy's wand into a high-prestige area of London. It will take a lot of work on the part of a lot of people to make the most of Kennington—Stockwell—Vauxhall.

FULHAM — PARSON'S GREEN

Local council
London Borough of Hammersmith

Postal areas
S.W.6, S.W.10

Type of housing
Victorian
Edwardian
Cottages

Approximate number of flats and houses in district
25,000

Local estate agents
Acland & Co., 193 King's Rd,
S.W.6, 736 1368
Aylesford & Co., 440 King's Rd,
S.W.10, 351 0121
Cowley & Andersen, 13 Langton
St, S.W.10, 352 0201
Friend & Falcke, 293 Brompton
Rd, S.W.3, 584 5361
Johnson & Pycraft, 228 Fulham
Rd, S.W.10, 352 6533
Lofts & Partners, 123 Sydney St,
S.W.3, 351 0077
P. & J. Phillips, 64 New King's Rd,
S.W.6, 736 4422
Redfearn & Redfearn, 109 New
King's Rd, S.W.6, 736 7127
Wheeler & Atkins, 4 Harwood Rd,
S.W.6, 736 7066

APPROXIMATE COST OF HOUSING

Long lease unfurnished flats
price
£10–16,000

(non commercial)
Houses freehold or leasehold
price
£17–22,000

Amenity society
The Fulham Society,
6 Edenhurst Ave, S.W.6

Citizens' Advice Bureau
Cobbs Hall,
Fulham Palace Rd, S.W.6
385 1322

TRANSPORTATION

Tube stops
Fulham Broadway
Parson's Green

Bus service routes
14 Piccadilly Circus—King's Cross
22 Hyde Park Corner—Bank

Resident parking
No permit required

Tube lines
District

Travelling times
West End 12–15 mins
City 20–30 mins

Fulham – Parson's Green

A Bit of History . . .

In 1086 Fulham was identified as a manor of 1560 acres, well-wooded, with a wood for 1000 pigs. The Bishops of London were granted the Manor of Fulham, which included the area now known as Hammersmith, early in the eighth century. Exactly when the Bishop of London began to reside in Fulham is not known. The present Fulham Palace is a Tudor mansion house built in the sixteenth century.

Where Putney Bridge now stands was once a busy ferry boat, used by Londoners on their way to Surrey. This traffic resulted in the growth of the village of Fulham. In 1729 Fulham Bridge was built at this crossing. Financed by tolls, it stood to 1886, when Putney Bridge was opened a few yards upstream.

Parson's Green

The main concern of Fulham in the eighteenth century was its market gardens. During the first half of the nineteenth century, Fulham farm land was gradually built over.

The real Fulham building boom came between the 1870s and 90s. In 1899, the Vicar of St Peter's Church, Varna Road, Fulham, said the gulf between the clerks (middle class) and the working class was such that they would not meet socially, or even in church! Labourers who were displaced by the railways from their homes in central London moved to Fulham, for the prospect of employment in the building trade.

There were never very many merchants or professional people in Fulham, largely labourers attracted to the Victorian terrace houses, which when built in the 1880s went for rentals of £30—60 per year.

Fulham is thriving with small industry today. But it was not industry that caused the growth of Fulham. Industry was the result rather than the cause of the residential growth of the area.

The Atmosphere . . . The People . . .

Every Londoner knows the Fulham Road these days, because the rise in the number of trendy shops and restaurants is a hint that it might take over some of the glory which was once exclusive to the King's Road. That part of the Fulham Road which is so well known—the Great American Disaster, Hollywood Road—isn't even in Fulham; it's in Chelsea, or S.W.10. Lionel Bart had a home here, in this part of Chelsea known as 'off the Fulham Road'.

Part of Fulham is very appealing, with newly painted-cottages with window boxes—the Chelsea bit. Some other terraces of workmen's cottages are so uninteresting that they will probably never rise above their present forlorn state. Basically, Fulham is yet another working man's area, with a minimum of amentities, that is being invaded by the aggressive middle-income people who prefer owning a house in central London to renting one, or owning one in the suburbs.

A Look at the Buildings, Outstanding Streets and Squares . . .

Drive past World's End on the King's Road, and follow the New King's Road. South of New King's Road are Fulham and Hurlingham. To the north, Parson's Green and Walham Green, and to the north-west, more of Fulham. You will hear Parson's Green, Walham Green and Hurlingham named as separate residential areas, but it is wise to wrap them up in one package called Fulham, for each area borders so closely on another.

High-price Fulham is that area nearest the Fulham Road, the part which parallels New King's Road; and also the area round Parson's Green, heading toward the Thames and the Hurlingham Club.

Low-price Fulham? The streets off Fulham Palace Road. There is also an 'in-between' price area in Fulham right now—around Walham Green (Fulham Broadway tube stop). Walham Green is now what the Moore Park Estate, just a little way from Chelsea's World's End, was two to three years ago— houses going at reasonable but not rock bottom prices in a still scruffy area, an area where you must have a vivid imagination in order to see what the neighbourhood could look like. Two tree-lined streets have already soared in popularity—Clonmel and Barclay Roads.

Fulham is solidly Victorian. Most of the houses in the heart of Fulham were built for factory workers, and so there is little architectural splendour in this part of the world. The grander houses to be found here and there were built for the factory owners! One couple looking for a moderately priced house in London chose Islington in preference to Fulham 'because the gardens of Fulham houses are a joke—they're smaller than the kitchens'.

The Moore Park houses were almost destroyed by the council at one point, to make way for new tower blocks of flats. Tenants were pushed out of the houses and relocated. Then the council surprised everyone and placed the houses on the market. They were grabbed up by a new type of Fulhamite— the man who could not afford Chelsea, but could afford to buy and do up a lower-priced Fulham house.

Just a few yards from Moore Park, where there is no such thing as a park, is Parson's Green, which is a very mixed bag of Victorian cottages, and Victorian giants. One family living at the bottom of Broomhouse Road in a grand old Victorian villa, have been approached four times during the past year by different estate agents, who inquired whether they would like to sell the house. Their house, which is so mouth-watering to estate agents, is one of two gems in an otherwise uninteresting road of small terrace houses, all rented as bedsits.

The best of Parson's Green roads are those leading south of the New King's Road toward Hurlingham—Foskett Road, Napier Avenue, Peterborough

Seymour Walk off Fulham Road

Broomhouse Road Victoriana

Road. Nearer to Hurlingham Park and the shops of Putney High Street are popular roads like Cortayne Road and Bettridge Road.

Fulham is houseland, not flatland, with the exception of the area round the entrance to the Hurlingham Club. Three huge blocks of flats are there, overlooking the river: Napier Court, Napier Road; Ranelagh Gardens, West Hill Road; and Rivermead Court.

Wandsworth Bridge Road is the most unattractive part of Fulham, and has the least potential for rehabilitation.

Amenities of the Area

Very good shopping in the New King's Road. Quaint shops like the Merchant Chandler for kitchen goods, and a smattering of antique-cum-junk shops. A very good selection of antique shops way out on the Fulham Road. Economical lively shopping of all sorts in the North End Road.

The Hurlingham Club: beautiful grounds; tennis, swimming, tea parties, and dances. The waiting list is anywhere from two to four years, and you must be nominated for membership by two members.

Great residential area for football fans. The Chelsea Football Club lives here—kick-off on Saturdays is at 3 p.m.

Chelsea Football Club's home ground

Disadvantages?

Sameness of architecture means a lack of character or personality in many parts of Fulham. None of the builders of Fulham was exactly inspired in his work.

Few really good parks for children. Eel Brook Common and part of Hurlingham Park are two of the few green spots.

235

HAMMERSMITH

Local council
London Borough of Hammersmith

Postal areas
W.6

Type of housing
Victorian
Georgian
Pre-war
Modern houses

Approximate number of flats and houses in district
14,000

Local estate agents
W. Herbert Dunphy & Son,
53 Shepherd's Bush Green, W.12,
743 1100
Green & Son, 172 King St, W.6,
748 4256
J. Harding Marsh,
133 Hammersmith Rd, W.14,
603 2780
Morton & Waters, 310 King St,
W.6, 748 1080

APPROXIMATE COST OF HOUSING

Long lease unfurnished flats
price
£9–13,000

(non commercial) Houses freehold or leasehold
price
£15–22,000

Amenity society
Hammersmith Society,
28 St Peter's Square, W.6

The Brook Green Association,
13 Luxemburg Gdns, W.6

Citizens' Advice Bureau
Cobbs Hall,
Fulham Palace Rd, S.W.6
385 1322

TRANSPORTATION

Tube stops
Hammersmith Broadway

Ravenscourt Park

Bus service routes
27 Kensington—Marylebone Rd
73 Oxford Circus—Euston

Resident parking
Yes. Permit £7·80 per year

Tube lines
Piccadilly
District
Metropolitan

Travelling times
West End 10–15 mins
City 20–30 mins

Hammersmith

A Bit of History . . .

All of the medieval hamlet of Hammersmith lay within the great Manor and Parish of Fulham. Hammersmith was not a separate parish until 1834.

In the 1720s, Defoe described the well-to-do village of Hammersmith as a wood of great houses and palaces, and a noble square (Broadway) built in the middle of several handsome streets, as if the village seemed inclined to grow up into a city. Both Hammersmith and Fulham had market gardens which supplied Londoners with vegetables, from the time of Charles II onwards.

What is to be seen in Hammersmith today is the growth of the mid-nineteenth century. At that time, many people who prospered in Victorian England came to live in the clean air of Hammersmith. The arrival of the railways, from 1864 to 1880, brought an even larger influx of people, and a great wave of speculative building.

The first bridge at Hammersmith opened in 1827 as a toll bridge, and was the first suspension bridge to be built over the Thames. The present beautiful bridge is built on the foundations of the original.

Hammersmith Bridge

The earliest industry in Hammersmith was its brickfields, which provided materials for the terraces and squares of Georgian London.

The Atmosphere . . . The People . . .

The air of Hammersmith today is heavy with industry and the fumes of the cars which roar by on the Hammersmith Flyover. There are 400 factories, all considered light industry, within the borough of Hammersmith.

More than 5000 families are on the waiting list for council housing in Hammersmith; and one quarter of the borough's housing is owned by the government. So it is obvious that Hammersmith will never quite acquire the status of its neighbour, Chiswick. Yet it surely could and will rise above its other neighbour, Shepherd's Bush, which has very little architecture of merit, and a greater transient immigrant population.

The atmosphere in Hammersmith, with the exception of the St Peter's Square area, is solid blue collar or factory worker. The area round the tube is rough round the edges, and dirty. However, there are all sorts of rumours about the redevelopment of the heart of Hammersmith—the Broadway—in the seventies.

Many people who are moving in to save Hammersmith housing from the blow of the council are B.B.C. employees, who want to live near their work in the White City. Other young professionals, too, are seeing the advantages of Hammersmith's convenient location, so well connected by public transport to central London. Certain conveniences of life tend to make grime and noise less noticeable!

A Look at the Buildings, Outstanding Streets and Squares . . .

The buildings of Hammersmith are either Victorian, or council-built in the current century! The only star shining in the vast firmament of Hammersmith is St Peter's Square (closer to Stamford Brook tube station than to Hammersmith) and its Victorian four-storey houses. The square itself, and the small streets which surround it—Black Lion Lane and Standish Road—are very smart, as the description of very acceptable residential areas goes. Across King Street from St Peter's Square is Westcroft Square, which is not 'smart' as yet. Latymer Court is a well known huge block of flats in Hammersmith.

The Upper and Lower Mall of Hammersmith provide an elegant living area. Hammersmith Terrace, the group of red brick houses built around 1775 of Hammersmith brick, has always had distinguished residents. Here you are removed, in a way, from the traffic and the rest of the busy world—one could pass life by in a cottage on the Mall, watching the boats, and the cars roaring over the bridge.

A few words about some slightly interesting areas which border Hammersmith.

BROOK GREEN: the one-time Catholic colony of Hammersmith, home of Irish immigrants, who flocked to Hammersmith to construct the canals and railways in the nineteenth century. Three-storey Victorian terrace houses, a few roads back from the Green itself, are reasonably priced. Two-storey

St Peter's Square

terraces, closer to Shepherd's Bush, are even lower in price. And everyone knows what can happen to a London area filled with two-storey cottages! Chelsea forever.

SHEPHERD'S BUSH: because of the nearby B.B.C. studios and Hammersmith Hospital, and also because of a tremendous new shopping centre sprouting up at the Holland Park end of Shepherd's Bush Green, many people say this area is certain to move up. The architecture is so uninteresting, and the area so heavily populated with immigrants, that it is difficult to truly believe what people are saying about Shepherd's Bush. The houses on Hammersmith Road, Overstone Road and Southerton Road could be large beautiful one-family homes, but the conversions seem to be more to bed-sits than anything else.

WEST KENSINGTON: a bit like its sister North Kensington (across Hammersmith Road) which, with all its conveniences in location and transport, has never really lifted itself or been lifted above a certain very mediocre level. Lillie Road to Talgarth Road is the area served by the West Kensington and Barons Court tube stops, close enough to the 'real' Kensington to be considered as central London. Yet the Kensington-style tall white pillared terrace houses are in a deteriorating state. Comeragh Road and Barons Court Road are considered to be in the best condition, and you will see that they are not in the least inspiring. These houses are not cheap. Barons Court Road backs onto the railway line to boot. These West Kensington properties are probably riper for conversion to family flats than to one-family houses.

Amenities of the Area

King Street, with a Marks and Spencer, and a lane of barrow boys selling fruits, vegetables and almost everything. The council plans an £8 million redevelopment of this King Street shopping centre, which really isn't bad as it is. Superb low price shopping around Shepherd's Bush Green and North End Road (West Kensington).

Excellent private schools: St Paul's School for Girls and the Latymer Foundation School (for boys); Godolphin and Latymer Girls' School.

The White City Stadium, built for the Olympic games in 1908.

The Queen's Club, the second best known tennis club in London. Private membership only.

Disadvantages?

Masses of noisy and dirty traffic, which is almost impossible to escape. The Hammersmith Flyover, Hammersmith Bridge Road, Great West Road. Ugh!

Serious doubt among many people as to whether Hammersmith can ever rise above its present state of dilapidation. Look how long it's taken Islington to get away from its purely industrial run-down image. And Islington has far more basically interesting houses than Hammersmith.

Brook Green

CHISWICK

Local council
London Borough of Hounslow

Postal areas
W.4

Type of housing
Victorian
Cottages
Georgian
Neo-Georgian
Modern houses
Edwardian

Approximate number of flats and houses in district
12,000

Local estate agents
Raymond Bushell & Co.,
70 Turnham Green Terrace, W.4
994 1032
Cole & Hicks, 42 The Broadway,
W.5, 567 4014
A. J. Fowkes, 150 Chiswick High
Rd, W.4, 994 1244
Michael Richards, 401 Chiswick
High Rd, W.4, 994 8512
Rodney Scott & Co., 1a Sutton
Court Rd, W.4, 995 9609
Sturgis & Son, 155 Chiswick High
Rd, W.4, 995 3443
Tyser Greenwood & Co.,
386 Chiswick High Rd, W.4,
994 7022
Whitman Price & Coleman,
273 Chiswick High Rd, W.4,
995 2345

APPROXIMATE COST OF HOUSING

Long lease unfurnished flats
price
£9–13,000

(non commercial)
Houses freehold or leasehold
price
£14–22,000

Amenity society
Old Chiswick Protection Society,
Swan House, Chiswick Mall, W.4

Citizens' Advice Bureau
16 Heathfield Terrace,
Chiswick, W.4
994 4846

Tube stops
Gunnersbury
Chiswick Park
Turnham Green

Bus service routes
27 Marylebone Rd—Camden
Town
88 Shepherd's Bush—Notting Hill
—Oxford Circus

TRANSPORTATION

Tube lines
District

Travelling times
West End 15–25 mins
City 25–35 mins

Resident parking
No permit required

Train services
British Rail, Southern Region to
Waterloo

Travelling times
Waterloo 25 mins

Frequency
Every 20–30 mins

Chiswick

A Bit of History . . .

Some of the seventeenth-century Chiswick, the riverside village, still stands.
Hogarth's House, in Hogarth Lane, for instance. (Though it is a miracle his
house has been permitted to stand, for an industrial laundry hovers over it on
one side; a motorway roars by the other.) In Chiswick Mall are beautiful
Georgian double-fronted houses, all vine-covered.
could be seventeenth century citizens.

In the eighteenth century, Chiswick became the centre of a dignified way
of living, with lavish entertainment at houses by the Thames. Chiswick House
is the epitome of the spacious elegant living of the day—there the Earl of
Burlington collected his tapestries and pictures, and entertained the likes of
Alexander Pope.

Strand-on-the-Green

The Atmosphere...The People...

Once you depart from the revered riverside houses of Chiswick Mall and Strand-on-the-Green, Chiswick becomes sadly suburban. You could walk for half an hour on a winter's day and not see a single person. Everyone is snug inside his detached house, or his flat in the big block of flats, or his car on the road. Most of these houses and flats are far from the river so that you have no feeling at all of being in a riverside town. The atmosphere is that of a safe, secure, well-to-do suburban community.

A Look at the Buildings, Outstanding Streets and Squares...

A person must be reasonably affluent to live in Chiswick. And yet a Hartington Road family house, with lawns running down to the riverside,

Thames Road

may cost a lot less than a large family house in the heart of Kensington. Hartington Road is not for walking—it's long and wide, made for chauffeur-driven cars—the smartest road in Chiswick (Eamonn Andrews lived in this road for a while.)

There is nothing wrong with the suburban sections of Chiswick: they're fine for the family with a car. But if you require any sort of charm in your daily life, stay close to the river. Strand-on-the-Green is the kind of place where one could decide to spend the rest of one's days: authentic Regency and Georgian houses sitting right on the riverbank, gulls floating outside the front window, the tide rising and falling. Some modern two-bedroomed houses here, on a site called Magnolia Wharf, sold for £13,000 each. Chiswick Mall's houses are grander than those of Strand-on-the-Green. But the Strand has the advantage of being near Kew Bridge, and several public transport stations. Chiswick Mall is rather isolated.

You'll find parts of Chiswick that are not posh. The properties of Turnham Green are rather dreary. Chiswick Common, near Turnham Green tube, can be deserted on a Sunday afternoon. Even the cottages, which sell so well in almost any area of London, show no sign of being snatched up or modernized.

Bull's Head pub, Chiswick

Windmill Alley and Road, both rows of workmen's cottages off Chiswick Common, stand ignored.

If you like three-storey Victorian terraces, such houses abound near Chiswick House, the Palladian masterpiece which is Chiswick's landmark.

Amenities of the Area

Hogarth's House, his home for fifteen years, filled with 150 of his works. Chiswick House, and its grounds, great for walking.

Two well-known schools: St Paul's Girls' School and the Latymer Foundation Schools.

Kew Gardens and Richmond Park, just over the river.

The Thames, with lovely old riverside pubs, like The Doves, the Old Ship, the Blue Anchor.

Good location near the airport for jetsetters or Common Market commuters.

Disadvantages?

Would be very difficult to get along without a car.

The noise—from both the air traffic overhead and the road traffic heading to the airport.

Thank goodness for Hammersmith. For without it as a neighbour, Chiswick residents would be hard put for shopping facilities. Chiswick High Road, wide and lined with shops, is completely lacking in vitality. Hammersmith is alive.

Around Chiswick Station are a few shops, for the executive who was told not to forget to bring home some salt, or Schweppes. If Chiswick is such a fine place to live, why cannot it support a better shopping centre? The first thing one notices about an improving area, *vis a vis* Canonbury, is that the shops get better, to fit the requirements of the 'new' residents.

BARNES

Local council
London Borough of Richmond-on-Thames

Postal areas
S.W.13

Type of housing
Victorian
Modern houses
Neo-Georgian

Approximate number of flats and houses in district
5000

Local estate agents
Rodney Scott & Co., 82 Church Rd, S.W.13, 748 2641
Sturgis & Son, 133 Church Rd, S.W.13, 748 8483

APPROXIMATE COST OF HOUSING

Long lease unfurnished flats
price
£10–15,000

(non commercial)
Houses freehold or leasehold
price
£18–35,000

Amenity society
Barnes Amenity Committee,
8 The Mall, Fife Rd, S.W.14

Citizens' Advice Bureau
Barnes Municipal Offices,
Sheen Lane, S.W.14
876 1513

TRANSPORTATION

Bus service routes
9 Hammersmith—Piccadilly—Bank
72 Hammersmith

Resident parking
No permit required

Train services
British Rail, Southern Region
Travelling times
Barnes—Waterloo 15 mins

Frequency
Barnes—Waterloo
Every 10–15 mins

Travelling times (bus and tube)
West End 15–20 mins
City 20–30 mins

Barnes

A Bit of History . . .

The Manor of Barnes was given by King Athelstan in the eighth century to the Dean and Chapter of St Paul's, who still hold it.

The present day community of Barnes sits on the site of what was once Barn Elms, a great manor, which was sold to the Hammersmith Bridge Company in the 1820s. When the bridge was built, a new road was cut across the Barn Elms estate to form Castelnau. Castelnau was developed by the Boileau family, and named after their ancient site of origin in France. Prior to that time, Barnes had been a small village, with a few large houses in gardens, a village pond, and houses facing the river in Barnes Terrace. All the larger houses have perished, but the general layout of the village survives, and the area round the village pond has been designated for conservation.

The Atmosphere . . . The People . . .

It is surprising how few Londoners know about the charms of Barnes.

Barnes is a lovely rural setting in the city, with its own village duckpond in fact. Barnes Common is smaller than her sister commons of Putney and Wimbledon, to which she is contiguous. And the whole feeling of Barnes is a cosiness that is not prevalent in London neighbourhoods in general.

The people who live in Barnes seem as attractive as the village. Youngish couples with children as well-dressed as their parents. These are for the most part families who've taken advantage of the opportunity to get the most for their money when they buy a home. If you can't have Chelsea or Hampstead, there's always Barnes, where houses sell for half the price. Barnes still has a number of long-time residents, whose fathers and grandfathers were born in the very cottages or houses in which they were born. So Barnes is not all newcomers, by any means.

Barnes is bordered on the north and north-east by the Thames; east and south by Putney; and west by Mortlake, which is by no means as attractive as Barnes. The brewery in Mortlake gives it an industrial aura.

A Look at the Buildings, Outstanding Streets and Squares . . .

Cross Hamersmith Bridge and you are in Castelnau, a wide road of Regency-like early Victorian villas which sell for more than £30,000. Even with the traffic streaming by, these houses can command a high price. They are set back from the road, with front gardens and driveways, which soften the noise somewhat. The enormous red brick Victorian houses further along Castelnau are not nearly as attractive.

Castelnau is really an independent little area, which is part of Barnes but not really. Lonsdale Road, facing the new St Paul's School, has houses as generous and costly as those of Castelnau itself.

Castelnau Row, Merthy Terrace, and several roads with ladies' names—St Hilda's Road and Lillian Road—contain some of the prettiest artisan cottages this side of Chelsea. As recently as 1956, these cottages were selling for as little as £500. Now they're priced like Chelsea. Not so charming but none-the less attractive is the Lowther Estate—similarly shaped semi-detached houses, basically rectangular in shape, of a grey-sandy colour exterior. The houses are spacious, and have good gardens. Without a garage, many of them would go for more than £15,000.

The village part of Barnes, which is off the top of Castelnau, via Church Street, is somehow separate from Castelnau. The heart of the village of Barnes is its green, with duckpond and common. Beyond the green is the High Street of small shops, leading to the river.

The properties in the village are solid Victorian/Edwardian, with the exception of the Homestead and Homestead Cottage, beautiful Georgian buildings in Church Street. Barnes Terrace, on the river, boasts some Georgian and Queen Anne houses, going for more than £30,000. Barnes' little Chelsea, a group of artisans' cottages, is located at the bottom of White Hart Lane, between the common and the Thames. This is pricey Barnes, perhaps an omen of things to come. Some of the not yet pricey roads off the common are

Barnes Green

A house on Barnes Common   Castelnau Victorian Villa

Woodlands Road, Westwood Gardens, Ranelagh Avenue and Hillersdon Avenue. Even with the aircraft noise overhead, Barnes has nowhere to go but up.

Barnes is not made up entirely of romantic old houses. Property developers get in when they can. On the site of a derelict laundry on Glentham Road, twenty-three new town houses have been built, starting at £19,750 each! A small number of blocks of flats are located near the river. Elm Bank Mansions flats had ninety-nine-year leases which sold for £6000 and up in 1971. Elm Bank Gardens, under Barnes Bridge, is a cul-de-sac of new and Victorian properties. Riverview Gardens is a former Key Flat block, all red brick with white paintwork, located on the Barnes side of Hammersmith Bridge.

Amenities of the Area

Acres of green to roam in, for not only Barnes Common, but Putney Heath and Wimbledon Common are nearby. Barnes Green has a day centre for community doings.

The shops offer everything on a village scale. The superstores—Tesco and the Co-op—are across the bridge in Hammersmith.

St Paul's School is certainly an amenity, but one resident says it looks like a crematorium from a distance.

Disadvantages?

Aircraft noise. Worse at the village end of Barnes than at the Castelnau end.

Poor public transport. No tube stop. Numbers 9 and 73 bus to Hammersmith tube.

Motorway threat, 1981–91: would bisect the common. Check with Richmond Town Hall.

PUTNEY

Local council
London Borough of Wandsworth

Postal areas
S.W.15

Type of housing
Tower blocks
Victorian
Modern houses
Edwardian

Approximate number of flats and houses in district
20,000

Local estate agents
Ellis Copp & Co., 210 Upper
Richmond Rd, S.W.15, 788 4533
H. A. Mawer, 322 Upper
Richmond Rd, S.W.15, 788 2882
Redfearn & Redfearn, 109 New
King's Rd, S.W.6, 736 7127
Sturgis & Son, 188 Upper
Richmond Rd, S.W.15, 789 2124

APPROXIMATE COST OF HOUSING

Long lease unfurnished flats
price
£12–20,000

(non commercial)
Houses freehold or leasehold
price
£20–35,000

Amenity society
Putney Society,
6 Chartfield Square, S.W.15

Citizens' Advice Bureau
Welbeck House,
43 Wandsworth High St, S.W.18
874 0488

TRANSPORTATION

Tube stops
East Putney

Bus service routes
14 South Kensington—Piccadilly
—King's Cross
30 Baker St—King's Cross—
Islington
74 Marble Arch—Camden Town

Resident parking
No permit required

Tube lines
District
Piccadilly

Travelling times
West End 20–25 mins
City 25–35 mins

Putney

A Bit of History . . .

At the time of the Domesday Survey in 1086, Putney had a ferry which yielded twenty shillings a year to the Lord of the Manor, and there was also a fishery there.

With the growth of travel in Tudor times, Putney grew too, for travellers heading for anywhere in the south or south-west of England passed through Putney. During the golden age of the stage coach, in the late eighteenth century, Putney grew, with blacksmiths and inns jostling for frontage on the High Street. In those days, Putney became a rich man's suburbia, with huge houses built in great gardens. But the big building boom in this area came with the opening of the railways, in the mid 1800s.

Even with two buildings booms—at the height of stage coach travel, and then again with the start of railway travel—Putney entered the present century with a lot of wide open spaces, most of which have been seized by property developers for the numerous modern town houses and flats you see in Putney now.

A tottering wooden bridge, the original Putney Bridge, was built in 1729. The present bridge of Cornish granite was built in 1886. It was, in fact, called Fulham Bridge.

Roehampton, on the south-west border of Putney, was once a paradise of country houses.

The Atmosphere . . . The People . . .

Here are two quotations about Putney, each of which contains a good deal of truth:

' . . . one of the pleasantest of the London suburbs, as well as the most accessible . . . there is still an almost unlimited extent of open ground which cannot be covered; and with wood and water, common and hill, there will always be an element of freshness and openness in Putney seldom to be obtained so near London'.

(That from a book called *Hammersmith, Fulham and Putney*, one of series called *The Fascination of London*, general editor Sir Walter Besant.)

'In modern Putney there is absolutely nothing of interest. . . . Everything is big, pretentious, costly, showy and utterly uninteresting'.

(From *The Way about Surrey*, Volume I in the *Way-About* series published by Gliffe and Son.)

The first of the quotes was made in 1903; the second, in 1891. So neither of the men was actually speaking about the Putney which greets you as you drive over the bridge today. And yet they said seventy or so years ago is still partly true today.

Putney is a very popular place to live, but it is definitely a suburb, no longer a village. Its picturesque qualities are difficult to discern apart from the riverbank, or the heath. Because Putney is so popular, its price tags are moving too high for some. We know one couple who moved to Richmond, not because they wanted to, but because they couldn't afford the house they wanted to buy in Putney. They had been long-time flat-dwellers in Putney, but reached the stage of wanting their own home. The suburban qualities of Putney are apparent in plot after plot of small new homes with communal gardens; and in an overdose of purpose-built blocks of flats.

Putney is at its prettiest by the river, and it is almost resort-like at Putney Pier, where the rowing clubs gather.

A Look at the Buildings, Outstanding Streets and Squares . . .

Putney is largely Victorian, or modern, Putney Hill contains the prestige blocks of modern flats.

Manor Fields, on Putney Hill, looks like a fortress. In reality it is a grouping of many big mock-castle blocks of flats with Scottish names like Baillol House and Glenalmond House. At one time for rent, these flats are now for sale. Kings Keep is another mock-Gothic flat complex near Manor Fields.

Putney Hill flats

Neo-Tudor house in Putney   Modern flats at Putney Hill

There are plenty of straight and stark modern blocks of flats in Putney as well. Look at West Point, just across the road from Manor Fields.

Highest prices in Putney are for the properties around the heath. And the 'high price square' is that within the boundaries of Putney Hill and Roehampton Lane, Upper Richmond Road and Putney Heath. This 'square' is a large area, and within it are many modern homes. Chartfield Avenue is typical—a sprawling wide road, with big houses sitting not on top of each other but still close enough together to be called suburban.

Lowest price Putney is near the river, west of Putney High Street, between the river and Upper Richmond Road. The small Victorian terraces are not very attractive, but more could be made of them. Lower Richmond Road, in the same area, is very run-down.

Amenities of the Area

A playground for all the family along the Thames: restaurants, rowing clubs, ice cream stands.

Two annual events, the Boat Race and the Head of the River race, take place within a week or so of each other. The Boat Race has been run on the same Putney to Mortlake route since 1851; the Head of the River race, with as many as 300 rowing eights taking part, is rowed in the opposite direction, Mortlake to Putney.

Putney enjoys a low density of population, due to its park, common and heath.

Superb shopping along Putney High Street. A Putney resident really need never venture beyond there. Parson's Green and Fulham people, in fact, got to Putney to shop!

Disadvantages?

Air traffic overhead makes a great deal of noise; other than that, it's a very peaceful suburb.

Most underground trains go to Putney Bridge, which is on the Fulham side of the river, not even in Putney! Most Putney residents want to go to the East Putney Station. So there is almost always an unpleasant wait for an East Putney train. This factor alone has influenced some young families to buy their houses in Islington or Fulham, rather than Putney.

A river scene in Putney

WIMBLEDON

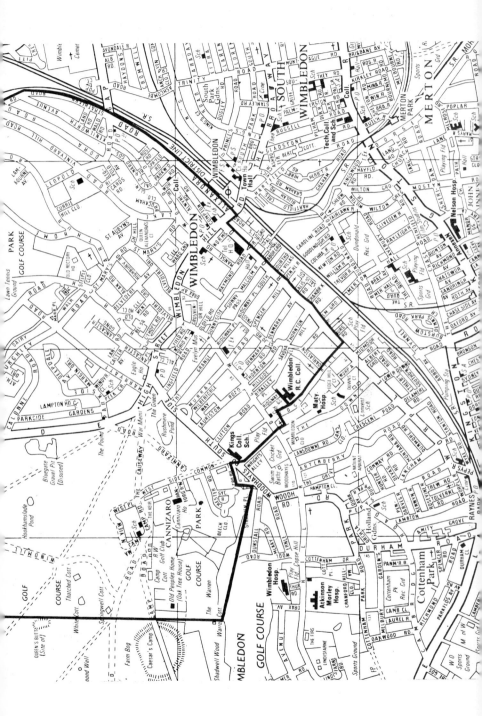

259

WIMBLEDON

Local council
London Borough of Merton

Postal areas
S.W.19

Type of housing
Modern houses
Neo-Georgian
Tower blocks

**Approximate number of flats
and houses in district**
23,000

Local estate agents
Frank N. Bateman, 81 High St,
S.W.19, 946 9811
Hampton & Sons, Hampton House,
High St, Wimbledon, S.W.19,
946 6464
Hawes & Co., Wimbledon Station,
S.W.19, 946 7676
Sturgis, 70 Wimbledon High St,
S.W.19, 946 5052

APPROXIMATE COST OF HOUSING

Short lease unfurnished flats
annual rent
£800–1300

Long lease unfurnished flats
price
£12–20,000

**(non commercial)
Houses freehold or leasehold**
price
£25–40,000
Mansions £50–100,000

Amenity society
Wimbledon Society,
109 Pepys Rd, Wimbledon, S.W.20

Citizens' Advice Bureau
30–32 Worple Rd, S.W.19
946 0735

TRANSPORTATION

Tube stops
Wimbledon

Bus service routes
77a King's Cross
155 Victoria Embankment

Resident parking
No permit required

Tube lines
District

Travelling times
West End 25–35 mins
City 30–40 mins

Train services
British Rail, Southern Region to
Waterloo

Travelling times
Waterloo 10–15 mins

Frequency
14 per hour

Wimbledon

A Bit of History . . .

Wimbledon was part of a grange in the Archbishop of Canterbury's Manor of Mortlake. The last Archbishop to hold Mortlake (meaning Wimbledon) was Thomas Cranmer, who exchanged it with Henry VIII for other lands in 1536. Henry granted it to Thomas Cromwell (whose father had been a brewer and blacksmith of Putney). After Cromwell was executed in 1540, many famous people owned the Manor. The owner, Sir Thomas Cecil, is credited with 'making Wimbledon', for he recognized the advantages of it as a place of residence and had the road from London to Wimbledon improved. Sir Thomas Cecil, his son, sold the Manor to the Crown. During the seventeenth century, the Manor House attracted notable residents to Wimbledon, and the village began to develop. The building of great mansions in Wimbledon continued well into the nineteenth century.

The railway reached Wimbledon in 1838, and led to the development of artisans' dwellings in South Wimbledon. Up the hill, mansions began to sell for redevelopment to suburban houses for London business men.

The Atmosphere . . . The People . . .

Putney Heath adjoins Wimbledon Common, and yet the two residential areas differ widely in character. Wimbledon still has an old village charm to it, in its central part; whereas Putney seems to have grown just because the rest of London came out to meet it and had nowhere to go except across the river.

There is more wealth in Wimbledon, a higher proportion of families who've reached their pinnacle of financial success, as opposed to Putney, which has lots of young families on the way up.

Wimbledon is one of the most prestigious areas of London in which to live, and it has been Up for so long that one has barely a chance of making a bad property investment there.

To live in Wimbledon is perfect, so long as you're near the common. Overheard at a cocktail party:

'Where are you living now?'
'Wimbledon'.
'Oh, on the common?'
'Well, not right on it, but near it'.
Silence.

A Look at the Buildings, Outstanding Streets and Squares . . .

The atmosphere in Wimbledon village is affluence. But there is this 'both sides of the track' thing about living in Wimbledon. To live up Wimbledon

A mansion on Wimbledon Common

Belvedere Drive

Wimbledon modern

262

Hill Road, near the common and the old village, is a far better thing than to live at the bottom of the hill, by the railway station. At the bottom are all the Victorian terraces, row after row of exactly the same thing. At the top of the hill are the old mansions and estates which remain; or the new and modern houses and estates which were carved out of or built on the sites of the old.

It's cheaper to buy a luxury flat or an average size family house in Wimbledon than it is in central London. But to buy a big house, sitting facing the common, would possibly cost you £100,000. That, however, is for the kind of mini-mansion you see in The Bishops Avenue in Hampstead, protected from the rest of humanity by brick walls or high green hedges. Parkside Gardens and Marryat Road also have £50–100,000 price tags on some of their houses.

Exemplary of the new wave of building taking Wimbledon by storm is the neo-Georgian town house, à la Newstead Way and Lincoln Road, over £25,000 for those four-bedroom townhouses. A new estate of forty houses has appeared in Welford Place, Church Road. Four-bedroom houses on one hundred and thirty-year leases went for £22,950, and residents have the added attraction of a fifty-foot heated swimming pool.

All over Wimbledon you will see signs such as 'Sold for Redevelopment' — which means that a property developer has purchased an old estate and will be putting up some new houses. Look at Castle Close, off Parkside, to see how elegant these new neo-Georgian town houses can be. A Jensen or Bentley in every garage. . . .

Wimbledon's well-known large blocks of flats prevail along Parkside. The Oakfield Estate, luxury flats overlooking Wimbledon Centre Court, slashed individual flat prices by about £2000 in 1971. Their original prices for flats in two eleven-storey blocks ranged from £13,000–19,000.

Belvedere Drive is the curving road to the left, off the hill leading down to Wimbledon Station. This is a very attractive 'central Wimbledon' location, between the station and big shops, and the village and its small shops. Other roads in that location are equally attractive.

Amenities of the Area

Wimbledon Common, with London Scottish Golf Club, riding facilities, 1200 acres of nature.

Wimbledon is the centre of the Lawn Tennis World during the last week of June and the first week of July. Londoners know Wimbledon as New Yorkers know Forest Hills—for its tennis courts.

Few far-out suburbs have such excellent connections with central London. Very, very good shopping around the station. A Safeway supermarket.

Disadvantages?

Some residents thereabouts believe the common is too wild, and too vast to be safe, particularly at night.

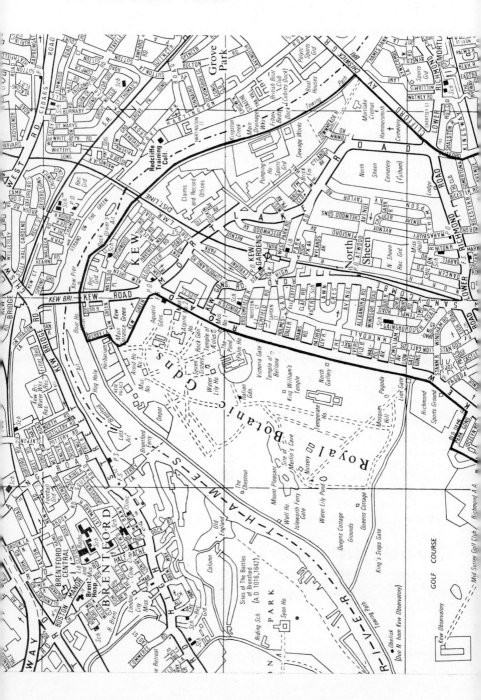

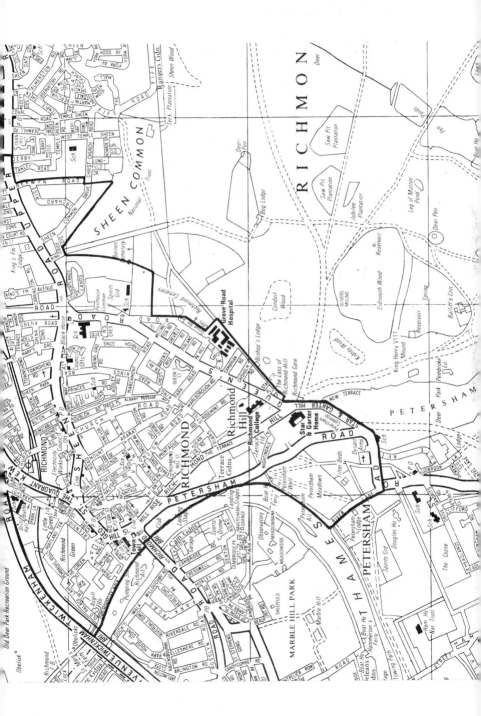

265

RICHMOND — KEW

Local council
London Borough of Richmond-on-Thames

Postal areas

Type of housing
Victorian
Georgian
Queen Ann
Pre-war
Modern blocks
Modern houses

Approximate number of flats and houses in district
13,000

Local estate agents
Acland & Co., opposite Richmond Station, 948 1122
Barnes & Barnes, 40–42 Hill Rise, Richmond, 940 0093
Breadmore & Webb, 44 The Quadrant, Richmond, 940 2211
Rodney Scott, 371 Upper Richmond Rd, S.W.14, 876 0152

APPROXIMATE COST OF HOUSING

Long lease unfurnished flats
price
£9–15,000

(non commercial)
Houses freehold or leasehold
price
£16–30,000

Amenity society
Richmond Society,
39 Church Rd, Richmond

Citizens' Advice Bureau
51 Sheen Rd, Richmond
940 2501

TRANSPORTATION

Tube stops
Richmond
Kew Gardens

Bus service routes
27 Kensington—Paddington—Marylebone Rd
65 Ealing
290 Hammersmith

Resident parking
No permit required

Tube lines
District

Travelling times
West End 30–35 mins
City 40–45 mins

Train services
British Rail, Southern Region to Waterloo

Travelling times
Waterloo 20–25 mins

Frequency
Every 10–15 mins

Richmond – Kew

A Bit of History . . .

Richmond is an historic riverside town, which grew up as a residential area around the Royal Palace of Henry VII, the former Earl of Richmond. The records of the Palace actually date back to Edward I, who lived there. Elizabeth I died there. The Palace was practically demolished early in the eighteenth century, so the families of the early Georges grew up at Kew, and their entourages overflowed into the houses round Richmond Green. Thatched House Lodge in Richmond Park is to this very day a royal home, for Princess Alexandra and her husband Angus Ogilvy live there.

The view from Richmond Hill has been painted by Gainsborough, Turner and Reynolds.

Kew, which is a part of the Greater London Borough of Richmond upon Thames, also dates back to the time of Henry VII. Many of the residences on Kew Green were at one time 'grace and favour' residences for friends of royalty or ladies of the court.

Richmond

The Atmosphere...The People...

Richmond town retains much of its rural village charm and beauty, and yet offers most of the advantages of a town. It is more a self-contained village than a suburb. And Richmond Hill has all the amenities of an artists' colony— galleries, antique shops, a potter's studio, book shop, restaurants, in addition to the essentials like chemist and greengrocer.

To the suburbanite, who lives further out in Surrey, Richmond is definitely the city, or part of London. But to the real central-city dweller, who never sees a rose other than those in Queen Mary's Rose Garden in Regent's Park, Richmond is the country. To a real city person, Richmond seems like a charming country town, where you can browse in antique shops, stop for tea and homemade cakes, and then stroll by the river or in the park.

Around Richmond Green live some film luminaries like Richard Attenborough. But most of Richmond seems to be populated by young families on the way up—who want the city, not the suburbs, and may one day move closer to the city—at that stage in life when they can afford a home in the country as well! Many older families have always lived in Richmond.

A Look at the Buildings, Outstanding Streets and Squares...

What's so nice about Richmond, from the antiquarian's point of view, is that there is no brand new property thereabouts. The houses in Kew are a mix of Victorian and Georgian, and the Georgians are most certainly the best.

Though Richmond is spotted with Georgian jewels, Victoriana predominates. Look at Mount Ararat Road and Church Road for the greatest variety: some houses huge and handsome; other, small unattractive grey brick and poor quality plaster, with decorative detail. Queen's Road has the handsomest Victorian villas of Richmond—real detached villas, not the string of adjoining terrace houses called 'villas'. And yet the council has purchased some of them, and no one is sure whether they'll be demolished, or restored.

The best and highest priced of the Georgian and Queen Anne properties are around Richmond Green, and at the top of Richmond Hill—The Terrace, a much loved promenade for Richmondites. On a clear day you can see as far as Windsor Castle.

Richmond Green was actually part of the grounds of Richmond Palace, once upon a time. Maids of Honour Row, facing the west side of the green, was built as accommodation for the ladies of the court of George I. There is one modern intrusion—town houses—upon this glorious green.

The Vineyard, a small street which is a left turning as you head up Richmond Hill, leads to the most charming villagey part of Richmond—Victorian cottages laden with vines and flowers. The Vineyard actually has three buildings which were once almshouses. The Alberts, tiny two rooms up and two down cottages, are very popular.

Kew is a favourite place to live because of its proximity to the Botanical Gardens, but Kew is distinctly more suburban than Richmond. Look at the new town houses and small blocks of flats which appear now and then on the

The river at Richmond

The Vineyard

Richmond Green

roads behind Kew Road. The main gate to Kew Gardens is in Kew Green; and the oldest and handsomest houses in Kew are those around the green.

Amenities of the Area

Richmond Park, ten miles in circumference, containing everything from roaming deer to a golf course. Pembroke Lodge, restaurant.

Kew Gardens, 270 acres, including a pagoda and greenhouses of tropical plants.

The area is rich in historic houses to visit on a quiet Sunday—Syon House and Ham House, for instance.

The Richmond Shakespeare Society performs on the upper lawn of The Terrace Gardens, off Richmond Hill.

Richmond Theatre, on Richmond Green, opened in 1899, and the theatre and its repertory are still alive and well.

Cricket on Saturday afternoons in summer, on Richmond Green.

An annual Georgian Fayre at St Ann's Church on Kew Green.

The Thames, of course: motor boats for rent, towpaths for wandering.

Ice skating rink, across the bridge from the shops.

Richmond is unusually rich in quality restaurants.

Shopping in Richmond is superb. Around Kew Station is a charming assortment of non-essential shops.

Disadvantages?

Aircraft noise: one couple who loved Richmond had to move away only because they could not live with it. Richmond/Kew sit directly under a fly-in route to London Airport. One retired air force officer is very happy in Richmond, for he is never far from his memories. Other people feel very differently about the noise.

Parking in the town centre is almost impossible. Very heavy traffic through the village.

Living on the Waterfront, or in the City

St Katharine Docks

Living 'on the waterfront?' On a twenty-five acre site, just behind the Tower of London, screened by a warehouse from the thundering traffic of Tower Bridge Road, lie St Katharine Docks.

This area, no longer needed by the Port of London Authority, is to have a new life—new housing, a hotel, primary school, shops, a cinema, restaurants and pubs. The G.L.C. bought the whole site, and leased it to a private builder, requiring him to find new uses for two historic warehouses—built by Telford and Hardwick in 1828, they are famous in the architectural world for their graceful iron pillars, rising from floor to ceiling. One of the warehouses will become a British Export Centre; the other, ships chandler's stores for the proposed yacht marina. Incredible imagination is being put to use on this site by Taylor Woodrow, the builders, and it may prove to be a most attractive place to live.

The borough of Southwark has plans for a new life for its four-and-a-half miles of derelict wharves and warehouses on the riverside (from Blackfriars Bridge to Surrey Docks); guidelines for the property developers and builders call for offices, hotels, flats, a riverside walk and a park. The plan is only at draft stage, to be presented for public discussion, but it is an omen of 'things to come' in London's dockland.

Small groups of adventurous individuals are moving into the riverfront area as well. Twelve Georgian houses at Wapping Pier Head, just down the river from Tower Bridge, were restored and put on the market at prices from £20,000—40,000. Ralph Pay and Ransom were the selling agents.

If you look carefully down by the riverside, you'll see all sorts of interesting conversions. A nineteenth century grain warehouse, called St Mary's Mills, has being transformed into thirty-five flats. Aylesford and Company are the agents.

On the other side of the river, at Deptford, an old rum warehouse has been converted to flats under the council's 'higher rented accommodation' scheme. The G.L.C. Housing Department at County Hall, London, S.E.1, holds the waiting list for tenants.

The Barbican

Not very far from Blackfriars Bridge is a housing development which has caused quite a stir in London, because there is nothing quite like it—the Barbican. The owners, the Corporation of London, call it: 'The latest concept in urban living' and indeed, with its goal of 7000 residents, the Barbican might be called a separate town within the City of London.

Originally the Barbican was a fortified tower protecting the northern approaches to the old walled city, Londinium. Today the Barbican consists of three forty-four-storey tower blocks of flats, some lower blocks, and town houses as well. These buildings, comprising 2500 flats, are arranged around their own lakes, fountains and gardens. The Barbican is to have its own arts centre as well, due to open in 1975—and with a hundred flats in it as well. The owners expect the flats to be filled by the middle of 1973.

Approximate rentals for Barbican flats are:

one room, from £375 per annum
two rooms, from £575
three rooms, from £700
four rooms, from £830
five/six rooms, from £1200.

Rates, payable by the tenant, are approximately 20 per cent of the rental. For further information, direct inquiries to the Manager, Barbican Estate Office, Barbican, London, E.C.2, or telephone 628 4797.

One couple, living in the Barbican at the start of 1972, said that there was very little sense of community about the place, and a sort of '2001' feeling around. However, only 800 of the 2500 flats were occupied at the time. The Barbican population consists largely of young professional couples with no children; or older couples now on their own, as their children are grown up. Roger Moore, 'the Saint', is one of the best-known tenants.

There are two tube stops—Barbican and Moorgate—but, as one tenant points out, the location is not as convenient as it sounds, for some parts of the Barbican are a fifteen- or twenty-minute walk from the tube.

The Barbican

The Motorway Problem

Any area definitely scheduled for motorway redevelopment should be avoided like the plague. The G.L.C. estimates that some 19,750 families will be displaced by the London motorways. A small price to pay for progress some would say. Even with all the rehousing at the expense of the council it won't be pleasant for those unlucky enough to be in the path. And it's even worse for those who live nearby and are not directly affected. If your house is in the direct path you'll receive its full market value from the government. But houses two or three streets from the motorway are not included in any 'blight' compensation. Before moving into an area scheduled for a possible motorway route, find out the exact plan, and make sure you don't choose a flat anywhere near it.

However, much of the motorway plan for London may never be a reality because of local opposition and financial problems. If the motorway does come to London, it won't be before 1990, or possibly even later. The Greater London Council is holding hearings to determine whether a motorway system is really necessary for London. If you have strong feelings one way or the other get on to your local amenity society or the G.L.C.

Areas in central or fringe London that may be affected by motorway redevelopment are:

Hammersmith and Chiswick—already affected by the M4 flyover and the Great West Road. Things could get worse. Chiswick is also in the direct path of a possible Ringway 2 route.
Barnes—possible Ringway 2 route.
Putney—possible Ringway 2 route.
Battersea and Clapham—possible Ringway 1 route (motorway box).
Blackheath—possible Ringway 1 route.
Holland Park, Earls Court, Kensington, and Chelsea—West Cross route (motorway box) affecting Holland Park Avenue, Earl's Court Road, Warwick Road, east of Stamford Bridge and western end of Cheyne Walk.
Highbury, Islington, Camden Town and Kentish Town—possible Ringway 1 route.
Belsize and Kilburn—possible Ringway 1 route.
Camberwell—possible Ringway 1 route.

Don't panic if you're living in these areas, or planning to move in. Only a small part of the area will be affected—the actual route and a few streets on either side. Of course the motorway for London may be a non-event. There is talk that Ringway 1 (motorway box) is a non-starter. In which case you may make a packet buying property near the proposed route at knock-down prices! But far better to be safe than sorry!

Projected London Motorways

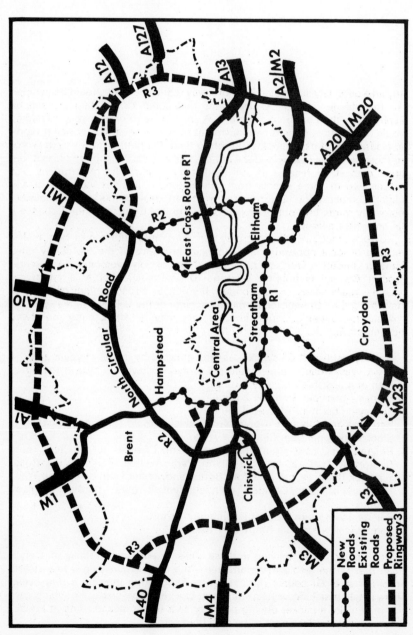

The Legal Maze

How to Use a Solicitor

While it's not the purpose of this book to take you through all the legal complexities of buying a house or taking a flat, an initiation may be helpful. If nothing else it'll help you to communicate with your solicitor and understand why things take so long. And a brief explanation of renting, buying and selling legalities now will save you having to ask later: 'Why didn't someone tell me about all those fine points?'

Basically, house purchase requires a deed because ownership is being transferred, assuming the house is a freehold property. With a flat, rented on a short-term basis, either furnished or unfurnished, a lease is involved. The hybrid of the two is buying a lease on a long-term basis of more than twenty-one years, which is similar to becoming an owner, except that someone else is the landlord or the freeholder. The legal considerations are different for each of the three.

Getting yourself through the complexities of deeds and leases requires a solicitor, the professionals' professional. It is much more difficult to become a solicitor than an estate agent. One must have a current practising certificate from the law society, earned after long, hard academic study. Solicitors can't advertise for business though they seem to have plenty of clients. A big reason for the demand for solicitors is that all property transactions, whether one buys or sells, require conveyancing—the transfer of ownership through a deed. And solicitors have a virtual monopoly over the business. Even if you simply rent a flat or house, a solicitor is required in the exchange of the lease.

Choosing a Solicitor

Your solicitor can be a real help to you. Choose him wisely and work closely with him and you'll never be sorry. How to find one?

Go by recommendation. Perhaps someone in the office where you work knows of a solicitor. Get the individual solicitor's name, rather than the firm. Ask your bank manager, surveyor, estate agent, or architect to suggest one. Get help from your local Citizen's Advice Bureau (see neighbourhood summaries).
The Law Society, 113 Chancery Lane, W.C.2, 242 1222, may offer assistance in helping you to find a solicitor. Or consult the law list at your local library.

Don't put off finding a solicitor, thinking you'll get once you've found your house or flat. You save nothing by delaying, and you may get some helpful advice early in the game, which could save you a lot of trouble later on.

Legal Points to Remember When Buying a House

The first thing to remember when you make any offer to buy property is to make it 'subject to contract'—that way you're not legally obligated to go through with the deal should you change your mind. But be aware that this freedom to back out works both ways. See 'Gazumping' in Glossary. Also be careful about giving deposits. If you must give a deposit, limit it to 10 per cent of the purchase price; and give it to the seller's solicitor, not to the estate agent. The proper moment for turning over the deposit is when contracts are exchanged.

Here's how the legal maze works, should you go ahead with your house purchase:

1. The buyer's solicitor gets a draft contract from the seller's solicitor.
2. Searches and inquiries are made by the buyer's solicitor; such questions as boundaries, rights of way and restrictive covenants are examined. Planning matters must be checked—maybe a hotel is going up across the road, or worse, a main road or motorway. Then there's always the question of whether the seller really has a legal right to sell the property.
3. The buyer's solicitor satisfies himself on the draft contract, and suggests amendments if necessary. The seller's solicitor works up a final form contract, which is then sent back to the buyer's solicitor.
4. The buyer signs the contract and exhanges his copy for a signed one from the seller. This is the appropriate time for any deposit to be paid.
5. Transfer procedure takes place at H.M. Land Registry Office, Lincolns Inn Fields, W.C.2 or at one of the London offices of the Land Registry.
6. Seller receives and approves draft transfer document.
7. Seller submits completion statement about any final costs which have to be paid by the buyer.
8. Final search certificate obtained at register office.
9. Purchase completed by the buyer handing over his cheque and obtaining key, documents, and best wishes from the seller.

A good solicitor can take you through this maze with few if any problems. And since in London all property is registrable at H.M. Land Registry it makes the job even easier. People with a flair for legal work often do the conveyancing themselves and save the solicitor's fee. It can be done, but complications can and do occur and it then pays to have a good solicitor representing you. Some of the problems you could encounter include:

1. Getting planning permission to modify the use or the size of the property.
2. Getting around some restrictive covenant imposed by the previous owner.
3. Understanding some special duties and rights that affect the property, like sharing driveways, rights of way and maintenance agreements.
4. Dealing with sitting tenants and understanding the provisions of the rent. acts where the ratable value of the property is under £400.
5. Handling an outstanding mortgage on the property.
6. Arranging a transfer, should the seller die or have to leave the country permanently, before the transaction is completed.

To get through this maze takes time. Seventy-five per cent of transfers take more than two months, and some can take up to six months to complete. So don't expect a fast transaction. And don't try to speed up the legal procedure, because you can't!

Legal Costs When Buying a House

Solicitors used to charge a scale fee approved by a committee consisting of the President of the Law Society, the Lord Chancellor and others. Charges are now subject to negotiation. The scale, still used as a guideline, varies depending on whether the house is registered or not at H.M. Land Registry. Scale fees on registered houses are far lower but land registry fees are payable which reduce the difference. Most, if not all houses in London are registered.

Cost of house	Registered house fee	Unregistered house fee
£12,000	£70	£115
£15,000	£78·75	£130
£20,000	£89·75	£155

If you want to save some money on legal fees, do-it-yourself, or try the National House Owners Society, 3 Railway Approach, Wealdstone, Harrow. The N.H.O.S. is devoted to short circuiting the solicitor's stranglehold on house transfer. It handles more than 1500 transfers a year. Once you become a member, which costs £1, you can save £20 to £40 on buying or selling a house and £40 to £60 when changing houses. The N.H.O.S. is not as personal as having your own solicitor, but not as costly as the latter either!

What's in a lease?

The Legal Side of Renting a Flat or House (Furnished Accommodation)

Most furnished accommodation is let on a weekly, monthly or quarterly basis, and there is often no lease involved. As long as you pay your rent and want to stay in the furnished flat, you can. If you want to leave you give the appropriate amount of notice—say a week, a month or a quarter—and when the time is up you're free to go. On the other hand if the landlord wants to get you out, either because he wants to sell the building with vacant possession or do it up so he can charge more rent, he'll give you 'notice to quit'. If you don't mind leaving, start packing. But if it's the middle of winter and you planned to stay until the following summer and you dread looking for another place to live, here's what you can do.

Furnished flats with a ratable value of under £400 in London (check the ratable value with the local council) are covered by the rent acts. All one has to do to delay a notice to quit is to apply to the Furnished Houses Rent Tribunal (again consult your local council) and apply for a reduction in rent and claim for security of tenure. Usually you can get a delay of up to six months. So don't be too hasty about packing your bags when your landlord wants you out: unless you have a lease for a fixed period which has expired, you've got a chance to fight. And don't be intimidated by harassment—see a solicitor. Who knows, you may get paid off handsomely to leave. A landlord must pay for relocation of tenants whom he forces to leave.

Some Points to Check on a Furnished Flat

1) Is there a fixed period on the lease, at a stated price or rent? Agree in

advance on what happens when the lease expires. Get an extension for another fixed period, at the same or an agreed rent.

2) Does the landlord supply electricity, gas and hot water at his expense or do you have to pay? And who's responsible for reading the meters? What about installing a telephone?

3) Make sure an inventory of the contents is taken while you're present. Any replacement or repairs are your responsibility. If something happens to one of the items, say the T.V. breaks down, and it's not your fault, reduce your rent by the appropriate rental value of the missing object until the landlord has it replaced.

4) What about animals? Can you or can't you keep them?

5) Is there an assignment or subletting clause?

6) What about deposit money? When do you get it back? What can be deducted from it? Do you earn interest on it?

7) Make sure the landlord pays the rates and does not ask you to contribute.

8) If you let your flat or house on a furnished basis for a fixed period while you're away, you're legally entitled to reclaim it when you return—unless you've sublet it illegally—then you're in trouble.

The Legal Side of Renting a Flat or House Unfurnished on a Short Lease

Getting an unfurnished flat on a short lease in London is becoming more and more difficult, especially for a flat with a ratable value under £400.

To get an unfurnished flat of any kind it's more than likely that you'll have to pay a 'fixtures and fittings' premium to the current tenant. While not strictly legal, on accommodations covered by the rent acts, it's almost the only way of getting into an unfurnished flat in central London these days. A few lucky Londoners whom you meet will tell you they paid no premium. But they are the exception, not the rule.

Usually the current tenant has to leave for one reason or another and the current lease has a few years to run, with the tenant having the right to assign. If you agree to buy 'fixtures and fittings' the tenant will recommend you to the landlord as a suitable tenant to take over his lease.

Some legal points to keep in mind and discuss with your solicitor:

1) Does the current tenant have the right to assign the lease to you, in fact? Is there a clause in the lease which states that the tenant must offer the lease back to the landlord or to the managing agent? Don't pay over any money unless the landlord has approved the assignment.

2) If the flat is covered by the rent acts, the fixtures and fittings charge must bear a true market value to what is actually left in the flat. You may like to itemize the fixtures and fittings that you are to receive, and get the tenant to put some numbers next to each item. If you've paid too much you may want to try to recover the difference after you've moved in.

What to Look for in a Lease

Check the lease for restrictive covenants, things you're forbidden to do. You may be able to get your solicitor to request some changes.

Normally on the standard lease the landlord is unmovable, and most solicitors will not even attempt to change a word. If you make trouble you may not get the flat at all, as the saying goes. Generally the more you're paying in rent the more leverage you'll have in lease negotiations.

As one estate agent said to us regarding our lease: 'You're not permitted to do anything according to the lease. But every tenant has a dog, sublets or doesn't carpet the halls—and gets away with it'. Yet another landlord will 'get the tenant on the slightest offence'.

Some of the covenants you should note and discuss with your solicitor are:
1) The right to assign—you should have this right. Some leases allow it with the consent of the landlord. Others do not.
2) The right to sublet—a very valuable right to obtain. Most leases forbid it. Landlords don't like their flats or houses let to people they don't know. Even if it's not allowed, some people get away with it for a short period of time. The landlord can ignore it or, if he wishes, evict you on a breach of covenant. Taking a boarder or lodger is acceptable unless strictly forbidden in the lease.
3) Dilapidations and internal repairs—could prove to be a big expense to you. Normally it's the tenant's responsibility to maintain the flat and make all necessary repairs.

The tenant has the responsibility, in many leases, of restoring the property to its original state of 'good and substantial repair'. Don't get caught holding the end of a long lease. If repairs are not done to the satisfaction of the landlord he can impose a dilapidations charge, allowing him to make all necessary repairs and decoration.
4) Use as business premises—find out how the property is zoned and abide by it. Usually there is a covenant in the lease that states the way in which the flat may be used—normally for residential purposes only. If you plan to run a business from your flat don't get caught. You could be evicted. A change to commercial status will increase the rates. And the G.P.O. will charge you commercial rates for your phone.
5) Maintenance of the communal parts—usually included in the service charge. The tenants collectively must pay a share of the cost of things like central heating, lifts, the porter, staircases, and common gardens. Check the service charges over past years as an indication of costs. The landlord usually retains the right to increase the charge as costs go up. See what control there is to prevent costs from spiralling to your disadvantage.
6) The rent review—best not to have one. Read the lease. Many landlords have a provision for rent reviews every three years. The review period should be accompanied by a chance to leave the flat without penalty. The increase at rent review time can vary depending on whether the flat is or is not regulated by the rent acts.

Legal Costs for Flats and Houses on Short Leases

On a short-term lease of under one year, a solicitor can charge what is 'reasonable' for his work, depending on the time and complexity of the agreement. Probably £5–10 would be appropriate. For a longer lease of say, three, five, or seven years there are scale fees set by the Law Society depending on the annual rent. For example:

Annual rent	Scale fee
£400	£22·50
£750	£30·00
£1250	£37·50

Higher fees can result if the solicitor has to pay certain costs on behalf of completing the lease: searches, stamp duty, and other charges are passed on to the client. Stamp duty is a tax on financial transactions and property transfers, for example:

Annual rent	Stamp duty (leases not more than 7 years)
£400	£2·00
£750	£3·75
£1250	£6·25

The Legal Side of Flats or Houses on Long Leases

Long leases provide excellent security of tenure and can be an excellent form of investment depending on the length of the lease, the tenant's rights as guaranteed in the lease, and the costs exacted on the leaseholder by the landlord or freeholder.

When you're buying a flat or a house on a long lease, of more than twenty-one years, you'll want the legal protection of a freeholder along with all the rights of a leaseholder. But the problem is you're not a freeholder: you have a landlord and sometimes more than one. They'll want to protect their interests and will exact ground rent and maintenance charges, and have their solicitor insure their interests in the lease.

The Leasehold Reform Act doesn't protect the flat dweller on a long lease. It does give to a tenant of a long-lease house the right to buy the freehold, provided the ratable value of the house is under £400 in London. The tenant must have lived in the house for five out of the past ten years.

There are some legal problems with the premiums charged for long leases. If the ratable value is over £400 in London, there is no restriction on the premium a seller can ask. However, on a flat or house protected by the rent acts there can be a restriction on the premium, or it can be illegal. If the lease includes rent reviews and forbids assignments or subletting you may find that charging a premium is illegal.

Some people who paid premiums of up to £15,000 discover, when they want to sell, that a premium is illegal. You can ask only a proportional value, based on what you originally paid for the lease. It's calculated in proportion to the years remaining on the lease on purchase, to the years remaining on the lease on sale. For example if you paid £10,000 for a lease with thirty years unexpired and now you want to sell it with fifteen years unexpired, and it's protected by the rent acts, you'll be able to ask £5,000.

A solicitor can make the complexities of long leases understandable, and help to draw up a lease that protects you. Make sure you have the right to assign and sublet, and check the rent reviews on the ground rent and the determination of the maintenance charges. No matter how you look at it, long leases are messy and more complicated than a simple freehold situation; and financing may be more difficult on a long lease as against a freehold purchases.

Solicitors Charges for Long Leases

Their fee is based on the ground rent and the premium. For example:

Annual ground rent	Premium	Scale fee	Total
£100	£15,000	£28·50 and £130	£158·50
£200	£20,000	£39·75 and £155	£194·75
£400	£10,000	£54·75 and £105	£159·75

For Non-British House Hunters

There is no nationality restriction imposed on property owners in Britain. Anyone who can pay the price can own land or houses.

All purchases must be in sterling, and are restricted to sterling on sale. Sterling transactions for foreigners are subject to the same regulations of exchange control as for nationals. Non-nationals are permitted to maintain external accounts, in the currency of their homeland, and are not subject to exchange control for a period of up to three years. Transfers between resident sterling accounts and external non-sterling accounts are forbidden. Under certain conditions one can get Bank of England permission to convert sterling to other currencies when one leaves the country permanently.

The Rent Acts

The biggest bargains in the property market in London are those flats and houses that somehow come under the jurisdiction of the rent acts. Because the various pieces of legislation are so numerous and complicated one often needs a solicitor just to help in reading the information produced by H.M. Stationery Office about the rent acts. Many people currently living in dwellings that come under the control of various rent acts may not know their rights. So whether you are a flat or house hunter, a rent payer or a landlord, this section should give you some valuable tips.

The first instance of rent control in England occurred during the First World War. Another wave of controls preceded the Second World War in 1939. Apart from the fact that rationing and price controls are a normal part of war, it's probably thought bad for morale if the troops hear about landlords raising rents back home, while they are fighting to keep the landlords in business.

The introduction to the Rent Act of 1968 makes for interesting reading:

An Act to consolidate the Rent and Mortgage Interest Restrictions Acts, 1920 to 1939, the furnished Houses (Rent Control) Act 1946, the Landlord and Tenant (Rent Control) Act 1949, Part II of the Housing Repairs and Rent Act 1954, the Rent Act 1957, the Rent Act 1965 and other related enactments.

Add to that the Leasehold Reform Act of 1967 and the Housing Act of 1969 and you've got a real headache on your hands if you intend to study all the information yourself. As one of the officers of the National Association of Property Owners related, 'It's all written down somewhere. It's the piecing together and interpreting that's really impossible'.

Currently 300,000 houses and flats exist as controlled tenancies in London. The average rent each tenant pays is £1·50 a week. A bargain! Not really. Most do not have toilet facilities, heat, or hot water. Slowly these controlled

RENT ACT PROVISIONS (If the ratable value of your house or flat is over £400 in London, disregard the table, the rent acts do not apply. Your only protection is what's agreed to in the lease.)

Type of Accommodation	Rents that can be charged	How can rents be increased or decreased	Security of Tenure
Unfurnished	If the tenancy is controlled (ratable value of under £40 as of November 1956) rents cannot be increased until the property comes into the Fair Rent System, slowly being implemented around the country. Under a regulated tenancy (flat or house has to meet certain minimum standards) the rent officer arbitrates a fair rent. The 1969 Housing Act specified how a landlord can transform a tenancy from controlled to regulated. A new 'fair rent' must be phased in over a five-year period. If you're moving into a regulated flat the rent can be no greater than the last registered rent. Check with local rent officer.	Once a fair rent has been agreed to and phased in over five years it becomes the registered fair rent. The registered rent can be reviewed every three years. An increase can be agreed to by the rent officer at that time. The landlord can charge an increase, due to a rise in services provided. Rents can also be decreased if certain repairs are not carried out by the landlord. The tenant can apply for a reduction because of disrepair. Your local council can give complete instructions for obtaining a certificate of disrepair.	As long as you continue to pay your rent you can't be evicted. Once your lease expires you become a statutory tenant with complete protection. The courts will not grant an order to quit unless suitable alternative accommodation is available. The landlord would also have to show why his hardship in not regaining possession is greater than what the tenant would face on having to leave. So pay your rent and don't break any rules or covenants in the lease and you'll have nothing to worry about.
Furnished	Tenants in furnished flats do not have the same protection as those in unfurnished flats. Basically you pay the rent that the landlord specifies, the rent agreed to in the lease. You can ask the local rent tribunal covering your area to determine whether you're paying a fair rent. A great majority of the applications received by the rent tribunals result in lower rents on furnished flats. Because of the difficulty in comparing fair rents on furnished accommodation, especially in central London, you're pretty	Rent can be increased when the lease expires. No real control on lengths of leases or frequency of increases. You could theoretically go to the rent tribunal for an assessment of a fair rent every time it is increased. To get rent reduced you must apply to the local council's' rent tribunal for a fair rent assessment.	If you're on a fixed term lease, when that lease expires you can be asked to leave. Likewise, on a month-to-month agreement, one month's notice is all a landlord has to give to get you to go. If you're not on a lease, or if the lease has expired, you can get up to six months security of tenure by applying to the rent tribunals to set a fair rent.

much at the mercy of the landlord. You can always shop around for furnished accommodation, if you believe your rent to be unfair. Also remember that if the flat or house has a ratable value of over £400 it doesn't come within the protection of the Rent Acts. There's no limit to what the landlord can charge.

Leasehold Reform Act 1967

The provisions of this act do not apply to tenants living in a flat unless the tenant has a lease on an entire house and he is just living in one part of it. The Leasehold Reform Act permits a house dweller, on a lease that was originally more than twenty-one years, to buy the freehold or extend the lease for another fifty years. Tenant claiming the freehold must have lived in the house for five out of the last ten years.

You don't have to wait for the lease to expire to extend or ask to buy the freehold. And it pays to buy the freehold rather than extend the lease because the courts have been fairly liberal in arriving at a price the leaseholder has to pay for the freehold. The leaseholder, according to the Housing Act of 1969, does not have to bid as if he were on the open market. So the price one would have to pay is extremely fair.

Doesn't apply to houses where the ratable value is over £400. Nor does it apply to houses where the rent payable is more than two-thirds the ratable value.

Unfurnished

Furnished   Same as unfurnished.

accommodations will be converted to regulated status, provided the landlord makes necessary improvements. Many won't: the cost of the improvements, compared to the rent increases possible, aren't enough of an incentive for many landlords. So while the paint is chipping, the walls crumbling and the ceiling leaking the tenants go on paying the same rents they did in 1939. There are exceptions of course. One lady in a mews house, with a leaking ceiling, found a kindly neighbour—who threatened to take the case to the health officials if the landlord didn't mend the old lady's roof. The roof was repaired!

Housing is a hot political issue and over the years various governments have enacted legislation to protect the tenant against the landlord. But landlords have not been sitting back idly. Under a number of different organizations, landlords have been spending quite a bit of money lobbying to get Parliament to soften things.

Landlords know how to use the courts to get possession of a flat or house, even though the tenant is supposed to have security of tenure. Landlords also have found ways of increasing rents in regulated blocks of flats. One ploy used is to get a new tenant to agree that his starting rent is fair and to sign a statement to that effect. The landlord then uses this as a basis for convincing the rent officer that the rents of everyone else in the building should be increased. The Rent officer is not obliged to register a rent even if this has been agreed between the landlord and the tenant.

What are the landlord's and tenant's responsibilities? Well, as one estate agent said half jokingly: 'The tenant has the responsibility to pay the rent, the rates, the service and maintenance, make necessary repairs, not let any one else sublet unless granted special permission, and leave the premises as he found it. And the landlord, well he has to let the tenant enjoy what he's paying for, and make arrangements to collect the rent . . . quarterly in advance of course'.

Selling Rent-Controlled Flats on a Leasehold Basis

The big trend in some of the best rent-controlled flats is to offer them for sale on long leases to the current tenants. Many specialist finance companies, property companies or merchant banks, known in the trade as 'break-up merchants', have been taking over large blocks of residential flats from the established property companies. The established property companies are steadily de-emphasizing the residential part of their assets in favour of commercial property.

Since few professional merchant bankers or finance companies want to manage flats, the trick is to convince the tenants that it makes more sense to 'own' their flats than to go on paying rent to a landlord. Estate agents are brought in by the 'break-up merchants' to 'sell' the tenants on the advantages of the long lease arrangement.

The argument goes something like this:

1) Why go on paying rent for the rest of your life to a landlord? The rent is likely to be increased every three years.
2) Buy the lease and you know the rent can't be increased. And any improvements you make benefit you, not the landlord. With property values going up all the time because of inflation, you'll surely be able to sell your flat at a profit, should you decide to sell.

3) In addition you'll convert the rent you're paying into a mortgage repayment and you'll get tax relief on the interest; and if the repayment is in the form of an insurance endowment plan you'll get tax relief on the premium.

4) If you can't get a mortgage we'll arrange one for you, with total payments coming to little more than you're currently paying in rent.

5) Because you are the present tenant in the flat we'll offer it to you at a price 10–15 per cent less than the market value.

This sounds like a good sales line; it is and it has been successful. The 'break-up merchants' are stepping up their activities. But before you jump at the chance of buying the lease on your rent-controlled flat, if it's offered, determine:

1) Are the total payments under the new arrangement, with tax relief, about the same as you're now paying? Remember, if it's a rent-controlled flat the rent increases are limited to one every three years, and usually no more than 10 per cent.

2) How long is the lease? If it's not more than sixty years, it's going to be a decreasing asset. A ninety-nine- or one hundred and twenty-five-year lease is ideal. The Leasehold Reform Act does not apply to flats. So you can't extend the lease or buy the freehold when the lease expires.

3) What other charges will you have to pay? Maintenance or service charges and ground rent are various ways in which 'break-up merchants' may attempt to make a capital gain when they sell the lease, and also a continuing income after the sale. Or the managing agents may be charging high maintenance to set up reserves for further improvements to the property.

4) Do you have to put in your own capital? This could cause hardship to many people who shouldn't have all their cash assets tied up in their flat. Older people should be extremely cautious as should young marrieds who may prefer to own their own house, and will need a deposit. And remember you'll have to pay stamp duties on the premium for the long lease plus solicitors fees and mortgage costs. On a £20,000 flat this could come out to £500 or more.

5) When you get ready to sell, how do you know you'll be able to find someone with enough cash to buy you out? Remember a new tenant may be unable to get a mortgage. If the lease is under fifty years you'll have to supply the mortgage because it's unlikely that a building society would.

6) To legally charge a premium for your lease, it must have been written originally for more than twenty-one years. The lease must have no provision for a rent increase within the first twenty-one years, and must permit the tenant to assign or sublet without the permission of the landlord.

If you're in a rent-controlled flat you have the upper hand. You've got security of tenure and you can't be forced to leave if you decide not to buy the lease. Just go on paying your rent. For many people buying their own flat or house is a wise decision. But not for everyone.

In any event if you are interested in buying your own flat get your solicitor to go through the leasehold agreement with you so you understand what you're buying and the terms thereafter.

If you would like to find out how other tenants are dealing with their 'break-up' problems, contact The Federation of London County Residents' Associations, Playfair Mansions, Queen's Club Gardens, West Kensington.

Improvement Grants

Improving older houses is much in vogue since the 1968 White Paper, 'Old

Houses into New Homes'. The 1969 Housing Act improved the size of existing grants and gave local councils the incentive to get on with rehabilitating districts heavy with decaying houses.

What are They?

Basically there are two kinds of grants that you can get to do up your house— standard grants and improvement (discretionary) grants. A standard grant allows various amounts ranging from £10–50 to pay up to half the cost of the installation of such things as baths, showers, sinks, wash-hand basins, and water closets. Standard grants are automatically paid upon completion of the installation.

Improvement (discretionary) grants are more comprehensive. You can qualify for money if you are the owner-occupier, or if you are converting a house to flats for other people. The amount of money that you can get is half of the expenses up to £1000. If there are more than three storeys, including a basement, to be made into separate flats you can qualify for up to £1200 per flat. Improvement grants do not have to be repaid. You can use grants to improve the value of your house and then sell the house a few years later. The profit's all yours.

How Does One Apply?

Application must be on a prescribed form that you get from your local council. You must apply before you start the work. You must be the freeholder or have a lease with more than five years unexpired. There is no restriction based on your financial situation; the objective is to rehabilitate older houses, although the money is not intended for the rich.

Some of the Drawbacks

1) The steps that have to be taken and the supporting material that has to be submitted for approval of an application are complex and time consuming. You can't start any work until the application has been approved. You may not think it is worth the trouble.
2) If you're thinking of letting off the improved flats the rent you charge may be regulated.
3) Basement flats must conform to the underground room regulations, and may or may not qualify for paying tenants.
4) You must maintain the property in a good state of repair and all work must conform to certain standards. Inspections are often made.
5) The grant is discretionary and basically intended for those who can't afford to pay the cost of making improvements, or to help restore decaying houses. Don't expect the local council to help you make improvements to your Nash terrace house in Regent's Park.

The Financial Side

Where to Find the Money to Make it all Possible

The money borrowed to finance a house or flat is popularly known as a mortgage. A mortgage is specifically a loan made by some lender, where the collateral is the house or flat purchased with the loan. In some cases one can mortgage or pledge some other asset as collateral for the loan, but for most people the home purchased is the collateral. If the loan is not repaid the lender can foreclose or take over the asset given as collateral, and dispose of it to recover the amount of the loan outstanding.

To insure that there is no difference, in case of default, between what the house will bring when it is sold and what is outstanding on the loan, a lender will often lend up to a percentage of the surveyed value. In reality most mortgages are repaid. And lenders rarely have to or want to foreclose. It's too messy and creates bad feeling. Most people in financial trouble will sell their house, pay off their mortgage and rent accommodation with the remaining cash until things improve.

Where Does the Money Come From?

Money for a mortgage is rarely easy to come by. The 1971—2 easy mortgage money period was exceptional and the prime cause of the boom in house prices. When capital is in short supply, very few people or institutions have it to lend out over a long period of time at relatively low rates of interest. There's usually a far greater demand for mortgages than there is money available; and not every house qualifies for a mortgage. Age, length of lease, and the condition and location can make some properties almost impossible to finance.

There are three major sources of mortgage money in England. The major source is the *Building Society*. Lending money for house purchase is the building society's main business, depending on the state of the stock market, credit in general, interest rates, and business conditions. Building societies either have a lot of money to lend out for house purchase or very little.

Local Government Councils are the second biggest lenders. They normally lend out money to encourage people to buy old property in their area, with a view to improving the value of the house and the attractiveness of the area. Local authorities normally lend small amounts at reasonable rates of interest. Some councils, like Islington, have raised the maximum they're willing to lend from £6000 to 9000, and have also cut their interest rates slightly. The Greater London Council makes home loans of 100 per cent of the valuation of the house. Normally small amounts are loaned. Over 70,000 families have G.L.C. loans. Local council loans are difficult to come by, can take up to three months to arrange, and are rarely given for amounts over £10,000.

Insurance Companies are the third biggest lenders of mortgage money. They lend the highest individual amounts, but also charge the highest rates of interest on the loan, which remains level throughout the term. Insurance companies expect you to pay back the loan with an endowment insurance policy.

Types of Mortgage

There are three main types of mortgage:

1) A building society or council loan with a mortgage repayment scheme. The borrower makes regular payments which include interest plus repayment of the loan (amortization principle). No life assurance is included.

2) Building society loan at a fixed rate of interest, with repayment using an endowment policy approved by the society. Interest rates charged with this type of repayment are normally higher than with a building society repayment scheme.

3) Insurance company loan at interest, with an endowment policy of the same company used for repayment.

Which Type of Mortgage is Best?

Theoretically the best loan is the one where you get the most money, at the lowest rate of interest, repayable over the longest period of time. In reality what you'll have to accept in central London is something a little bit less than ideal. *Building societies* often give the best terms at the most favourable rates but prefer to lend amounts under £13,000 although there is talk of increasing the maximum to £20,000. And they will only lend in proportion to what you earn—normally two-and-half to three times your income plus a proportion of wife's income. Building society mortgages are best for people whose income isn't likely to rise much in the years ahead. Also best method for older people who may be uninsurable. The annual outlay is less than an endowment policy yet you get good tax relief in the early years.

Insurance Companies don't mind lending more than £13,000, provided the loan is repaid with an endowment policy. So the chances are that an insurance company will be your mortgagee on your central London home because prices normally start at around £13,000. Insurance companies demand a flat rate of interest on the amount borrowed. The rate of interest can vary between $8\frac{1}{2}$–$10\frac{1}{2}$ per cent depending on the age of the house, amount borrowed, length of lease, and status of borrower. The interest stays in effect on the original amount borrowed throughout the term of the mortgage, even though you are paying premiums on the mortgage repayment policy. You do, of course, qualify for tax relief on the interest and on the insurance premium, which reduces the net cost of the mortgage.

Which Mortgage Best Suits Your Needs?

1) Do you need as large a mortgage as possible, perhaps as high as 95 or even 100 per cent of the value?

Get details of option mortgage schemes offered by building societies.

Many local councils or the G.L.C. offer no deposit mortgages.

Avoid old houses or flats. Stick to new freehold houses.

2) Do you want to limit your outgoings to the lowest possible monthly repayments?
Avoid high interest rates normally charged by insurance companies. Insurance company rates remain level throughout the term. Not such a good feature when interest rates in general are declining.
Building societies tend to offer the lowest rates.
Try to get the longest term of mortgage, twenty-five or thirty years if possible.
Avoid high premium with profits endowment policies.
3) Are you a high taxpayer or even a surtax payer?
Use a with-profits endowment mortgage.
4) Do you earn income abroad and prefer not to remit income into this country?
Try to use capital accumulated prior to entering the U.K. to buy your home.
See if you can arrange a loan payable abroad.
5) Is sudden relocation a possibility?
Avoid endowment policies which have little surrender value in the first few years.
6) Do you want to use the discipline of paying off a mortgage to enable you to save as well?
Use an endowment mortgage with profits which both pays off the mortgage at maturity and also provides a cash sum free of tax.

Some Points to Consider on the Financing Side

Building societies are a good choice for *leasehold flats* selling for under £15,000. In general leases of under forty years should be avoided as they are difficult to finance. Most societies aren't keen on freehold flats. Getting a loan for a flat in a converted property is difficult. Some societies refuse to consider flats above the fourth floor in blocks of more than eighteen flats. And if you're looking for a mortgage on a flat be prepared to pay up to 20 per cent of the purchase price.

The *company* for which you work may offer *money for house purchase* at a lower rate of interest than the market rate. In effect they are subsidizing your house which is good as long as you remain with them. If you should leave the firm you will have to find a new source of finance probably at less favourable rates. Some firms subsidize the interest rate but arrange the actual financing through another source, which is by far the best arrangement.

Mortgage brokers are very ingenious at arranging financing for houses. But remember that they make their money on commission from the insurance policies used to repay the mortgage. So they'll be more than likely to proclaim the virtues of insurance company mortgage plans. For a building society repayment mortgage they'll expect a fee from you of about 1 per cent. Most estate agents can recommend a mortgage broker or you can get a list from the Corporation of Mortgage Brokers.

Insurance brokers tend to have high professional standards, more so than mortgage brokers, providing you use one who is a member of the Corporation of Insurance Brokers, C.I.B. or the Association of Insurance Brokers (A.I.B.). An Incorporated Life Assurance Broker is in the same league. Membership of the C.I.B. requires a solvency certificate, a proper balance sheet, and a sizable fee. Insurance brokers do the job mortgage brokers specialize in doing, finding sources of mortgage money linked to endowment repayment. They can also arrange other types of coverage such as 'buildings and house contents'. Your insurance should start when contracts are exchanged, not after you take possession. You can't back out once the deal is done and the house burns down.

Since building societies provide the most money for mortgages—about 80 per cent of money lent—it's best to open accounts with a few of the larger ones and one or two of the smaller ones. The *societies tend to give depositors preference* so that the more societies in which you're investing the better. Do this well in advance of looking for a house or flat to buy.

Don't Limit your Choice of financing to one source. Many deals fall through and its better to be negotiating with several sources at the same time. *A good time to apply* for a building society loan is when no one else is. From November to the end of February is best, when fewer houses change hands than in the autumn or spring.

Be prepared for disappointment on getting a *loan for an old house*, say pre-1920. Only 17 per cent of mortgages are on old houses, yet the demand for mortgages on old houses is staggering, especially in central London. If you do get an offer of a mortgage it may be for only sixty per cent of the value; and then you may have to pay off the mortgage in fifteen or twenty years. Some building societies may permit you to repay your mortgage with a *property or equity-linked insurance policy*. This is generally an excellent way of repaying, if you can take advantage of the tax reliefs. Check the past performance of the plan and whether a maturity value is guaranteed.

Many insurance companies have launched insurance policies linked to a *building society investment*. Part of the premium pays for the life cover and the remainder goes to a building society in a special link. After tax relief the return on this policy is quite good. Don't buy one with the expectation of getting a mortgage, however. There is no guarantee, although you will get the same preference for consideration as would a depositor with the building society in the link. The policies are also a bit inflexible if you intend to use them to repay a mortgage which you haven't as yet obtained.

Bridging Finance is an expression that refers to the raising of money for a short time, to bridge the gap between the time one has to make expenditures on a house, and the time one gets money from the financier of the mortgage. Bridging finance often is needed when one buys a new house before getting money from the sale of the old one. A bridging loan is also needed when one is making extensive renovations. Often the lender may not give the entire loan until all the work has been completed. The problem is that in the meantime money is needed. Where to get bridging finance? Ask your solicitor. Money may be available from his trust funds. You will have to pay a high rate of interest and a fee for the consideration, or your bank may be able to arrange an unsecured overdraft. Again the rate of interest is high, and possibly a fee will be required as well. Some of the larger finance houses also offer bridging loans.

Mortgage protection policy is nothing more than a decreasing term insurance policy which insures the repayment of the mortgage in the event of the mortgager's dying. It pays to have such a policy if you're paying off a mortgage through a building society. You don't need one if you're repaying with an insurance endowment repayment mortgage.

Repayment of a mortgage before the term ends can be expensive. Most mortgage deeds provide for penalties from three to six month's interest if you decide to repay early. It may be better to try to transfer the mortgage to your new house. Or have the purchaser of your old house take over the mortgage and pay you the difference between the sale price and the outstanding mortgage account.

Foreign nationals may have trouble getting a building society loan. You may have to obtain Bank of England permission to borrow sterling, confirm that you have a resident account for exchange control purposes, and show the amount of income you're earning or remitting into Britain. Americans should first try branches of American banks in Britain, especially the First National City Bank, for house purchase loans. You may be able to repay the loan abroad.

The largest National Building Societies get the most deposits, so it stands to reason that they should have the most to give out for mortgages.

The smaller societies normally charge more to do what the larger societies do for less though they tend to be more flexible and often consider propositions that the larger Building Societies will not touch. The largest building societies are: Halifax, Abbey National, Woolwich Equitable, Nationwide, Alliance, Provincial, Leek and Westbourne, Bradford and Bingley, Anglia, Burnley, and Leeds Permanent.

Option mortgage—the government-backed option mortgage is designed to provide inexpensive mortgages for those people who have few or no savings, and who pay little or no tax. Up to £7500 is available from building societies or insurance companies participating in the scheme. No tax relief is available on an option mortgage although you are permitted to switch to a tax relief mortgage if your financial situation changes.

Indispensable Helpers

The Surveyor – the Professional Property Expert

Who Are They?

A surveyor is a professional property expert. He's not an estate agent, although many estate agents are also surveyors. And he's not a property developer. But he's someone you should know more about if you're planning to buy a house and invest money in it. It's likely that you'll be using his services.

The best surveyors belong to the Royal Institution of Chartered Surveyors. Prior education, experience, plus an examination are required for membership. A surveyor with F.R.I.C.S. or A.R.I.C.S. to his name is the true professional — be wary of the others. Most of the professional surveyors work for the big property companies, estate agents, or as partners in their own business.

What do They do?

Surveyors basically do three things for the flat and house hunter:

1) Inspection—a survey of a piece of property to determine if there are any defects. (The surveyor will recommend what to do about them.)

2) Valuation—based on current market conditions and the nature and location of a house or flat, a surveyor can determine an independent value. Useful when trying to select a sale price, or deciding what you should offer someone when buying.

3) Preparation of specifications when building or renovating—a quantity surveyor works for a client and translates an architect's plans into a description of what has to be done, and the material that has to be used for the job. This 'bill of quantity' is then given to several builders or contractors so they can prepare bids. There is a considerable time element involved but it is worth it.

What it Costs?

1) Inspecting or surveying—there is no specific scale. A preliminary survey could cost £20–30. A proper survey, which would include inspecting the beams, walls, drains, electric wiring, pipes, roof, structural brickwork and other essential parts is really essential if you intend to spend a large sum on an old house. A thorough survey could cost between £100 and £200.

2) Valuation—freehold Property:

1 per cent on the first £1500

0·5 per cent on the next £11,000
0·25 per cent on the residue of the valuation

Example:

	Valuation	Fee
	£10,000	£57·50
	£15,000	£76·25
	£20,000	£88·75

On leasehold property the scale is the same. But there is an additional charge on the ground rent. The charges are:

7·5 per cent on the first £300
4·5 per cent on the next £700
3·0 per cent on the next £1500
2·0 per cent on the residue

Example:

	Ground rent	Extra fee
	£50	£3·75
	£100	£7·50
	£300	£22·50

3) Quantity surveying—computed on a percentage of the total cost or the lowest accepted bid on a job.

Value of work	House scale where alteration or renovation form majority of the work
up to £30,000	3·0 per cent (minimum fee £150)
£30,000–60,000	£900 plus 2·5 per cent on the balance over £30,000

How do you Find a Surveyor?

1) Recommendation.
2) Consult the Royal Institution of Chartered Surveyors for names of surveyors located in your area.
3) Ask your architect. He would work with them often. Some architects are chartered surveyors as well.
4) Ask your estate agent. Make sure the surveyor recommended is a member of the Royal Institution of Chartered Surveyors.

Tips on Using a Surveyor?

Don't rely on the value the building society surveyor places on your intended house. He is interested only in determining possible resale value, and not in discovering structural defects. Have an independent survey done.

Make clear to your surveyor exactly what you expect him to do, and the nature of the report you expect. Agree on all extra fees and charges beforehand.

If you are having major renovation and conversion done to your house—over £8000 worth—hire a quantity surveyor to work for you and obtain competitive bids from contractors. You may save a lot in the end.

The Architect — the Designing Man

If you are buying an old house in London you'll probably be needing an architect. Why? Because most old (period) houses need extensive conversions and renovations. You may need central heating, enlarged rooms, a redesigned kitchen and bathroom, eradication of damp or dry rot, or even a new roof. And you may want to put in a self-contained flat in your basement or an additional nursery floor on top. This is a job for an architect.

You could buy an old house with everything modernized, but then you'll be paying heavily for the work someone else has done. Rather than pay £20,000 to £25,000 for a totally modernized house, it may make more sense to buy a house for £10,000–12,000, in need of extensive repairs of say £7,000–10,000. In this way you'll end up with exactly what you want in the finished house.

While some people try to get by using only contractors in making renovations or conversions, it's not recommended unless the job is a small one, say under £3000. It's better to hire an architect and have a professional job done. You'll probably save money in the end. One couple regrets making what could have been a spare bedroom into a large quiet bathroom. An architect can help you avoid making such a mistake.

How do Architects Work With Clients?

To qualify as a professional architect requires a specialized five-year education and a written examination. The aspiring architect then works for another professional and eventually takes an examination from the Royal Institute of British Architects (R.I.B.A.), the architects' professional orgainization. The letters A.R.I.B.A. or F.R.I.B.A. after an architect's name indicate a fully-qualified architect. Architects can handle the whole conversion, renovation, and decoration including:
1) Specifying what has to be done—the Brief
2) Design
3) Town planning
4) Contract drawings
5) Co-ordination of contractor and suppliers.
Architects also work with quantity surveyors who convert the actual design to a specification, called a bill of quantities, for a builder's bid or tender. This is the most sensible approach because it sets the cost and provides control as to what is to be done, how, and with what materials. If you're planning to spend over £8000 don't be in a hurry. Use a quantity surveyor (see p. 000).

How do you Find an Architect?

1) Personal recommendation.
2) Look for architects doing work on houses in your area. Usually they'll put up their sign on the site.
3) Use the advisory service of the Royal Institute of British Architects, 66 Portland Place, W.1.
4) Ask your estate agent or solicitor.

What do Architects Charge?

Many architects work on commerical properties and try to avoid residential work on new houses because fees are too low. They don't mind doing alterations to existing houses. Normally any alteration work of under £8000 is small stuff and most busy architects won't touch it. This doesn't mean that if you have a £5000 job in mind you won't be able to find an architect, but your field will be limited. Young architects with young practices are more likely to consider small jobs. Ring up the University pf London's Bartlett School and ask to be put in contact with a student who may want some work.

The scale fees are:

Total amount spent:	fee expressed as a percentage of total cost
up to £2500	13 per cent

Total amount spent:	fee expressed as a percentage of total cost
£2500–8000	12·5 per cent
£8000–14,000	12 per cent
£14,000–25,000	11 per cent
over £25,000	10 per cent

Fees are payable in stages:
  15 per cent of total when brief is completed
  35 per cent of the total when initial design is completed
up to 75 per cent of the total when detail design is completed.

Tips on Using an Architect

1) Get a qualified surveyor to do a thorough survey even before you contact an architect. It's better to know the condition of the structure before you set about beautifying it.

2) Make sure you understand completely the fees you'll have to pay the architect. It's most important to come to an understanding on whether the cost of fixtures, fittings and furnishings are to be included in the total amount spent on the architect's fee. No matter who picks out the materials the architect may be entitled to a percentage.

3) Get your architect to recommend a reputable builder or contractor. You may be sold on the services of a builder only to find that he goes bankrupt before completing the job.

4) An architect can open doors at suppliers of fixtures, fittings and furnishings —you may even get a discount by just mentioning that you're using a certain architect. Normally the contractor gets the discount, and charges you for the full amount.

5) Don't overdesign or overspend architecturally on a house, thereby making it our of proportion investment-wise to other houses in your area. You may find that when you decide to sell, people won't pay the premium for your architectural work, preferring to buy a less expensive house down the road.

6) You must make all your decisions about the details of the conversion right at the beginning, and stick to them. Changes of mind halfway through the job are extremely costly, difficult, inconvenient, and cause tremendous delays.

7) A major renovation can take from six to twelve months. So don't be impatient to move in right away.

Builders or Contractors

Once you've completed all the legal steps in taking possession of a house or flat, you still may not be ready to move in, because now comes what's called 'making the place livable'. This could just involve decorating—paint, paper and the like; but if you've chosen an old house or flat because it's a 'good shell', you may have to rebuild the interior—install central heating, build cupboards, cure rising damp, repair a leaking roof. This is the sad truth about living in a city where most of the dwellings are old.

Depending on the extent of your 'inside job', you'll either hire a contractor, or do it yourself! For a job requiring more than one craftsman, it's best to use a contractor.

You will find more and more small, independent or self-employed contractors these days. Many of the largest contracting firms have broken-up. The cause of that break-up? S.E.T. This tax, which is being phased out and gradually replaced by another type of indirect tax, was paid by the employer for each person salaried by his firm. Self-employed persons, however, were not taxed. Thus, many contractors, in order to avoid the taxes, began working with craftsmen on a 'consulting basis', in preference to having them on salary.

The contractor can save you many headaches. He knows the best people for specific jobs, and he motivates them to finish work on time. Many workmen, as is well known, spend as much time taking tea and lunch breaks as they do working. A contractor is a sort of combination of film producer and sergeant major.

How to Find a Contractor

1) The best way is through a personal introduction, by someone whose house has recently been completed, and the job well done! All you have to do is ask a friend or acquaintance: 'Who's well known for restoring Georgian houses?' You'll probably get a few recommendations.
2) Look at the classified 'yellow pages' telephone directory under 'building contractor' and do some extensive telephone interviewing.
3) Check with the Master Builders Federation, 33 John Street, W.C.1., 242 7583, or the National Federation of Building Trades' Employers, 82 New Cavendish Street, W.1., 580 4041.
4) Ask your trusted estate agent, surveyor or architect for a recommendation.

Tips to Take into Consideration Before you Choose a Contractor

1) Make sure the contractor is reputable and well established. As for references, ask for the names of former clients for whom jobs have been completed. Then phone the clients and ask how their job turned out. A disreputable contractor—and there are some—may not do what he promised, and may co-ordinate a sloppy job, which you'll live to regret.
2) Do not take the first contractor who comes along. Ask for written estimates from five or six, and make sure that you give each contractor the same specifications. (And be forewarned about changing specifications midway through the job: such changes could cost you dearly. A contractor's profit comes from the margin between what he charges you, and what he has to pay for his men's time, and the supplies they use. It's on this basis that he gives you his estimate).
3) Do not necessarily hire the contractor who gives you the lowest estimate.

Find out, in a discreet way, why his price is low. If his reasoning is sound, he may well be your best choice. Estimates may vary by as much as 40 per cent.
4) Be very specific about when you want your work to start. Make sure the dates for the beginning and ending of the job are clearly stated in the estimate. Some contractors will price a job, hoping that they'll have the men to call on when they need them. But if for some reason the key man is not available when needed, all the schedules slip. A job then can take three to six months longer than expected.
5) If you can avoid springtime, when craftsmen are busiest, you're apt to be better pleased by the swiftness with which your job is completed. Christmas time is the slackest in the building trade, and may be the best period, from the customer's point of view.

To Save Money—Do It Directly

Some people do decide to work with individual carpenters, plumbers, painters, hiring them individually—in order to save the 10 per cent surcharge which the contractor usually collects. But surely one must have quite a lot of courage, and some previous experience in doing up flats or houses to operate this way. One woman who took charge of the job on her house in Montpelier Square, Kensington, said she did so only because she had done up another house a few years earlier with a contractor; and only because she had a personal recommendation for every craftsman she hired. Even then, she said, it wasn't easy.

An important point to remember before you charge into any major conversion or renovation is that any such major work increases the ratable value of your property, and of course the rates you'll have to pay the council increase as well. The property will either be revalued on completion, or whenever the next valuation is made in your area.

At Home Problems

Moving Day

Moving day is one of life's traumatic experiences, no matter how many times you go through it. Even if you actually look forward to the move, and the new life, moving day generally turns out to be anything but a pleasure.

When you hire a mover, don't just take pot luck from the classified yellow pages of the telephone directory. Write to the National Association of Furniture Warehouseman and Removers Ltd, 39 Victoria Street, S.W.1. They will send you the names of their members who work in your area. They'll also send you a brochure with 'Some Hints for Your Removal Day'. Any tips that will make moving day easier are welcome, especially if they come from the professionals.

A removal firm which is a member of the N.A.F.W.R. does not necessarily have higher qualifications or a better reputation than a mover who is not a member—so don't make membership a requirement before you hire. But somehow one feels more relaxed, knowing a removal expert, or any other home service agency, is a member of an association which strives to maintain high standards of service.

Be sure to talk to friends, acquaintances or business colleagues who have moved, for they offer excellent though biased recommendations or condemnations of a removal firm.

Be certain to call on several removal firms asking each to give you estimates of the cost of your move. They will give you these free of charge, and you can learn something about each firm as you talk to the estimator who calls at your home. Don't be surprised if one estimate is as much as twice as high as another one. One friend received an estimate of £1000 for a move from London to Brussels; and an estimate of £500 from another firm. Upon further inquiries, she found that the £1000 estimate was for a 'complete wrap'—every piece of furniture individually wrapped, mostly in cartons. Whereas the other firm had not thought it necessary to individually wrap all furniture, but simply give it the standard treatment. She decided on the more expensive firm, when she learned of its fine reputation in the shipment of antiques.

Be certain that your contract with the removal firm specifies packing, loading, shipping, unloading and unpacking. A very low estimate may possibly mean that the mover will unload boxes from the van, but will not unpack them, or carry each object to its proper room in your new home. Double check the damage insurance clause in the contract. You may have to take out an extra insurance policy as protection.

Once You've Chosen your Removal Man . . .

Some Hints for Making Your Pre-Moving Days and Moving Day Itself Easier:

1) Give three weeks' notice of 'turn-off' to your gas and electricity boards.

2) Write to the Water Board and Rating Authority—you may get a rebate on both water and rates, if you've paid them six months in advance.

3) Make an application to the G.P.O. for a telephone in your new home well ahead of your move; and give three weeks' notice to the G.P.O. about postal delivery cessation at one address and beginning at a new.

4) Removal men are not permitted to have anything to do with disconnecting electrical fittings or fixtures, gas cookers, water heaters and the like. You must arrange for the electrician, plumber or gas man to do so.

5) Likewise, line up the electrician, water, gas and carpet man well in advance for the work needing to be done in your new home. There's often a long waiting list for service.

6) Send anything small or valuable, like jewellery and silver, to the bank until you're settled in your new home.

7) To guarantee that underwear and other vital things like tin openers for cold drinks and toilet paper don't get locked away, pack a survival suitcase for yourself and tell the removal men to keep away from it.

Removal Men Who've Been Highly Recommended

Pitt and Scott, Ltd, London (20–24 Eden Grove, N.7, 607 7321), Liverpool, Glasgow and New York

John Lewis (Warehouse), 73 Pancras Road, N.W.1, 837 7302

John Barker and Co, Ltd, 18 Cromwell Crescent, S.W.5, 937 5432

Davies Turner, 326 Queenstown Road, S.W.8, 622 4393

Interdean Ltd, 150–2 Fenchurch Street, E.C.3, 623 5934.

Moving in to a furnished flat?

If you are moving into a furnished flat, be sure that the gas and electricity meters are read on the day you move in, so that you'll not be charged for weeks or months of the previous tenant's gas and electricity. Also be sure that the telephone has been disconnected. Then have it reconnected in your name so you can be certain that you won't be paying for any previous tenant's trans-Atlantic calls to his girlfriend.

Education

If state education for your children is your goal, you can find out the basics about schools in your area from your divisional office of the Inner London Education Authority. The office will not, of course, tell you which school is good, better, best or worst. This you must learn by word of mouth from your neighbours or acquaintances—sad but true, this is the only way to learn the merits or shortcomings of the local schools. Of course you may pay visits to the schools yourself, and talk to parents whom you meet there, either dropping off or collecting their children.

Inner London Education Authority, County Hall, Westminster, London, S.W.1
Divisional Offices

Division No. 1	33 Notting Hill Gate, W.11, 727 8012	Serving boroughs of Hammersmith, Kensington and Chelsea
,,	2	388–396 Oxford Street, W.1, 499 4141	Serving Camden, Westminster
,,	3	20 Compton Terrace, N.1, 226 4881	Serving Islington
,,	5	Harford Street, Mile End Road, E.1, 790 4231	Serving Tower Hamlets, City of London
,,	6	Riverside House East, Beresford Street, S.E.18, 855 3161	Serving Greenwich
,,	7	2 Greenwich High Road, S.E.10, 692 1042	Serving Lewisham
,,	8	83 Peckham Road, S.E.5, 703 6551	Serving Southwark
,,	9	50 Acre Lane, S.W.2, 274 8611	Serving Lambeth
,,	10	92 St John's Hill, S.W.11, 228 4104	Serving Wandsworth

Education Officer, London Borough of Barnet, Town Hall, Friern Barnet, N.11, 368 1101
London Borough of Haringey, Education Offices, Somerset Road, Tottenham, N.17, 808 4500
London Borough of Hounslow, Education Officer, 88 Lampton Road, Hounslow, Middlesex, 570 7763
London Borough of Richmond upon Thames, Education Offices, Regal House, London Road, Twickenham, Middlesex, 892 4466.

It is true that many young London families choose their house or flat because of the school district in which it is located. Though technically a child may attend any school in the I.L.E.A. area, the I.L.E.A. gives preference to local children, as it must pay travelling costs for children travelling three miles or more.

State schools in some sections of London are superb model or progressive or experimental—Brookfield School in South Highgate has its own swimming pool and nothing but praise for its educational programme; the same praise is known London-wide for the Bousfield Infant School in The Boltons, South Kensington.

But in some lower-income areas, there is nothing but bad news about the state schools, and that is the reason for the formation of so many Associations for the Advancement of State Education. As more professional couples with children move into once wholly working-class areas, they take a great interest in improving the schools. Both Camden and Islington have very active Associations for the Advancement of State Education.

If an independent education is more your family's preference, then probably the best way to gain guidance to the 'public' schools is through one of the Education Trusts (or Scholastic Agencies, as they are sometimes called), which offer advisory service free to the client. If you ultimately choose a school which has been recommended to you by the trust, then the school which you have chosen pays the trust a fee. There is no one educational trust which represents all the public or independent schools, but the Gabbitas—Thring Educational Trust, Broughton House, 6 Sackville Street, W.1, and the Truman & Knightley Educational Trust, 93 Baker Street, W.1, represent most of them, and publish some useful pamphlets for parents.

Once an educational trust has given you the names and addresses of several schools, fees, and names of headmaster or mistress, you personally call the school and aks for its prospectus, and then arrange a visit. (A few of the schools may send you the prospectus before you get round to phoning them.) You may also ask the school for the names of several parents to whom you may apply for references about the school.

(Ace)

The Advisory Centre for Education, an independent organization, runs an advisory service, which will offer members information and/or advice about choosing a public school. The advisory service has a stock of information (on more than 600 direct grant and independent schools) which provides parents with a quick, efficient method of comparing schools before they make a short-list of schools to visit. The information includes:

Size of school, age range of pupils accepted for day, weekly or termly boarding
Numbers and qualifications of teaching staff
Number of L.E.A. pupils, and pupils with parents resident overseas
Entry procedure, age, exams, scholarships, connections with prep schools, sixth form entry
Religious education
Admissions policy for children with special needs—high or low IQ, physical handicaps, etc.
Syllabus, subject options, external exam results
Facilities: laboratories, libraries, music, sports, dormitories
Activities: societies, visits and free time
Sixth form life, careers guidance
Parent-teacher relations.

To join ACE, write to Advisory Centre for Education, 32 Trumpington Street, Cambridge. Membership for a reasonable fee gives you a year's subscription to *Where*, the monthly magazine.

What will you pay for an independent education? Just under £900 a year is the top price, for boarding, but it's going up all the time. For the foreigner £1000 a year.

Prestige public schools are generally recognized by the annual number of their pupils who enter Oxford or Cambridge University, and by the names and reputations of 'old boys' or 'old girls'.

State schools are organized as follows:

Nursery schools—3 to 5 years
Infant schools—5 to 11/12

Junior schools—5 to 11/12
Secondary Modern or Grammar schools, gradually being replaced in most areas by Comprehensive schools—age 12/13—18+.

The state-maintained schools fall into two classes: 1) the county school, owned and run by the local authorities, who are responsible for the education of children in their respective areas, and 2) controlled voluntary schools, in which the local authority appoint two-thirds of the governors, and a voluntary body appoints the other third. All costs, however, are paid by the local authority, and two periods a week denominational study may be given. An aided voluntary school has two-thirds of its governors appointed by a voluntary body, and they are responsible for exterior repairs, alterations to the school building, and so on.

The local authority, however, pays the teachers' salaries, and the running costs of the school. Teachers are appointed by the governors and religious instruction is denominational.

The non-maintained schools, known as 'public' or independent, fall into two categories as well: those which receive no form of grant from public funds, and those which do—being known as direct-grant grammar schools. Direct-grant grammar schools have some free places available for students in return for a direct grant from the Department of Education and Science. The direct-grant grammar schools have very high academic qualifications.

The headmaster or headmistress of a public school belongs to either the Headmasters' Conference or to the Association of Headmistresses.

The Public Schools Commission has recommended that schools which charge fees should not be any part of the state system. If this recommendation is implemented, direct-grant grammar schools will be faced with two alternatives:
1) to become totally independent schools
2) to become schools owned or aided by the local authority.

The Chemical Bank of New York, Berkeley Square, publishes a booklet, *Education in England*, which is free—and very helpful for American parents in England.

Security Measures

London is among the safest of cities, yet crime in London, like the cost of living, is on the way up. Over the last ten years the number of crimes per year has doubled. And burglary is one of the fastest growing of crimes in London. It's a rare person who hasn't been the victim of burglary or doesn't know of someone who has been.

In 1970 there were more than 40,000 burglaries in flats and houses in London. That's more than a hundred a day. The most dangerous areas from a burglary point of view are those affluent areas bordering the less affluent ones. Prime examples would be Holland Park bordering on Notting Hill, and Swiss Cottage bordering on Kilburn. Some insurance companies charge as much as 50 per cent more for home contents insurance if you live in N, N.W, W.1, W.2, W.9, W.C.1, S.W.1 and S.W.3 compared to other London districts. A history of high claims is the prime reason.

The Pattern of Burglary

The average burglar is young, probably between fifteen and twenty-five, and he acts on impulse. If he sees an open door or window he may decide to go through it and see what he can find. Eighty per cent of burglaries are executed because the opportunity seemed right. The really professional thief sticks to the ultra wealthy in hotel suites, flats or houses, looking primarily for jewellery. The young burglar who strikes at the average house or flat takes on average £200 worth of property and does the job in approximately ninety seconds. Chances are the burglar will never be caught; nor will you ever see your property again. A friend who had a valuable violin stolen was lucky enough to discover it on a Camden Passage market stall, up for sale at a fraction of its true value.

Most burglaries occur when everyone is out of the flat or house. The favourite time is between 2 p.m. and 6 p.m. on weekdays, with Thursday and Friday the favourite days. The most popular items on the thief's list are: money, jewellery, radios, T.V. sets, cameras, clothes, silver, watches and clocks. The commonest way for a thief to enter is through a back window. Usually ground floor or basement flats are particularly attractive. When the front door is the target for entry it is usually forced or has a lock that is easily picked.

What to do to Protect Yourself

Which?, the Consumer Association magazine, recommends:

1) Thief resistant front door, mortise locks meeting British Standard 3621. Look for the 'kite mark'.
2) Locks should require a key to open them from the inside as well as the outside. Use Chubb, Banham or Ingersoll. Be sure the door is as strong as the lock.
3) For windows use locks that require a key. And the key should not be a standard type. The burglar may have one. Best are:

Locks Ltd 'Rola' for wooden sash windows
Squire Watchman for sash or casement
Yale window lock for sash or casement window
Banham w/109 for metal casement

Alarm systems come in three main varieties. Internal alarm which warns people inside the house; external, which ring outside the house; and '999' systems which ring the police or an alarm company office. Alarm systems can be expensive to buy, rent and install. *Which?* recommends the Granley TCU/5M, and the Sea-Bell Boat Alarm. Both come with external bells. Internal alarm systems don't make that much sense since burglars will rarely strike when someone is at home. '999' systems are much more expensive, you risk false alarms, and you miss the advantage of the bell ringing to frighten the burglar. Because most burglars spend just a few minutes in a home they're probably gone by the time the police arrive.

Ten Extra Tips

1) It always pays to change the locks in your new flat or house after you've moved in, there's no telling who has copies of the previous tenant's keys.

2) External alarm boxes may be big and ugly but they frighten away many would-be burglars. Internal alarms can't be seen and therefore lose some of their deterrent affect.

3) Whenever you go make sure that all windows and doors are properly locked. And don't leave keys under the front door mat, it's the first place a thief looks.

4) Leave lights on in the bedroom or living room when you're out. You can get lights controlled by an automatic time switch. A radio left on is also a good idea.

5) Be sure to examine the credentials of anyone who comes to install anything or survey your home. Professional burglars have been known to help secure a house only to unsecure it later with a break-in.

6) When you go on holiday don't let the world know it. Have post picked up by a neighbour.

7) Before you decide on a burglar alarm system get a number of estimates for different systems. Determine rental cost, purchase price, maintenance arrangement, and installation charge. The best systems have a combination of closed circuit contact points, pressure mat switches and shunt locks. Also determine the strength of the bell and how it can be deactivated once it's gone off.

8) It also pays to make a note of the serial numbers of your cameras, radios, binoculars and the like. Tracing them, if they are stolen, is much easier that way.

9) There is no way to make your home completely burglar proof. Best to get insurance for burglary and put your real valuables in a safe deposit box in a bank or at least while you are on holiday or business trips.

10) Be sure you have at your finger tips the phone number of the local police. Your area may have a Crime Prevention Officer at the local police station. They normally give free advice and may even come to examine the premises.

Addresses of Recommended Companies

Banham Burglary Prevention, 233 Kensington High Street, W.8, 228 6801.
Chubb & Sons: Locks, 68 St James's Street, S.W.1, 493 5414.
　　　　　　Alarms, 29 Enford Street, W.1, 262 3250.
Granley Burglar Alarms, 46 Great Eastern Street, E.C.2, 253 3186.
Ingersoll Locks, 89 Kingsway, W.C.2, 405 0961.
Yale Locks, 207 The Vale, W.3, 743 1200.

Security Through Insurance

As soon as you're legally responsible for your home, when you've exchanged contracts or signed the lease, be sure you've got insurance. Don't wait until you've moved in. Houses have been known to burn down or suffer damage between contract signing and moving in.

The best type of insurance is a comprehensive houseowner's policy. With one policy you're able to insure against:

*Destruction or damage to your building

*Destruction, damage or loss of contents
*All risk cover to protect your possessions, no matter where loss or damage occurs.
*Claims by a third party for damage to his property from something that happens in yours (essential for flat dwellers).

Each type of coverage carries its own premium. If you're in a flat you don't need buildings coverage. Normally if you take a mortgage on a house you've very little choice on building insurance. It'll be arranged for you by the building society or insurance company. Contents, 'all risk' insurance and third party cover are essential and it's surprising how many people don't have them. And it pays to shop around. The premium charges can vary quite a bit. Also read the small print and look for exclusions. Some insurance companies won't pay a claim if you haven't insured your contents for their full value.

What to Watch for

1) Does the policy exclude the first £5, £10 or £15 worth of a claim?
2) Are there limits on a per item basis on a claim for money, or other home contents? Are other valuables not included?
3) Is the 'all risk' cover for anywhere in the world or just in Britain or Europe?
4) Is the premium higher for certain areas of London?
5) How important is it to have a proper valuation on buildings and contents filed with insurance company?
6) Must you show that you've contacted the fire brigade or police to claim for destruction or theft?

What it Costs (example)

	Cover	Approximate annual cost
Home insurance (buildings)	£10,000	£10–13
Contents	£3000	£9–15
'All risks'	£750	£8–11

Some Companies with Competitive Policies

Albion Insurance Co. Ltd, 34 Leadenhall Street, E.C.3, 481 8151.
Coronet Insurance Co. Ltd, 32 Seething Lane, E.C.3, 109 9811.
Crusader Insurance Co. Ltd, Vincula House, Tower Place, E.C.3, 626 8031.
Eagle Star Insurance Group, 1 Threadneedle Street, E.C.2, 588 1212.
Guardian Royal Exchange Assurance Group, 14 Bonhill Street, E.C.2, 283 7101.
London & Edinburgh Insurance Co. Ltd, Albany House, Petty France, S.W.1, 222 3011.
Welfare Insurance Co. Ltd, 35 Cannon Street, E.C.4, 236 0781.

Selling Time – Selling the Roof over your Head

Anyone who leaves London becomes involved in sales. Even disposing of a rented unfurnished flat can become a big sales operation, for what tenant will move away without claiming the premium for fixtures and fittings—which is his due in the present property market.

For every buyer there's a seller. You've been through the house or flat renting or buying phase, but now the tables have turned.

Maybe you've found something better—you're moving up in the world. Or perhaps your company is transferring you to another location. And then there's the possibility of an economic reversal in your life and you're cutting back to a less costly life style. Whatever the reason, you'd like to move as soon as possible, with the least inconvenience and the maximum return on your investment.

Three Ways to Get Out

1) Use an estate agent.
2) Sell it yourself.
3) Go to auction.

Using Estate Agents

Estate agents charge the seller for his commission: here's what you pay (R.I.C.S. scale):

Freehold and Leasehold		Short Lease	
Sale Price	Commission*	Premium	Commission
10,000	£212·50	1000	£50
15,000	£287·50	3000	£100
20,000	£362·50	5000	£150

*R.I.C.S. scale charges are no longer mandatory. Some estate agents charge a flat 2 per cent of sale price. Others a sliding scale of $2\frac{1}{2}$ per cent of the sale price up to £10,000 and 2 per cent from £10,000 to £20,000, and $1\frac{1}{2}$ per cent for sales over £20,000. Under current practice the seller is free to negotiate a fee. (Since the Restriction on Monopolies (Estate Agents) Order 1970, became law, 'Scale Charges' as such for the sale/letting of unfurnished dwellings, i.e. houses/flats became illegal—hence the disparity in the rates quoted by firms.)

Ways of commissioning agents

'*Sole agency*' or '*sole selling rights*': giving a particular agent sole right to try and sell your house. Normally the exclusive rights last for three months. The sole agent gets the commission no matter who sells the house during this exclusive period. And even if the house is not sold you'll be charged for the agent's expenses (trying to sell through adverts). It's best to use sole agency arrangements on only the very expensive houses or properties that can't be sold easily.

'*Multiple agency*': giving a number of agents the opportunity to find a buyer. The agent who succeeds gets the commission. The aggressive agents don't mind this arrangement. In fact, they may even go out looking for it. The more traditional or conservative agents frown on this competitive system.

'*Joint agency*': in this arrangement you instruct two agents to co-operate over the sale. Done frequently on out-of-the-way properties where you might want a local agent *and* one closer to the central area. You normally have to pay scale-and-a-half for this arrangement. The agents usually split the commission on sale, and thereby each gets 75 per cent of the normal commission.

In a seller's market many people prefer the multiple agency method. The added exposure tends to move the property faster. Using a number of different agents presents opportunities for a 'Dutch auction'. In this legal but unethical practice, you get the interested buyers to bid against each other and thereby substantially raise the selling price.

Using an estate agent is probably the most convenient way to sell. It's best to work with the same agent who found the house or flat for you in the first place. He is most probably dealing with people who are looking for just your type of property.

Some agents specialize, for example, in finding unfurnished flats on short leases where premiums are involved. These agents have clients who may want exactly what you're wanting to sell. Use them for a quick convenient sale: it's worth the commission you must pay the agent.

Some estate agents (the less reputable ones, of course) don't always aim to get the highest possible price for you. They're trying to move your property quickly. Selling for a few hundred pounds less doesn't reduce their commission very much. Moral: comparison shop and find out for yourself what the true market value of your property is. When money is tight and mortgage money is nearly impossible to get there may be more people trying to sell than there are buyers who are able to buy. Then you may have to drop your price. When mortgage money is easy to get there will be more interested buyers than sellers. This is the time to raise your offer price and hold fast.

Be sure to clarify, when dealing with an estate agent, who pays the advertising cost and other fees.

To help you decide on a selling price, you may want to pay for a valuation by a surveyor.

Value of Property	Valuation Fee (minimum fee £10)
£10,000	£57·50
£15,000	£76·25
£20,000	£88·75

Selling it Yourself

Probably a quarter of the 500,000 houses sold every year in Britain change hands without estate agents. If the house or flat is in a good area, large enough for a family, in reasonable condition and not extravagantly priced, sell it yourself, and save the commission.

Best way to sell? Advertise in *The Times, Sunday Times* or *Observer, Evening Standard* or local paper. Also tell all your friends. And finally if you can, put up a sign or board outside, just as estate agents do.

When you've found a prospective buyer instruct your solicitor to handle all the details like deposits, contracts, transfer of ownership, assigning leases and other headaches. If you want to do it all alone and save the solicitors fees read the Consumer Association's book, *The Legal Side of Buying a House*.

Keep on showing the house or flat even though you've received an offer, for many offers fall through. Remember, make any agreement and accept a deposit only 'subject to contract' to protect yourself.

The Auction Route

The auction method is best for selling the very expensive and unusual house, which has received a number of serious offers. Try not to go to auction unless you have a definite number of interested bidders. The atmosphere of an auction often stimulates a higher price. Make sure enough advertising and publicity have been done in advance to attract additional prospective buyers. Also, advertising an auction often creates interest leading to an early sale before auction.

Ask your solicitor to instruct the auctioneer as to the terms and ask him for help in the preparation of the particulars. Your solicitor should also prepare the contract for the buyer's signature.

Make sure you set the reserve carefully. Some auctioneers may not want to agree on a reserve until the day of the auction. This is the price that must be reached, otherwise the property will be withdrawn. Good auctioneers often use techniques to ensure that this price is reached.

Fees for selling a house by auction are the same as in using an estate agent to sell. Most of the estate agents can arrange an auction. In addition you'll find firms of auctioneers who specialize in arranging auctions of houses. If no sale is reached you pay an agreed-upon fee as well as the cost of advertising and other related presale publicity. Some agents in exchange for sole selling rights for an auction chip in 10 per cent of the anticipated expenses as a sign of goodwill.

Make sure can cancel an auction if you sell the house at a price *you* accept. Don't let the auctioneer force you into taking an offer prior to auction. And don't cancel any auction until you've got the signature on the contract.

Another way to sell your house is through a tender, sort of a secret ballot auction. It's cheaper than a public auction but doesn't offer the excitement of a public auction.

General Points on Selling

While it doesn't pay to spend a great deal of money making extensive repairs or decorating, it does pay to touch up the appearance as best you can.

Make sure the house and the windows are spotlessly clean.

It's best to show the house or flat with furniture in it. It gives the house a lived-in look.

Don't be afraid to add a little to the price to allow for bargaining.

If you make a profit on the sale over and above what you originally paid for it and what you spent improving it, don't worry about capital gains tax. It's not payable on a person's principal private residence.

If you've got a mortgage or financial problems because you're negotiating on a new house or flat, consult your bank manager, building society or insurance company. See *The Financial Side* Chapter of this book.

Appendix I
Home Loans from Insurance Companies

The Following Insurance Companies Normally Provide Mortgages to the Public (list furnished by Life Offices Association)

British National Life Insurance Society Ltd, Spencer House, 4 South Place, London E.C.2.

*Equitable Life Assurance Society, 4 Coleman Street, London E.C.2.
*Friends Provident and Century Life Office, 7 Leadenhall Street, London E.C.3.

Gresham Life Assurance Society Ltd, Barrington House, 59 Gresham Street, London E.C.2.
Life, Casualty and General Insurance Co. Ltd, 7 Fenchurch Street, London E.C.3.
* London Life Association Ltd, 81 King William Street, London E.C.4.
National Provident Institution, 48 Gracechurch Street, London E.C.3.
* Norwich Union Insurance Group, 51 Fenchurch Street, London E.C.3.
Provident Life Association of London Ltd, 246 Bishopsgate, London E.C.2.
* Scottish Amicable Life Assurance Society, 17 Tokenhouse Yard, London E.C.2.
Scottish Equitable Life Assurance Society, 13 Cornhill, London E.C.3.
Scottish Life Assurance Company Ltd, 36 Poultry, London E.C.2.
Scottish Mutual Assurance Society, 6 Bell Yard, Law Courts, London W.C.2.
* Scottish Provident Institution, 3 Lombard Street, London E.C.3.
Sentinel Insurance Co. Ltd, 11–13 Holborn Viaduct, London E.C.1.
* Standard Life Assurance Co., 3 Abchurch Yard, London E.C.4.
Sun Life Assurance Society Ltd, 107 Cheapside, London E.C.2.
United Friendly Insurance Co. Ltd, 42 Southwark Bridge Road, London S.E.1.
* University Life Assurance Society, 4 Coleman Street, London E.C.2.

*   Insurance companies with the best with-profits endowment policies based on past performance or best current bonuses *(Money Which?)*.

Appendix II

The Extra Costs of Home Buying (Fees and Taxes)

PURCHASE PRICE—LOAN	SOLICITOR'S CHARGES			STAMP DUTIES		LAND REGISTRY FEES		SURVEY FEE	ESTATE AGENT'S COMMISSION
	unregistered	registered	building soc's solicitor (loan basis)	purchase deed stamp	mortgage stamp (loan basis)	first registration	already registered	based on valuation	paid by seller
£	£	£	£	£	£	£	£	£	£
7000	82·50	51·25	39·00		7·00	11·80	17·40	15·00	167·50
7500	86·25	53·13			7·50	12·50	18·50	16·00	175·00
8000	90·00	55·00			8·00	13·20	19·60	17·00	182·50
8500	93·75	56·87			8·50	13·90	20·70	18·00	190·00
9000	97·50	58·75			9·00	14·60	21·80	19·00	197·50
9500	101·25	60·63			9·50	15·30	22·90	20·00	205·00
10,000	105·00	62·50		55·00	10·00	16·00	24·00	21·00	212·50
11,000	110·00	66·25	by	60·00	11·00	17·40	26·20	23·00	227·50
12,000	115·00	70·00	arrangement	65·00	12·00	18·80	28·40	25·00	242·50
13,000	120·00	73·75		70·00	13·00	20·20	30·60	27·00	257·50
14,000	125·00	76·25		75·00	14·00	21·60	32·80	29·00	272·50
15,000	130·00	78·75		75·00	15·00	23·00	35·00	31·00	287·50
16,000	135·00	81·25		160·00	16·00	24·40	37·40	33·00	302·50
17,000	140·00	83·75		170·00	17·00	25·80	39·40	35·00	317·50
18,000	145·00	85·75		180·00	18·00	27·20	41·60	37·00	332·50
19,000	150·00	87·75		190·00	19·00	28·60	43·80	39·00	347·50
20,000	155·00	89·75		200·00	20·00	30·00	46·00	41·00	362·50

A Flat and House Hunter's Reading List

Ardron, S. and Zager, N., *Hang Your Hat in London*, First National City Bank, 1970.

Bartholomew, M., *Where To Live in London*, Comindus, 1971.

Blackheath Centenary, 1871–1971, Greater London Council Publication 7168 0350 0, 1971.

Boultbee, M., *New Guide to Buying and Selling Houses*, Homefinders (1915) Ltd, 1967.

City Assurance Consultants, *House Purchase*, 3rd edition, 1970.

Colville, R., *London, the Northern Reaches*, Robert Hale, 1951.

Consumers' Association, *The Legal Side of Buying a House*, 6th edition, 1968.

Consumers' Association, *Which?—Loans for Buying a House*, December 1968; *Buying and Selling a House*, November 1969; *Conveyancing*, March 1970.

Dalrymple, R., *England is a Foreign Country*, Birn, Shaw & Co. Ltd for Chemical Bank, 1970.

Do You Care About Historic Buildings?, Greater London Council Publication 7168 0324 0.

Fletcher, G., *London Overlooked*, Hutchinson, 1964.

Fulham History Society, *A History of Fulham*, Sherren & Son, Weymouth, 1970.

Gladstone, F. and Barker, A., *Notting Hill in Bygone Days*, T. Fisher Unwin, 1924.

Hancock, A. and Berrigan, F., *Buying a House*, BBC Publications, 1969.

Kitchener, S. W., *Old Highgate*, Fisher and Sperr.

London's Canal, its Past, Present and Future, Greater London Council Publication 7168 0264 3.

MacRobert, S., *The Development of Putney* (thesis).

Ministry of Housing and Local Government, *Choosing Your House*, H.M.S.O., 1968.

Nairn, I., *Nairn's London*, Penguin Books, 1966.

Norrie, I., *The Book of Westminster*, High Hill Books, 1964.

Norrie, I., *Highgate and Kenwood, a Short Guide*, High Hill Books, 1967.

Official Guides to the Boroughs of: Kensington and Chelsea, Westminster, Hammersmith, Camden, Southwark, Haringey, Lambeth, Merton, Richmond, Greenwich, Hounslow, Lewisham.

Piper, D., *The Companion Guide to London*, Fontana Books, 1970.

Register of Local Amenity Societies, Civic Trust, 18 Carlton House Terrace, London S.W.1, 1970.

Senior, D., *Your Architect*, Signet.

Shea, C., *The Times Guide to Buying a House*, Times Newspapers, 1970.

Summerson, J., *Georgian London*, Penguin Books, 1969.

Whitting, P. D. (ed.), *A History of Hammersmith*, Hammersmith Local History Group, 1965.

Williams, H., *South London*, Robert Hale, 1949.

Wittich, J. and Phillips, R., *Off-beat Walks in London, a Discovering Guide*, A Shire Publication, 1970.

NOTES

NOTES

NOTES

NOTES

NOTES

NOTES

NOTES